Governing the
Global Economy

Governing the Global Economy

International Finance and the State

ETHAN B. KAPSTEIN

Harvard University Press

Cambridge, Massachusetts

London, England · 1994

ACE - 1898

Portions of Chapter 5 originally appeared in: Ethan Kapstein, *Supervising International Banks: Origins and Implications of the Basle Accord*, Essays in International Finance no. 185, December 1992, copyright © 1992, reproduced by permission of the International Finance Section of Princeton University; Ethan Kapstein, "Resolving the Regulator's Dilemma: International Coordination of Banking Regulations," *International Organization* 43 (Spring 1989), reprinted by permission of the MIT Press; and Ethan Kapstein, "Between Power and Purpose: Central Bankers and the Politics of International Regulation," *International Organization* 46 (Winter 1991–1992), reprinted by permission of the MIT Press. This last article is also the source of the figure on page 90, reprinted by permission of the MIT Press.

This book is printed on acid-free paper, and its binding
materials have been chosen for strength and durability.

Library of Congress Cataloging-in-Publication Data

Kapstein, Ethan B.
  Governing the global economy: international finance and the state
  / Ethan B. Kapstein.
      p.   cm.
  Includes bibliographical references and index.
  ISBN 0–674–35757–4
  1. Banks and banking, International.   2. Banks and banking,
International—Law and legislation.   3. International business
enterprises—Finance.   4. International finance.   I. Title.
HG3881.K286   1994
332.1'5—dc20

93–50895
   CIP

Preface

With increasing frequency, public officials, journalists, and scholars are referring to the "globalization" of economic activity. Though rarely defining this term with precision, they seem to be alluding to the inability of governments to control their nation's economic destiny, as the international marketplace for goods, services, and even people presses down on domestic societies. To complicate the problem of economic governance, the major players in this drama seemingly do not possess any national identity at all; they are multinational enterprises which make corporate decisions solely on the basis of overall profit maximization. In short, the world economy has liberated itself from territorial fetters, and it now operates on a global instead of an interstate basis.

My objective in this book is to provide a contrasting view of globalization. I argue that nation-states have created a regulatory structure for international economic activity and that they remain the single most important players. States have created these political structures in order to provide the global economy with its underpinning, its safety net. Public officials and business executives agree that such structures are necessary, for without them markets might produce outcomes that are in nobody's interest.

I focus here on international banking, since no sector has become more global in its operations and thus more difficult to monitor. If—as I shall try to demonstrate—international banks are highly supervised and regulated, then we are likely to see nation-states playing a prominent role in other areas of economic life as well. By showing how governments have responded to new developments in the international economy, I hope to turn public attention back to the state's role as regulator of the marketplace.

This work is the product not just of my academic background in international economic relations, but also of my past experiences as an international banker. As a banker, I became interested in the role of the state in regulating our firm's activities. As an academic, I have been particularly intrigued by the development of cooperation among states to supervise financial institutions and provide a level international playing field on which banks from different countries could compete. Indeed, I began on this long road with a short article about the Basle Accord, an agreement on bank capital levels that had both supervisory and competitive objectives.

Along the way, I have accumulated enough debts to face a crisis of my own. A significant portion of this debt is owed to the hundreds of public officials and bankers in the United States, western Europe, and Japan who have responded to my requests for interviews and information over the past five years. In most cases, these interviews were held "off the record," and I have respected the usual request for anonymity. I am also happy to thank my academic colleagues and the institutions that have given me a home. For their overall support of my work, I am grateful to Benjamin J. Cohen, Samuel Huntington, and Raymond Vernon. For financing this project I thank the John M. Olin Institute for Strategic Studies at Harvard, the Bernstein Fellowship Fund at Brandeis, and the European Community and European Parliament through their jointly sponsored European Community Visitor's Program. For their comments on all or part of the manuscript, I thank Benjamin Cohen (whose review was especially painstaking), Andrew Cortell, John Goodman, Randall Henning, Andrew Moravcsik, Louis Pauly, David Spiro, Raymond Vernon, and Nicholas Ziegler; I am also grateful to the reviewers of my previously published work on international banking, especially Peter Kenen and Stephen

Krasner. Useful comments that forced me to sharpen my discussion were provided by participants in seminars at Brandeis, Harvard, McGill, and the Massachusetts Institute of Technology. For his early support of this project, I wish to thank Michael Aronson of Harvard University Press. I must also express my appreciation to Amy Englehardt for the administrative (and moral!) support she provided during her years at the Olin Institute.

My largest debt, however, is to my wife, Claire, and the book is dedicated to her in partial repayment.

Contents

Governing the
Global Economy

1 | Governments and Global Markets

Ideas, knowledge, science, hospitality, travel—these are things
which should of their nature be international. But let goods be
homespun whenever it is reasonably and conveniently possible,
and, above all, let finance be primarily national.

—JOHN MAYNARD KEYNES

Every age has its defining terms. In our day, one of those terms
is "globalization," which conveys the widely held belief that we
are living in a borderless world. Sovereign states appear incapable of controlling transnational flows of goods and services
(much less flows of people), and in many places the state itself
is collapsing. One can visualize globalization every night, as the
Cable News Network broadcasts its latest reports from Somalia
and the former Yugoslavia to television viewers around the
world.

The idea of globalization challenges public officials, who are
responsible to their societies for ensuring economic welfare
and national security. In an international system which lacks
any higher authority, citizens must look to the state for the
protection of their well-being. Likewise, globalization challenges scholars of international relations, most of whom continue to believe that states remain the most important actors in
the international system. If this is no longer the case, it means
that we must develop new theories of world politics.

I have written this book in the hope of contributing to both
the academic and the policy debates concerning changes in the
global economy. I approach the topic by examining the role of
the state in an issue-area where its power, by most accounts,

appears to be relatively unimportant or ineffective. That area is international finance. If I can show that states are responding to the challenges posed by globalization in this area and that they remain the single most important actors, then we will expect to find them playing a key role in governing other sectors of the global economy as well.

In this chapter I argue that states have responded to financial globalization through the development of *international cooperation based on home country control*. "International cooperation" refers to the myriad formal and informal agreements that states have reached with one another in an effort to supervise the financial marketplace; "home country control" refers to the responsibility that states have taken for defining their national financial institutions and for regulating them. In this way, every international bank is ultimately accountable to a single, national regulator.

This formula—international cooperation based on home country control—suggests that state policies must be understood in terms of a "two-level" approach. At the international level, agreements among states to regulate and supervise the activities of financial institutions are the product of intensive negotiations among central bankers and other financial regulators, and officials from the most powerful countries usually have the most significant voices in the final outcome.

The specific policies that states try to advance on the international level, however, are also the product of *domestic* political negotiations, especially between financial institutions and their regulators. Policies do not simply reflect the "national interest" as perceived by senior government officials, since in many cases several competing policies could serve that interest. In this book I demonstrate that regulators consult and negotiate with the regulated in formulating public policies. This two-level approach reminds us of the enduring importance of domestic politics, even in an increasingly interdependent world.

It has become a commonplace in recent years to speak of the "globalization" of the world economy. Increasingly, we are told, industries of all kinds are losing their national identity as they roam the planet for capital, markets, labor, and technology.[1] With this international expansion, the ability of states to control domestic economic activity has been eroded and sovereignty undermined. A prescient Charles Kindleberger took these developments to their logical extreme when he asserted in 1969 that "the nation-state is just about through as an economic unit."[2]

This tension between states and international markets is hardly of recent vintage. Writing on the eve of World War II, a professor at the Fletcher School of Law and Diplomacy, Eugene Staley, asserted that "fundamental technological changes are pushing mankind in the direction of world-wide economic integration and interdependence, but . . . political tendencies . . . have strongly resisted that trend."[3] He called for "the creation of a permanent International Economic Organization in which economic groups as well as governments would be represented" as a first step toward ameliorating that tension.

Thirty years later, Richard Cooper renewed interest in the conflicts between nation-states and the international economy with his classic work, *The Economics of Interdependence.*[4] Cooper argued that states were finding it difficult to strike a balance between increasing economic interdependence on the one hand and the pursuit of legitimate national objectives on the other. He concluded that the achievement of domestic goals in an international economy would require increased policy coordination among the major industrial powers.

The management of economic policy in the postwar period has been further complicated by the rise of the multinational corporation, the organizational form that now dominates world trade. These firms, which are at the cutting edge of product development for both goods and services, have created business structures that appear to put them beyond the reach of any single public authority. As Raymond Vernon and I have written elsewhere:

> By the late 1980s it was evident that the multinational network had become the dominant form by which enterprises of any size conducted their business in world markets; even firms headquartered in late-industrializing countries such as Brazil, Korea, Taiwan and India were beginning to develop multinational networks. And in practically all countries, the trend toward multinationalization seemed strongest in enterprises with advanced technological capabilities.[5]

The commanding role of the multinational in world commerce was clearly demonstrated by trade statistics. By the late 1980s, for example, "it appeared that US-based multinational enterprises were responsible for about 65 percent of total US merchandise exports, while the US subsidiaries of foreign-based firms may have been accounting for another 25 percent of US merchandise exports."[6]

No sector of the economy, it seems, is more global in its orientation and operations than finance. As Stephen Kobrin of the Wharton Business School has argued, "The financial market is global in the sense that transactions are linked in an electronic network and borders and territoriality are virtually irrelevant." Drawing support for this view from such experts as former Citicorp chairman Walter Wriston and consulting business guru Keniche Ohmae, Kobrin asserts that "government control over flows of funds and thus the value of currencies or monetary policy is very limited."[7]

The data would appear to support the view that finance has gone global, operating outside the framework of nation-states. International bank lending grew from $40 billion in 1975 to well over $300 billion by 1990, while bond lending rose almost tenfold, from $19 billion to over $170 billion during the same period.[8] Banks have placed branches worldwide, and many now accumulate the bulk of their earnings outside their home country. By 1990, London was host to more than 500 foreign banks, which held more than 87 percent of the international assets booked in that city.[9] In addition, the capitalization of foreign stock exchanges grew dramatically during this decade and a half, with major markets emerging in Tokyo, London, Paris, and Frankfurt; in 1992, the United States accounted for only 35 percent of all stock market capitalization.[10]

As international financial markets spread and deepened, money went speeding from one place to another in search of higher returns. With the liberalization of capital flows, these transfers of funds became virtually unregulated. They were creatures of investors and the private sector, and they responded solely to the profit motive. Allen Myerson of the *New York Times* emphasized this point when he asserted that "the world's currency markets . . . are no longer governed by central bankers in Washington and Bonn, but by traders and investors in Tokyo, London and New York."[11]

The technological processes that spawned these markets and sustained their operations were also, apparently, beyond state control (although, as Janice Thomson and Stephen Krasner have emphasized, technological change itself has been consistently encouraged by capitalist states).[12] In many accounts of financial globalization, pride of place has been given to the "technological revolution," which made the growing sophistication of the marketplace a function of bringing to the banking sector the latest in information technology, including telecommunications and computers.[13] According to one scholar, "One of the basic forces behind recent global financial evolution is technological change. Underlying the revolution in global finance is a revolution in communications and information processing which if anything may accelerate over time."[14] This technological sea change, combined with the fact that "banks and non-banks have become considerably more sophisticated" in their operations, has allegedly promoted and encouraged the globalization trend.[15] Indeed, according to Professor Michael Dertouzos of MIT, "There are so many [computer] networks and subnetworks . . . It could mean that there is no longer any meaning to international boundaries."[16]

This combination of increasing interdependence, expansion of the multinational corporation, and technological change—in short, the globalization of the world economy—poses a major challenge not just to public officials, but also to students of international relations. It suggests that traditional approaches to analyzing world politics, with their focus on "power," "interests," and the "state," are missing a large chunk of contemporary reality, and must be revised or, perhaps, tossed into the dustbin of history along with many other theoretical relics. If the state is losing control of its economic borders, and if firms are losing their national identity, then maybe we do need, as John Gerard Ruggie has asserted, a "postmodern" vocabulary for describing the international system.[17]

One way of countering this assertion would be to deny the fact of globalization, or to minimize its importance. After all, as Thomson and Krasner remind us, "challenges to state-centric paradigms are nothing new in the study of international affairs." They demonstrate that the international *microeconomic* changes of the postwar world have been deeply embedded in political *macroprocesses*.[18] Regarding the global economy, to the extent that international integration has occurred (and by some measures the level of interdependence today among the major industrial nations is *lower* than it was at the turn of the twentieth century), it has been a consequence of political decisions taken by the United States and other industrial powers at the end of World War II. As evidence of this fact, Thomson and Krasner contrast the relative degree of integration of the communist and noncommunist worlds during the postwar years; clearly, the level of integration in terms of trade and investment was much higher in the latter case.

My approach, however, is somewhat different from those just described. Unlike Thomson and Krasner, I take seriously the challenges that changes in the international economy have posed for nation-states; unlike Ruggie, I believe our vocabulary for dealing with those challenges, and with the state response to them, is perfectly adequate. To be sure, I accept the proposition that states have created the political conditions which have made globalization possible. But having said that, I would also agree that the development of a global economy has had unintended consequences for those who promoted it, creating a fresh set of problems that could not have been accurately predicted by policymakers.[19] Furthermore, even in those cases where the problems associated with increasing interdependence could have been accurately predicted (for example, when the signing of a free trade agreement leads to the closure of a domestic industry), policymakers must still respond to that economic change by making the case that the societal benefits will outweigh the particular costs. In short, changes are always occurring in the international system, and states and their societies must adapt to them if they are to survive and prosper.

This book is about the state response to the globalization of finance, with a focus on the regulatory response to international banking. States do not trust the financial marketplace to produce outcomes that are always in their interests, and, as we will see throughout this book, multinational banks still depend on the state to gain market access and to "level the playing field" of international competition. Globalization may tax the creative powers of public officials as they engage in policy development, but it has not rendered the state irrelevant.[20]

For nation-states, financial globalization has complicated the formulation of both economic and foreign policy; indeed, it has largely eradicated the distinction between the two. First, on the economic side, public officials have discovered that it has become increasingly costly to defend economic policies against market pressures, given the unimpeded flow of international financial transactions. Such policies are immediately translated by foreign exchange traders into currency valuations, and consequently result in a money flight into or out of the country. Several European states—notably Great Britain—were reminded of this lesson during the summer and autumn of 1992, when the pound sterling was battered by currency markets and ultimately forced to leave the European Community's Exchange Rate Mechanism (ERM). These developments, in turn, created severe tensions within the Community, especially between Germany and Britain.[21]

Second, domestic financial systems can no longer be sheltered against the collapse of international banks or foreign stock exchanges, as is graphically illustrated by the developing-world debt crisis of the 1980s, and by the October 1987 stock market crash that began in New York and then quickly spread overseas. Wall Street economist Henry Kaufman has observed that the major disruptions to financial markets "have come repeatedly on the international side in the past 20 years."[22] In the regulatory arena, states have found that they can achieve their domestic objective of maintaining a safe and sound financial system only through information sharing and policy coordination with other countries—that is, through international cooperation.

Third, economic globalization intensifies competition among nation-states. As we have seen in recent years, a growing number of sectors throughout the industrial world have appealed to the state for assistance in coping with competitive pressures. States have responded to these calls for help in a variety of ways. Sometimes, industrial policies have been adopted; at other times, protectionism has been used. In still other cases, states have done little to help their domestic firms, allowing the principle of comparative advantage to decide the issue. In this book, I seek to explain why states have responded to the demand by financial institutions that a level playing field be created for international competition; the issue is developed in detail in the concluding section of the chapter.

Globalization also poses political challenges to states, especially in terms of their control over transnational, private sector actors. In the "neo-mercantilist" (and, indeed, Marxist) literature on the topic, multinational corporations have been traditionally viewed as extensions of the state; foreign direct investment became, to paraphrase Clausewitz, state policy by other means. In the words of a leading member of the neo-mercantilist school, Robert Gilpin, "American corporate and political leaders have in general believed that the foreign expansion of American corporations serves important national interests of the United States. American policies have encouraged corporate expansion abroad and have tended to protect them."[23] Gilpin notes that U.S. financial institutions have played an important role in this process of economic globalization, providing capital and loans not only to American-based multinational corporations, but also to the governments and enterprises of friends and allies.

In recent years, however, some analysts have questioned this neo-mercantilist perspective; ironically, Gilpin is among those who have raised a set of troubling questions about the long-term effects of foreign direct investment on American economic and political interests. As the pool of technology has spread around the world, the capabilities of other states relative to that of the United States has increased. Over time, America has lost many of the manufacturing industries that made it a great power, and as we face the millennium even its service industries are threatened by foreign competition. Owing to these trends, "the United States is moving to reverse the flow of global investment in the direction of greater investment in the United States itself."[24] American policies once served to promote globalization, but now they are being fashioned as a consequence of that phenomenon.

Concomitantly, the ability of states to use multinational corporations for the promotion of national interests has allegedly eroded. With these enterprises standing at the hub of the world's trade and investment networks, they have become less responsive to their national authorities, and may no longer possess a national identity at all. Robert Reich brilliantly captured this insight with his question, "Who is US?"[25] Reich asserted that large corporations take a global—as opposed to national—view in searching for markets, employees, and new technology, and as a result their national identity no longer matters to them. As proof of this statement, he cited a number of specific cases—including IBM, where foreigners make up 40 percent of total employment, and Du Pont, where "180 Japanese scientists" are working in Yokohama to develop "new materials and technologies." Reich pushed this argument to its limit, asserting that ownership and control over multinational corporations have lost importance, and that "American-owned corporations . . . have no special relationship with Americans."[26]

How have the industrial states responded to the challenges posed by financial globalization? They have done so, I argue, by promoting *interna-*

tional cooperation based on home country control.[27] As noted above, states that wish to enjoy the benefits of an open economy while shielding their national financial institutions from systemic pressures have found it necessary to develop an array of cooperative arrangements. These have included, since 1974, the founding of a bank supervisors' committee by the Group of Ten (G-10) countries; the convening of annual meetings and "summer schools" of bank regulators; and the articulation of internationally accepted principles and rules of banking supervision.[28] The net effect of international cooperation among banking regulators has been to promote policy convergence, including in some cases (notably bank capital) the development of uniform standards that all international banks must meet. Nonetheless, international cooperation remains far from complete, and tensions among states with respect to banking supervision remain; more on this in the following pages.

International cooperation among bank supervisors rests on the bedrock of home country control. "Home country control" refers to a model of governance in which the responsibility for defining national financial institutions (that is, for determining "who is us?") and regulating them is placed on the state. Under home country supervision, states look to one another, as opposed to some supranational or multilateral entity, to legislate and enforce any agreements that have been collectively reached. (In the European Community the concept is far more expansive, involving *mutual recognition* by each member state of the others' home country regulations; this issue is developed separately in Chapter 6.) As a result, the linkages between states and their national banks have not been broken by globalization, and in some respects they have even been strengthened.

The remainder of this chapter is devoted to unpacking the concept of international cooperation based on home country control, and showing how it applies to the specific case at hand. In the following section, I provide an overview of my argument. After that, I describe in greater detail the rationale for government regulation of banking. In the concluding section, I discuss the role of governments in promoting national competitiveness. Overall, I suggest that the "formula" of international cooperation based on home country control has been developed by public officials as a way of solving their globalization problem; but, as I will show, that solution remains incomplete.

The Politics of Home Country Control

This study is concerned with the regulatory actions that states have taken to cope with the consequences of financial globalization. In explaining state policies, I adopt a two-level approach, and argue that public officials face both systemic and domestic constraints as they shape foreign policy; that is, decisionmakers must confront both other states and their own societies during the policy process.[29] Systemic constraints are imposed by the relative position of the state in the international system, and small states are generally less capable of influencing international outcomes than great powers. In the case of banking supervision, powerful states are those, like Britain, Germany, Japan, and the United States, which possess large and dynamic financial markets. Their power resources include the ability to provide international lender-of-last-resort services, to grant market access to financial institutions, or, alternatively, to threaten market closure. To be sure, as the monopoly supplier of the world's reserve currency, and as home to the world's largest economy, the United States has held a unique position as "crisis manager" of the international financial system, giving it a singular voice in setting the global agenda and advancing its preferences. But the United States has not been alone in this respect. Owing to London's prominence as a global financial center, Great Britain has also played an enormous role in shaping international cooperation among banking supervisors, and several of the most important developments to date, such as the formation of the Basle Committee of Bank Supervisors, were British initiatives.

But there are limits to the exercise of even American or British power in the banking issue-area. Some limits are imposed by other states like Japan and Germany, but others are set by societal actors, and any account of national policymaking in the world economy would be incomplete without reference to domestic politics.[30] In conceptualizing domestic politics with respect to banking supervision, I adopt an "institutionalist" approach, and argue that the ability of societal actors, like banks, to influence public policy depends in large measure upon the formal and informal institutional networks that bind them to the central authorities.[31] An institutionalist perspective reveals that banks are uniquely situated in this respect, since they are "privileged" actors in the domestic political economy, given their roles and responsibilities in money creation, the granting of credit, and the harboring of household savings. Banks are able to draw on a set of formal, institutional linkages to the state in voicing their concerns and policy preferences (although it should be noted that financial actors do not always speak with one voice), since every state possesses regulatory structures that link banks with supervisory and monetary authorities. In the United States, for example, representatives of commercial banks serve among the directors of the Federal Reserve Banks in each district, giving them a voice in both monetary and regulatory policies. Raymond Vernon has labeled the institutional relationship that links government with privileged business enterprise one of "constrained capture."[32]

As Vernon's phrase suggests, it has long been recognized that regulators respond to the industries they supervise. Indeed, the traditional view in economic theory is that the regulators have, ironically, been captured by their industry. In George Stigler's famous phrase, "regulation is acquired by the industry and is designed and operated primarily for its benefit."[33]

Subsequent analysis has suggested that the story is more complicated than that. According to Sam Peltzman, a colleague of Stigler's at the University of Chicago, regulators are bureaucrats who attempt to resolve conflicting public and private sector interests in such a way as to maintain and enhance their positional power within the domestic political structure.[34] Central bankers, for example, are concerned with maintaining a safe and sound financial system, but they have also been forced by societal actors to accept policies, such as prohibitions on interstate banking, that appear to be at odds with that objective. The success of bank supervisors in maintaining or enhancing their positional power will be a function of their ability to solve complex regulatory problems, and judging from the relative growth of central bank authority in the field of financial regulation over the past two decades, we can conclude that these bureaucrats have, indeed, been successful.[35]

The external and domestic constraints that act upon public officials are not static, but change over time. In the literature of international relations, however, we have few works that analyze how state actors adapt to these changes.[36] From this perspective, globalization may be seen as just the latest of many challenges that the nation-state has faced, and an enduring puzzle concerns how and why the state has survived as a form of social organization. As Samuel Huntington wrote in 1973 in one of the classic articles on the phenomenon of transnationalism, "Predictions of the death of the nation-state are premature. They overlook the ability of human beings and human institutions to respond to challenges and to adapt themselves to changed environments. They seem to be based on a zero-sum assumption about power and sovereignty: that a growth in the power of transnational organizations must be accompanied by a decrease in the power of nation-states. This, however, need not be the case."[37]

Strong support for this analysis is found in the example of international banking. Specifically, I argue that states have continued to adjust to changes in the global economy over the past twenty years, largely by adjusting the terms of cooperation among them. As I will show, during the 1970s and 1980s the United States acted as the "hegemonic" leader of the international financial system, providing lender-of-last-resort and other managerial services in times of crisis, especially during the developing-world debt meltdown. By the late 1980s, however, the relative position of the United States in international finance had declined, and its banks had become less competitive. Domestic actors were no longer willing to pay all the costs associated with crisis management, and the U.S. Congress called upon American bank supervisors to develop a new "burden-sharing" formula with the other industrial states for propping up the weakened financial system.[38]

This history supports Robert Keohane's contention that international institutions and the principles they embody—in short, international cooperation—can facilitate states' adaptation to change in the international economy.[39] They are able to do so for what I call "cognitive" and "normative" reasons. First, in terms of their cognitive contribution, international institutions, such as the Basle Committee of Bank Supervisors and the International Monetary Fund, can help states adapt to environmental uncertainty through the development of consensual knowledge about particular issue-areas like banking, through the exchange of information among member states, and through the sharing of policy ideas. As a result of these activities, member states can increase market transparency and reduce uncertainty about market outcomes for public and private sector actors alike.

These cognitive contributions, it should be emphasized, are not merely academic but may also contribute to the normative task of developing "best supervisory practices" for complex sectors like banking. Furthermore, as such practices spread globally among bank regulators, international policy converges. This has been the case with bank capital adequacy, in which the United States ultimately adopted a British regulatory idea (which the British had developed after consultations with other Basle Committee members). In sum, institutions can help states define the rules of the game for sectors like banking by providing a setting in which policy ideas can be exchanged and debated, and best supervisory practices developed.

One common objection to international agreements is that they are difficult to enforce, since states may be tempted to cheat. But should a set of international standards be articulated, enforcement may evolve through the marketplace, without further government intervention; this point, I might note, has been little remarked in the academic literature on cooperation. For example, the Basle Accord's standard for bank capital adequacy gives market watchers such as debt-rating agencies a single measure of capital adequacy, and banks that wish to win high ratings for their debt issues will respond accordingly.[40] Similarly, once the International Monetary Fund (IMF) establishes an economic program for a given country, analysts in the private sector can examine the country's performance and determine whether or not it is achieving its targets.[41]

But despite these contributions to cooperation, there are limits to the effectiveness of international institutions, especially during periods of crisis. First, even if states shared a common interest in maintaining a safe and sound international financial system, differing views may exist regarding how that goal is best achieved. Certainly, as we noted above, cooperation among supervisors is likely to promote policy convergence, especially when coupled with the development of knowledge about financial markets.[42] But a complete harmony of views is unlikely to prevail in a world of nation-states, each with its own unique banking, legal, and accounting systems. A divergence in views over how to supervise international banking remains, for example, between the United States and the European Community, and this could become a growing source of tension in the future; this issue is treated in some detail in Chapters 6 and 7.

Second, even when states agree about policy means and ends, they rarely agree about the distribution of costs associated with international agreements. Indeed, no universal burden-sharing formula has ever been derived for international organizations.[43] In the absence of a dominant power that is able and willing to foot the bill for maintaining a safe and sound financial system, states will undoubtedly argue about how the burdens of system maintenance should be shared.

These problems of collective agreement and burden sharing are likely to become especially acute during periods of crisis.[44] At these times, decisive action is often needed to diffuse an eroding situation, and prolonged debates over how and when to respond may have grave consequences for international stability.[45] There was a marked difference, for example, between how the allies responded to the energy crises of the 1940s and 1950s, when the United States provided Europe with emergency shipments of coal and oil, and how they responded in the 1970s, when it could not. During the earlier period, market stability was maintained, but during the oil shocks of 1973–74 and 1978–79 panic ensued, despite the existence of an International Energy Agency, whose stated mission was in part to manage energy shortages.[46] In sum, institutions can contribute in important ways to international cooperation and policy convergence, but their record as crisis managers has been poor.[47]

One possible solution to the problems of international cooperation would be to develop *supranational institutions*. But the evolution of cooperation among banking supervisors has not yet reached the supranational plane, even in the European Community; surprisingly, even the European Central Bank has been given only limited regulatory powers by its framers.[48] Supranational cooperation would require that supervisors hand over their responsibilities to a global agency, which makes some intuitive sense in a world of global finance. Given that states still wish to maintain some control over their domestic financial firms in order to pursue national interests, however, supranational solutions lose their attraction; the quotation from Keynes that opens this chapter is suggestive of the policymakers' nationalistic view.

Far from developing supranational institutions to supervise global finance, national banking regulators instead have acted to strengthen home country control. It seems counterintuitive that home country control would be maintained, much less strengthened, in a world of global finance, but a deeper understanding of the issue reveals its logic. First, as finance has globalized, states have seen an increasing number of foreign banks settle on their territory. This forces the national authorities to ask whether or not they wish to provide discount window and lender-of-last-resort services to these foreign banks. In those cases where banking operations are being conducted out of branch offices, with the headquarters clearly based overseas, the answer is no: they would usually prefer that the banks' own national supervisors provide emergency assistance. The single most important reason for home country control is found in the lender-of-last-resort function.

Second, home country control forces states to take responsibility for the enforcement of those regulatory standards adopted domestically or in international forums. In the absence of a supranational central bank or regulatory agency with enforcement powers, only state authorities can punish banks for improper behavior and force them to conform to domestic and international norms. By demanding home country control of one another, states are seeking to ensure that regulatory agreements are enforced. The tacit threat that states are making to one another is that, in the absence of such enforcement, the national banks of that country will not be permitted to operate overseas. As a corollary, as the regulatory practices of home countries begin to converge, harmonization will develop from the "bottom up" rather than the "top down." This appears to be the hope that officials of the European Community have for the continent, as we will see in Chapter 6.

Third, to the extent that central authorities seek to use national firms for the advancement of broad domestic and foreign policy interests, they will wish to maintain control over these institutions. Money is a critical power resource in both domestic and international politics, and it is usually intermediated by financial institutions. Control over the allocation of credit, in the form of targeted loans or loan guarantee programs, for example, is an important tool of "economic statecraft."[49] The use of banks to advance the state's foreign policy objectives is clearly demonstrated in the chapters of this book that deal with petrodollar recycling and the debt crisis.

From the perspective of banks and other societal actors, home country supervision also has some advantages, especially when it is combined with international cooperation which leads to the establishment of certain common standards. Only the state can defend corporate interests in international negotiations over trade, investment, and market access.[50] Agreements over such things as the opening of banking establishments and the right to sell insurance are not decided by corporate actors; they are determined by diplomats and bureaucrats. Furthermore, given complaints in recent years, especially within western Europe, over the "democratic deficit" that occurs when international institutions assume the tasks once reserved for national governments, home country control ensures that domestic political actors will continue to have a voice in policy deliberations; in this regard home country control may be linked to the political demand for "subsidiarity," or to the fact that decisionmaking may devolve to the lowest possible political level.[51]

These comments should help us understand why the alternative regulatory paradigm of *host country control* has also been rejected by supervisors as a response to globalization. Under host country control, states treat each operating unit of a multinational as an independent subsidiary. In the case of banking, it means that foreign banks in a host marketplace are separate entities whose activities are monitored by local authorities. But this is not a satisfactory solution, for the reasons already mentioned. States do not wish to provide lender-of-last-resort services to foreign banks; regulators have found that it is impossible to analyze a subsidiary's condition simply by examining the local books, given the complex ties that normally exist with the headquarters (thus the demand by supervisors for consolidated accounting of banks, which presumes one regulator who has an overall picture of the institution); and public officials still wish to exercise some control over the foreign operations of their banks. From the perspective of the multinationals, host country control is also problematic: it means that they must adapt to the separate regulations of each country in which they do business, creating operating inefficiencies. To be sure, all states, in their role as hosts, have reserved at least residual authority for regulating the foreign firms on their soil (and some, like the United States, much more authority than that), but in the case of banking we find that they look first to the home country to provide adequate supervision.

Yet home country supervision also leaves critical problems of financial governance unresolved, and these may be called the problems of *control, capability,* and *competitiveness*. First, despite the emphasis placed on home country supervision, countries continue to disagree over the appropriate division of responsibility between home and host states when it comes to regulating international business. In the European Community, recent banking legislation has diminished the authority of the host; in the United States, especially following the BCCI scandal, the opposite has occurred. This conflict over where the dividing line should be drawn between home and host countries continues to animate international banking negotiations, as it has troubled all efforts to regulate multinational business.[52]

Second, home country control does not address the fact that different states have differing capabilities when it comes to international banking regulation: some states are more capable than others. Greece and Luxembourg have fewer resources than France and Great Britain when it comes to regulating complex financial institutions, and if this is the case it suggests that not all home countries will be regarded with equal confidence. In the European Community particularly, the differing capabilities of the member states may cause problems for regulators in host countries. Finally, home country supervision has competitive consequences for national firms that operate in the global economy. If state A imposes a set of unilateral regulations on its national firms, the less regulated firms in state B may gain a competitive advantage. One implication of this development is that firms have called upon state actors to level the playing field in the regulatory arena. This, in turn, has reinforced the need for international cooperation among banking supervisors. Still, in the absence of complete harmonization, differing regulations will continue to have competitive effects.

To summarize, the development of international cooperation and the strengthening of home country control exemplify the adaptations made by states in recent years to financial globalization. That response, however, is incomplete, since continuing differences in national and regional approaches to regulation, coupled with the limits of cooperation, suggest that this framework would prove incapable of withstanding a systemic shock on its own; as we will see, it has even proved incapable of coping with lesser scandals of the type posed by deviant financial institutions like the Banco Ambrosiano and the Bank of Credit and Commerce International. International cooperation based on home country control has certainly promoted policy convergence and contributed to the overall stability of financial markets, but my analysis also supports Charles Kindleberger's assertion that the international financial system requires a reliable lender of last resort during times of crisis.[53]

Governments and Banking Regulation

In some respects it is ironic that banking is characterized as a global industry, for no sector of the economy is so heavily regulated by domestic authorities. Banks are told how much capital they must hold, where they can operate, what products they can sell, and how much they can lend to any one firm. While regulations vary from one country to the next, some "essential" regulations, such as those on minimal capital levels, apply almost everywhere.

Two fundamental reasons have traditionally been given for banking regulation: first, that it is difficult for depositors to have sufficient information to gauge the safety of their bank; and second, that banking failures create negative externalities by reducing the money supply. A concomitant of each is that bank failures are prone to contagion: when one bank fails, a domino-like failure may ensue. While the contagion effect is apparently eroding in the presence of deposit insurance at the domestic level in most countries, it remains a concern of regulators in international wholesale markets.

According to a Federal Reserve publication, "the most basic reason for regulation of banking is depositor protection."[54] Individuals entrust banks with their savings, and it would be costly and time consuming for them to assess the quality of their financial institution; there are economies of scale and scope associated with information gathering and assessment. In essence, a depositor is a creditor of the bank—he or she has loaned money to the institution, but without full knowledge of the risks associated with the transaction. In few other business dealings do ordinary customers assume this role. Government regulations thus provide a protective wall between the consumer and his or her bank.

The second reason for banking regulation has to do with the role of banks in the monetary system. In modern industrial economies, banks are the major issuers of money. When banks fail, the money supply contracts. In short, banks provide broad social benefits, and when they fail the social costs of a shutdown outweigh the private costs.

The international interdependence of the payments system compounds this "externalities" problem, since a banking failure in one country could have severe repercussions for banks in another country. If a bank in country A has interbank loans outstanding to a bank in country B and the former bank fails, this could cause liquidity or even solvency problems for the latter, depending upon the level of exposure. Supervisors remain fearful that such failures could spread beyond their control.

Furthermore, as Federal Reserve Board chairman Alan Greenspan has pointed out, the financial marketplace is now crowded with new instruments of every kind, with uncertain risk profiles. Banks are filled with contingent liabilities that they could not possibly fund if a substantial number of them came due at the same time. In Greenspan's words, "A failure by one of these institutions to perform on its contractual obligations could impose serious losses on customers and could result in serious systemic problems."[55]

This fear of a global banking crisis has afflicted bank regulators since the Great Depression, and its influence on them cannot be exaggerated. During the 1930s, "more than one-fifth of the commercial banks in the United States suspended operations." In Europe, "major bank failures or payments moratoriums were common. Withdrawals of bank loans and deposits played a major role in the balance of payments crises of the period, particularly in Central and Eastern Europe." Overall, "the Great Depression of the 1930s could be defined in terms of financial collapse."[56]

To be sure, since the 1930s, central bankers have developed a set of regulatory safety nets whose purpose is to maintain the safety and soundness of individual banks and, when necessary, "to keep financial systems functioning in the face of economic shocks." These include (1) prudential measures to maintain bank solvency; (2) prudential measures to protect bank liquidity; (3) official assurances such as deposit insurance to convince depositors that their deposits are safe, even with troubled institutions; (4) orderly resolution of the problems of failing banks; and (5), in the last resort, official provision of liquidity to permit solvent institutions to keep functioning in the face of a loss of depositor confidence.[57]

A prominent question, however, is: Who provides the safety nets in international markets? In his classic work on the Great Depression, Charles Kindleberger argued that the financial crisis spread because no single central bank was willing to act as lender of last resort; in short, there was no hegemonic power which dominated the system and took a position of leadership in crisis management.[58] The history of the Great Depression may have been learned *domestically* by central banks; but has it been learned *internationally?*

In this book I argue that international leadership has been provided, mainly by the United States; the nature of that leadership, however, has changed over time as America has adapted to its relative decline in the financial marketplace. For most of the postwar period, Washington acted as a hegemonic leader, providing lender-of-last-resort services during periods of financial crisis. A parsimonious reason the 1970s and 1980s did not duplicate the 1920s and 1930s is found largely in the hegemonic role played by the United States. In recent years, however, the United States has sought to develop a burden-sharing formula in which the costs of financial system maintenance would be shared among its major trading partners; more on this below.

The need for a lender of last resort (LLR) in international financial markets has not been sufficiently appreciated by those who claim that finance has gone global and now exists on some supranational plane. But the growing international transactions of financial institutions did nothing to lessen the concern of banking supervisors about the safety and soundness of the payments system; perversely, some argued that systemic risks had *increased* despite the diversification of banking assets and liabilities.[59] Some of these risks were created by macroeconomic policy in the 1970s and 1980s, while others were a function of changes in banking practices over this period.

To begin with, international finance took off in the 1970s, which is hardly a coincidence. Unlike previous postwar decades, the 1970s were characterized by a unique combination of inflation, floating and erratic exchange rates, and volatile interest rates. The major commercial banks in the industrial countries, long accustomed to a benign macroeconomic environment, suddenly found it necessary to become more active in asset and liability management.

In an effort to protect both their customers and their own institutions in the face of systemic shocks, bankers responded by promoting three developments in financial markets. These were *globalization, innovation* of financial practices and instruments, and *speculation*. Accompanying and contributing to these developments was the *deregulation* of financial markets across the Group of Ten (G-10) countries and the European Community (EC). Deregulation, it should be emphasized, is no less an act of state policy than regulation. Globalization has created challenges for states, but the major powers have also viewed it as being in their national interest.[60]

The global spread of financial activity meant that banks increasingly engaged in international transactions on both the asset and liability sides of the balance sheet. By the early 1980s, American money center and super-regional banks had more than 800 branches overseas—up from 100 in the 1950s—and they were deriving anywhere from 30 to 60 percent of their profits from international operations.[61] At the same time, an increasing amount of deposit taking and lending was occurring offshore, in the Euromarkets. The Eurocurrency market increased from $57 billion in 1970 to $575 billion a decade later, fueled in large part by petrodollar deposits.[62] As a dense network of relations evolved within and among banks, the distinction between domestic and international finance became blurred, with net savers in one country becoming increasingly linked to net borrowers in another.

To be sure, the globalization of finance posed a multitude of new problems for bank supervisors, who had traditionally focused on the domestic marketplace; many of these problems could not be foreseen in the early 1970s. German supervisors, for example, were constrained by law from collecting information on the international operations of their financial institutions. Globalization also meant that the liquidity or solvency problems of a foreign bank or the foreign branch of a domestic bank could have serious repercussions in domestic markets.

As will be seen in the following chapters, this was borne out by the global ramifications of the failures of the Herstatt Bank in Germany, the Franklin National Bank in New York, and the British-Israel Bank in London, all in 1974, as well as the Banco Ambrosiano collapse of 1982. These failures led to the formation of a G-10 committee on banking regulations and supervisory practices, now known as the Basle Committee. This committee has been at the center of efforts to develop a new regime for financial supervision, as amply demonstrated by its promulgation of the Basle Accord on capital adequacy in 1987.

The second trend, innovation, or financial engineering, was evident in the introduction of new practices and instruments throughout the 1970s and early 1980s. Among these innovations, two of the most prominent have been securitization, in which traditional bank assets such as mortgages are transformed into marketable instruments, and the growing use of contingent liabilities or off-balance-sheet times. These include performance bonds (which ensure that firms, such as construction companies, will perform their contractual obligations to customers or the bank will pay the penalty), letters of credit, and various "derivatives" such as currency and interest rate swaps. By the late 1980s, the contingent liabilities of major banks constituted a large multiple of shareholders' equity, far outstripping third-world debt exposures. Furthermore, the growing importance of securitization meant that the traditional business of banks—

lending money—was decreasing in importance, leading them into new—and perhaps riskier—businesses.[63]

The third trend was the increasing importance of speculation in short-term financial markets as a source of bank profits. Given the macroeconomic instability of the 1970s, activities such as foreign exchange trading became increasingly risky, for currency values could swing sharply on a daily basis. This volatility offered the promise of large profits for banks that bet correctly on currency movements but the certainty of heavy losses for banks that did not.

Accompanying and contributing to these changes in capital markets was the widespread liberalization of capital flows and deregulation of commercial banking. During the 1970s and 1980s, many of the G-10 countries lifted controls on interest rates and widened the permissible scope for bank activities. This process opened up new opportunities for commercial banks, but it also exposed inexperienced bankers to fresh dangers.

On top of these changes were shifts in bank balance sheets which made the banks less able to withstand the systemic shocks that they now faced. Specifically, bank capital ratios dropped during this period to postwar lows, while claims against sovereign borrowers increased. It appeared that banks found the risk of loss on such loans to be minimal. When crises came, therefore, banks lacked the capital to maintain their solvency.

With globalization, banks also became more exposed to liquidity crises. The newfound ability of banks to borrow money in one currency and lend in another opened fresh arbitrage possibilities, but additional risks as well. A bank that suddenly had to meet a large demand in a particular currency could find itself in a liquidity crunch if the necessary funds were unavailable.[64]

All these changes led central bankers and bank regulators to question whether the new environment that they had helped to bring about in the 1970s and 1980s resulted in a more secure international payments system. If anyone had doubts before the eruption of the debt crisis in 1982, by that time it was painfully obvious that the answer was no. Unlike domestic financial systems, which were regulated according to long-established rules and procedures and which, if all else failed, had the benefit of a lender of last resort in the event of a banking crisis, the international payments system had nothing of the sort. Rules and procedures had to be established, and a lender (or lenders) of last resort had to be identified.

Yet in providing such a service, an international lender of last resort would create a massive "moral hazard" problem. Already on the domestic level, bank supervisors have seen how the lender of last resort and deposit insurance have combined to encourage imprudent behavior on the part of some financial executives; witness the savings and loan crisis in the United States. If bank depositors were more like shareholders, they would try to prevent management from engaging in careless banking practices. Regulators have argued, however, that depositors lack the information necessary to monitor either the prudence of bank management or the overall quality of the bank's portfolio. Naturally, the information problem is compounded in a global economy, in which depositors from country A may place their savings in a bank with operations in countries B, C, and D; indeed, they may do all their banking with the branch office of an international bank whose headquarters are in country E. As information problems grow, the rationale for financial regulation increases.

No country, however—not even the United States—wants to serve as lender of last resort for the entire international financial system. Thus, American policy has sought to shift the terms of international cooperation from hegemonic *crisis management* to *crisis prevention* based on home country control. Crisis prevention and crisis management differ in several fundamental respects. First, crisis prevention does not rely on one single state to serve as lender of last resort for the financial system; instead, it requires information about systemic risks and recommendations for maintenance of the system. Second, it shifts some of the costs of excessive risk taking from the public sector to the banks. In a crisis prevention system, emphasis is placed on monitoring financial institutions and ensuring that they have sufficient capital and internal controls to weather financial difficulties. Third, it demands that states refrain from competitive deregulation. Under hegemonic crisis management, with an international lender of last resort, states may be tempted to "free ride" on the guarantor and deregulate in order to capture financial business. When crisis prevention is the focus, in contrast, home country control of national financial institutions, adequate regulations, and a level playing field must be established. The United States has, of course, served as crisis manager—notably during the debt crisis—but in the intervening years it has sought to promote burden sharing among the industrial powers by developing international regulations which would restore public confidence in the world's banking system, and in turn reduce the risks of a global crisis.

National Regulations and International Competition

This burden-sharing exercise has been both encouraged and made more complicated by growing concerns over the competitiveness of national financial institutions; this concern mirrors a longer-standing worry among the advanced countries on the industrial side. Indeed, since the mid-1970s, economic debates in the United States and western Europe have largely centered around the theme of international competitiveness. As one traditional sector after another fell victim to foreign manufacturers, firms have turned to their governments "for support and protection."[65] In more recent years, service industries have also been under pressure from foreign competitors, and they, too, have sought "support and protection" in a number of ways. Thus, not only are contemporary bank regulators paid to worry about safety and soundness, but they are expected to worry about competitiveness as well.

In the words of a leading student, Laura Tyson, who has served as chairperson of the Council of Economic Advisers, competitiveness "has become a buzzword."[66] As a buzzword, it means all things to all people, and precise definitions of the term are difficult to find. According to economist C. Fred Bergsten, competitiveness is "largely synonymous with productivity."[67] This leads one to wonder why that more precise term isn't used with greater frequency, especially when contrasted with the vague definition employed by a U.S. presidential commission. The commission has referred to competitiveness as "the degree to which a nation, under free and fair market conditions, produces goods and services that meet the test of international markets while simultaneously maintaining and expanding the real incomes of its citizens."[68] Behind this vapid-sounding phrase are two important observations: first, competitiveness has to do with market access—the ability of national firms to sell their products in domestic and foreign markets; second, countries that are competitive in the global economy need not engage in currency depreciation and suffer, as a consequence, the erosion of real incomes.[69]

In recent years a number of studies have pointed to the declining competitiveness of U.S. financial institutions. According to a Cato Institute study, "The U.S. banking industry has seen better days . . . At a time when European and Japanese banks are emphasizing expanding international services, U.S. banks are being forced to retrench."[70] Noted financial economist David Hale writes: "The United States may soon face the same market erosion in financial services that has afflicted its producers of machine tools, automobiles, and semiconductors. There is already ample evidence of a Japanese challenge in financial services."[71] A recent report by the U.S. Congress asserts that "the relative competitive position of U.S. banks has deteriorated significantly . . . The relative prominence of U.S. banks in both foreign and domestic markets has diminished."[72] And taking note of congressional and broader public concerns about the safety and soundness of the financial system, the American Banking Association has written that "public attention has recently focused on the decreasing international competitiveness of U.S. financial institutions."[73]

The data would seem to support these assertions. Whereas in 1983 the United States was home to three of the world's twenty largest commercial banks, today it is home to none of the top twenty (see Table 1.1), and the

Table 1.1. The world's twenty largest banks, 1991 (by assets, in millions of U.S. dollars).

Rank	Company (country)	Assets	Capital	Net income
1	Dai-Ichi Kangyo Bank (Japan)	480,081	29,902	734
2	Sumitomo Bank (Japan)	458,352	28,460	1,158
3	Sakura Bank (Japan)	453,353	26,344	689
4	Sanwa Bank (Japan)	451,656	29,693	906
5	Fuji Bank (Japan)	447,736	35,023	809
6	Mitsubishi Bank (Japan)	428,418	21,170	819
7	Industrial Bank of Japan (Japan)	325,197	190,273	529
8	Crédit Agricole (France)	307,203	68,211	952
9	Crédit Lyonnais (France)	306,370	32,625	610
10	Deutsche Bank (Germany)	295,114	42,986	913
11	Norinchukin Bank (Japan)	280,550	57,020	369
12	Tokai Bank (Japan)	280,015	14,005	351
13	Sumitomo Trust (Japan)	278,092	7,750	367
14	BNP (France)	275,876	28,269	568
15	HSBC (Hong Kong)	270,117	19,627	637
16	Mitsubishi Trust (Japan)	269,712	8,991	330
17	Barclays (U.K.)	258,146	17,959	452
18	Bank of Tokyo (Japan)	248,943	61,597	393
19	Kyowa (Japan)	245,940	13,747	406
20	Amro Bank (Netherlands)	243,168	29,362	900

Source: Wall Street Journal, 24 September 1992, p. R27. Reprinted by permission of the *Wall Street Journal*, © 1992 Dow Jones and Company, Inc.; all rights reserved worldwide.

largest American bank, Citicorp, is only number twenty-six in terms of assets. Similarly, American investment banks are now exceeded in size by their Japanese counterparts (see Table 1.2).

A comprehensive study by members of the Federal Reserve Bank of New York, however, points to a more nuanced picture of competitiveness. Looking at U.S. financial institutions in terms of four broad categories— size, profitability, productivity, and capitalization—they argue that their sample group of firms "turned in a mixed performance during the mid- to late 1980s, showing strength in some areas but achieving only fair results in others. However, a few U.S. firms exhibited considerable overall

Table 1.2.   The world's twenty largest securities firms, 1991 (by capital, in millions of U.S. dollars).

Rank	Company (country)	Capital	Assets	Net income
1	Nomura Securities (Japan)	17,829	49,005	887
2	Daiwa Securities (Japan)	11,529	38,295	490
3	Salomon (U.S.)	11,097	70,157	507
4	Nikko Securities (Japan)	10,366	26,829	351
5	Yamaichi Securities (Japan)	9,739	31,851	320
6	Merrill Lynch (U.S.)	8,899	59,084	696
7	Goldman Sachs (U.S.)	6,869	46,150	n.a.
8	Dean Witter (U.S.)	6,442	20,698	345
9	Shearson Lehman (U.S.)	5,702	38,757	228
10	Morgan Stanley (U.S.)	5,422	34,988	475
11	Hees International (Canada)	3,992	4,578	154
12	Kokusai Securities (Japan)	2,834	4,881	133
13	Kankaku Securities (Japan)	2,563	5,167	25
14	New Japan Securities (Japan)	2,163	5,515	5
15	Wako Securities (Japan)	1,960	4,086	67
16	CS First Boston (U.S.)	1,912	18,294	186
17	Paine Webber (U.S.)	1,791	17,347	151
18	Bear Stearns (U.S.)	1,754	15,850	143
19	S. G. Warburg (U.K.)	1,746	26,007	153
20	Sanyo Securities (Japan)	1,588	3,671	16

N.a. = not available.

Source: Wall Street Journal, 24 September 1992, p. R27. Reprinted by permission of the *Wall Street Journal,* © 1992 Dow Jones and Company, Inc.; all rights reserved worldwide.

strength and must be counted among the world's leading financial institutions."[74] In 1992, for example, four U.S. banks counted among the world's ten most profitable: Banc One; State Street Bank; Bankers Trust; and Norwest.[75] At the same time, the study admitted that Japanese, Swiss, British, and German banks "were formidable in a few categories."

An important question that arises from all these studies of competitiveness is: So what? Why should the government (as opposed to the firms) be concerned about the competitiveness of the banking sector? Does the state *qua state* have a national interest in the health of its financial firms? Should it act to promote the competitiveness of national banks?

A task force appointed by the U.S. Congress asked these and related questions about competitiveness, and concluded that there were "no definitive answers."[76] Indeed, the task force commented that "some legitimate areas of concern have been identified *by industry observers* [my italics] that should be recognized and assessed by the public and U.S. policymakers." That should come as no surprise; obviously, industry actors will lobby for policies that give them marketplace advantages. The question is whether public officials, in the absence of political pressure, would feel moved to promote financial competitiveness for reasons of state.

In making the argument for state intervention, one would either have to show that foreign firms had some kind of "unfair" advantage in the marketplace, or demonstrate that dependence upon foreign financial institutions is actually or potentially harmful to national security and/or economic well-being. To be sure, many countries have refused to provide American firms with market access on the basis of national treatment—that is, treating American firms like domestic firms—and the promotion of national treatment has been a centerpiece of U.S. international financial policy.[77] Nonetheless, few observers believe that American financial firms have faced the kind of subsidized competition that is commonplace in such industries as electronics.

On the contrary, when comparing the performance of U.S. and foreign financial firms, most analysts have focused on macroeconomic issues. These include the U.S. budget and trade deficits, with their impact on the cost of capital and the value of the dollar, and differences in regulatory systems. It is American macroeconomic policies, not unfair trade practices, that must assume primary responsibility for the decreasing competitiveness of American banks.[78]

Nor would national security rationales be adequate to justify government intervention on behalf of competitiveness. It is difficult to imagine, for example, a situation in which the United States could not finance a war or large-scale mobilization owing to an absence of capital. History suggests, in fact, that countries have often depended heavily upon foreign sources of capital during periods of conflict.[79]

A rationale for intervention based on economic welfare during periods of economic downturns or crisis is perhaps more compelling. The problem here is that, during a "credit crunch," banks tend to allocate capital among their customers; market imperfections are such that markets do not clear at any price. As a result, customers tend to queue up for credit.

What some analysts fear is that, during a crunch, the queue could be determined by governments rather than banks. Foreign industrial firms could be favored in the allocation process, leaving American firms without needed liquidity. Although such a threat seems highly unlikely, a congressional task force has concluded that "the potential cannot be totally disregarded."[80]

Additional concerns arise out of monetary policy. Given the role of banks in the money creation process, a working relationship between commercial banks and the central bank is commonplace throughout the industrial countries. (To be sure, some view this relationship as benign, or helpful to the economy as a whole, while others view it as malign, or a battle between financial, industrial, and agricultural interests in which the latter two are usually the losers.)[81] Control over monetary policy could, it is argued, be lost if a country became overly dependent upon foreign banks.

These "national interest" arguments, however, always provide tempting cover for special interest groups. When industry members call upon the government to act in the cause of international competitiveness, they usually are seeking state support for something that benefits them as a group rather than the nation as a whole. Competitiveness, in many cases, has simply become a euphemism for protectionism.

In sum, the state response to globalization has been shaped by both systemic and societal forces. In a global economy, states will seek to enjoy the benefits of financial interdependence, but they will also be fearful of the havoc that international contagion effects could bring, since a bank failure in one country could create solvency problems for banks in other countries. At the same time, unilateral efforts to regulate financial markets are likely to be opposed by domestic political groups, especially financial institutions, which would be placed at a competitive disadvantage as a result. The challenge for public officials has been to strike a balance between these competing systemic and societal demands, and in so doing they have hit upon the formula of international cooperation based on home country control. In Chapter 8 we will have an opportunity to gauge that formula's success.

2 | The Collapse of Bretton Woods

When no other appealing solutions are evident, "coordination" seems the natural panacea.

—JAMES TOBIN

During the early 1970s, a number of structural changes occurred in the world economy that profoundly altered the manner in which banks conducted their business. In this and the following chapter, two of the most important changes are highlighted: the collapse of the Bretton Woods regime of fixed exchange rates, and the oil crises of 1973–74 and 1978–79. These systemic shocks ushered in an era of economic volatility, to which banks responded by diversifying their assets and liabilities on a global basis, creating new financial instruments (or "financial engineering"), and speculating in financial markets. Bank supervisors, for their part, obliged the banks' efforts at diversification by ushering in an era of sweeping deregulation.

Regulators hoped that the combined actions of governments and firms would lessen the risks that faced the international payments system, but this proved not to be the case. On the contrary, some banks took risks that threatened the stability of the system as a whole, necessitating renewed vigilance on the part of public officials. Indeed, banking supervision in the 1970s would take on an international character in response to the changes in financial markets, as central bank governors from the Group of Ten (G-10) nations created a new bank supervisory committee, based at the Bank for International Settlements (BIS) in Basle, Switzerland.

The end of the Bretton Woods monetary system, coupled with the oil shocks of 1973–74 and 1978–79, placed enormous strains on the international financial system. In the case of exchange rates, the end of Bretton Woods brought unprecedented volatility to currency values. Given the sharp movements in exchange rates, speculators who bet correctly on a currency could make substantial profits; tremendous losses, however, could also be suffered. Two of the great bank failures of the 1970s—those of Germany's Bankhaus Herstatt and New York's Franklin National Bank—were due largely to losses from foreign exchange trading.

Further shocks to the financial system were initiated by the oil crises and price hikes of the 1970s. The oil crises led to the biggest short-term income transfers in history, as consuming countries sent billions of additional dollars to producing states. At the same time, the oil crises created a sharp division between financial "have" and "have-not" states. These financial developments threatened the economic and political stability of almost every nation, including the oil-producing countries themselves, and governments did not trust the international financial markets, acting on their own, to produce outcomes that promoted their domestic and foreign policy interests. This belief, in turn, led governments to play an active role in the financial marketplace.

The pool of dollars that attracted special government attention during the 1970s and early 1980s was that which had been deposited outside the United States by oil-producing countries: the so-called petrodollars. Indeed, the takeoff in international banking is closely associated with the rising level of petrodollar deposits placed in the "offshore" markets for dollars and other foreign currencies, known as the Euromarkets; these markets, which bring foreign borrowers and foreign savers together outside their home market, are described in the following section. The Euromarkets became the single most important source of loans for public and private sector agents from many countries, including those of the developing world. That borrowing, of course, met its end with the explosion of the debt crisis in 1982.

The Origins of the Euromarkets: Alternative Explanations

Before proceeding with our study of how states responded to the crises of the 1970s and 1980s, it will be useful to survey the development of global financial markets during the prior decade, focusing on the so-called Euro-currency markets, or Euromarkets for short. It is an analytical challenge to describe this marketplace, especially in light of the conventional view that sees it as anational and beyond the reach of the nation-state. How do we conceptualize a market that appears to be seamless and shapeless?

Perhaps the best way to proceed is by defining the Euromarkets and suggesting why banks would loan their national currencies offshore. We must then ask why governments would permit such a development. If we find that the Euromarkets are operating against the interests of the great powers, we have a tremendous puzzle to explain.

Simply stated, the Euromarkets are "an organized market for foreign currency deposits."[1] To take the example of dollar deposits, a Eurodollar deposit is no more and no less than dollars deposited in a bank outside the United States. The bank could be the branch of an American financial institution, or it could be a foreign institution which accepts dollar deposits. The source of the dollars could be firms, central banks, or individual investors. On the other side of the transaction, borrowers would include governments, enterprises, or individuals that require access to dollars in order to pay their bills. The major borrowers in the marketplace, however, are generally other banks that require foreign exchange; this is the so-called interbank market.[2]

There are a number of theories that purport to explain the origins and growth of this marketplace, drawn from both economics and political science. Economists have focused on three paradigms: first, that the Euromarkets are an outgrowth of real-sector transactions; second, that they exist for purely financial reasons, with little connection to the real economy; and finally, that they are a product of efforts by firms to escape regulation and taxation.[3] Political scientists, in contrast, focus on the role of governments in creating and supporting these markets.

A prominent explanation for the development of a global financial market is found in the real economy. During the 1960s, U.S. direct investment abroad climbed sharply. As American firms went abroad, their banks followed. In later years, European- and Japanese-based multinationals copied this pattern and increased their own foreign direct investment; in response, Japanese and European banks established global branch networks. Indeed, the "traditional" answer to the question of why banks establish overseas branches is "to serve their domestic customers who have gone abroad, which is sometimes called the gravitational-pull effect."[4] Tables 2.1 and 2.2 provide some relevant data on the American case.

Additional support for this "gravitational-pull effect" is found in recent data on the Euromarkets. If one looks at the "lead managers" of bank loans to foreign corporations, one finds that they are generally of the same nationality as the firm that is the borrower. Thus, even in the offshore Euromarkets, Japanese firms tend to borrow from Japanese banks, German firms borrow from German banks, and French firms borrow from French banks. This suggests that strong national ties remain between banks and their industrial borrowers.[5]

Brookings Institution economist Ralph Bryant, in contrast, emphasizes the second explanation, which derives from the changing nature of financial transactions. Bryant argues that "new developments in communications technology" created "entirely new possibilities for financial transactions."[6] Foreign exchange transactions, for example, could be conducted on a "real-time" basis, providing banks with new opportunities for profit. Simultaneously, new financial instruments were created for sophisticated investors, including both individuals and corporations. By establishing offshore branches, banks "were able to facilitate their collection of funds

Table 2.1. U.S. direct investment abroad, 1960–1972 (in billions of dollars).

Year	Investment outflows
1960	1.7
1961	1.6
1962	1.7
1963	2.0
1964	2.3
1965	3.5
1966	3.7
1967	3.1
1968	3.2
1969	3.3
1970	4.4
1971	4.8
1972	3.3

Source: International Economic Report of the President, March 1973.

Table 2.2. U.S. bank branches in London, 1960–1972.

Year	Number of branches
1960	13
1961	13
1962	14
1963	14
1964	17
1965	21
1966	21
1967	24
1968	32
1969	37
1970	41
1971	45
1972	49

Source: Janet Kelly, *Bankers and Borders* (Cambridge, Mass.: Ballinger, 1977), p. 69. Copyright © 1977 by the Harvard Center for International Affairs; reprinted by permission of HarperCollins Publishers, Inc.

from and their lending of funds to the residents of foreign countries." Bryant provides us, in short, with an explanation grounded in technological determinism.

Still another explanation focuses on the Euromarkets as an escape valve from financial regulations and controls. In this view, firms responded to the needs of their borrowers and depositors by establishing offshore branches that were beyond the legal reach of any nation-state. In these unregulated markets, banks could pursue the type of financial transactions that were either prohibited outright or more costly in their domestic marketplace. In the words of a congressional report, "The motivation underlying the inception of the Eurodollar markets was the desire to avoid regulation, either regulations already in effect or additional restrictions that depositors feared might be imposed."[7]

Examples in support of this view are drawn from developments in Russia, Britain, and the United States. During the 1950s, the Soviet Union feared that its dollar earnings, if deposited in the United States, could be attached in the event of a crisis. As a result, the Russians deposited their dollars either in the European branches of Moscow-based banks (for example, the Narodny Bank in London) or in European banks that would accept the dollar deposits. In this way, Russian dollars could not be frozen by American unilateral actions.

The British added fuel to the Euromarkets in 1957, during a currency crisis that was triggered by balance-of-payments problems. The British government "imposed tight new restrictions on foreign trade financing denominated in pounds sterling. In response, British banks sought to preserve their sizable overseas business by actively soliciting and lending U.S. dollar deposits instead."[8] Benjamin Cohen argues that, "once started, a regular market for foreign currency deposits quickly developed."[9] Indeed, the market grew from nil in the late 1950s to $132 billion by 1973.

The United States further sparked the Euromarkets during the 1960s, the ironic result of programs designed to keep capital at home and reduce upward pressure on the dollar. Specifically, in 1965 the Federal Reserve instituted a "Voluntary Foreign Credit Restraint Program" which curbed borrowing by foreign firms and governments in U.S. markets; at the same time, a "Foreign Direct Investment Program" was announced which limited the amount of capital U.S. firms could ship abroad. In response, banks loaned money to their multinational and foreign clients from offshore branches. Banks also went offshore in an effort to escape the interest rate ceilings—the limits on interest rates they could offer to depositors—imposed by Regulation Q of the Federal Reserve Board.[10]

The notion that banks can escape national regulations by seeking refuge in a global market has undoubted appeal, but it, too, is lacking. Political scientists have thus sought to understand why governments would allow the development of such a market. Is it true that governments were incapable of regulating their transnational firms, or did they permit these markets to grow because they believed it was in their interest to do so?

The answer I develop here tends toward the latter perspective. I will show that public officials believed that the promotion of international financial markets was consistent with the state's broader economic and political goals, despite the potential regulatory costs associated with this evolution in terms of control over economic policy and the banking sector. For European states, the offshore financial markets provided their internationally active firms with a source of capital at a time when domestic capital controls and controls on interest rates were still widespread; the Europeans could thus segment their domestic and international financial markets. As we will see, the United States shared this perspective.

But the United States also had a "hegemonic" interest in international finance—namely, a desire to maintain the dollar as the world's reserve currency. This gave it tremendous freedom in the formulation of both domestic and foreign economic policy.[11] During the early postwar years, the dollar was not only the major source of international liquidity; it was a store of value, "as good as gold." The dollar thus provided two functions that are necessary in order to maintain an international monetary system: liquidity and confidence.[12]

By the 1960s, however, the dollar's domestic and international roles were coming into conflict. As Jeffry Frieden points out, "The Kennedy Administration had inherited a stagnant economy, and needed desperately to revitalize it. Yet the balance of payments deficit was growing, and the most important set of measures needed to reverse it was recessionary."[13] At the same time, American officials were committed to maintaining the value and role of the dollar. In an effort to meet both domestic and international demands, a policy decision was made to separate the American and foreign financial markets.[14] Controls of capital outflows would ease the credit crunch at home; at the same time, the pool of offshore dollars in the Euromarkets would serve the needs not only of U.S.-based multinationals, but also of friends and allies abroad who needed access to American currency.

As the years went on, foreigners lost confidence in the value of the greenback. With the Vietnam War, the outflow of dollars reached record levels, despite the capital controls. During fiscal year 1968, the war led to a direct deterioration of the country's balance-of-payments position by somewhere between $1 billion and $1.5 billion.[15] It no longer seemed possible that all those dollars in circulation could really be backed up by gold reserves. As early as 1960, Yale economist Robert Triffin had identified the contradiction in U.S. policy of providing both international liquidity while maintaining confidence, a finding that became known as the "Triffin dilemma." By 1971, President Nixon feared that a tidal wave of dollars would crash upon the U.S. Treasury.[16]

On August 15, 1971, Nixon announced that the U.S. dollar was no longer freely convertible into gold. Although several attempts were made over the ensuing years to maintain something like a system of fixed exchange rates, the end of dollar convertibility to gold at $35 per ounce meant that a new era of volatile currency values had begun. At an International Monetary Fund (IMF) meeting in Jamaica in 1976, the assembled leaders made de jure what had already been de facto; floating exchange rates were now officially accepted as the basis for valuing currencies. With Jamaica, it became the responsibility of individual governments to maintain their currency values; they could no longer look to the external discipline of gold, the dollar, or some other international standard.[17]

Floating exchange rates, however, had really been unleashed as early as 1973, when efforts to maintain rates through artificial "pegs" were virtually abandoned. And with the dawning of this new age, economic agents faced a host of new challenges, many of which would be poorly understood for years to come. Policymakers had established a new economic structure, but they could not predict all the consequences of their actions for international financial stability.

Floating-Rate Crises

Banks do not create the macroeconomic environment in which they operate; rather, they must adapt to it. For financial actors, the age of floating exchange rates brought with it a new problem: *exchange rate or currency risk*. This term "refers to the magnitude and likelihood of unanticipated changes in exchange rates and inflation rates; i.e., in the value of foreign and domestic money."[18] For importers and exporters, sharp changes in currency values could wipe out profits. For investors, such movements could quickly change the book value of foreign assets. It must be remembered that most business people do not want to speculate in foreign currency markets; a dealer who imports Japanese cars is in the business of selling Toyotas or Hondas, not in betting on the value of the yen.

There are economic agents, however, who specialize in financial transactions: banks. With the change in foreign exchange markets, it became only natural for banks to develop their capabilities for buying and selling foreign currencies. Over time, a number of new instruments were developed which shielded customers from excessive foreign currency movements, such as forward contracts, which enable a customer to be certain today of the price she would pay for a foreign currency tomorrow. Banks became quite adept at servicing the worldwide currency needs of their clients, and in so doing they facilitated international trade.

Some banks also saw in sharp currency movements the possibility of enormous profits. During the 1970s, foreign exchange trading became a major source of revenue for such money center banks as Citicorp.[19] A bank that had an uncovered position in foreign exchange—that is, a bank that was speculating on the direction of a currency movement—and bet correctly would enjoy a huge windfall; with a bad bet, however, a bank could find that its shareholders and depositors had taken a substantial hit. While most banks tried to monitor their risk position and limit any downside risk, some—generally owing to either fraud or incompetence—played a more speculative game that they could not control.

Yet a further complication arose for bank managers and regulators in the foreign exchange market. Normally, banks kept little foreign exchange in their vaults. In order to meet customer requests, they borrowed needed funds from other banks, both foreign and domestic, through the interbank market. With the growth of foreign exchange trading, the international interdependence of the banking system expanded greatly, since commercial banks in one country would have to go to those of another to obtain foreign currency. The problem that this system posed was that a commercial bank failure in one country would inevitably spread overseas, sparking financial problems in several countries. As is usually the case in politics, it would take an actual crisis before bank supervisors became fully cognizant of this problem and sought the appropriate remedies.

Indeed, it is somewhat ironic that flexible exchange rates increased this mutual sensitivity to bank failures, since economists and central bankers believed that the new regime did the opposite when it came to macroeconomic policy. Under fixed rates, central bankers had little autonomy; their policies had to be formulated with respect to those being set abroad, in order to maintain the value of the currency. Under floating rates, in contrast, it seemed that economic policies could be set independently, so long as the government and central bank were willing to accept the exchange rate consequences. With the benefit of hindsight, we now recognize that interdependence has important implications for macroeconomic no less than banking policy, and policy coordination has been promoted by Western governments in recent years as a way of advancing common objectives, such as the reduction of inflation levels.[20]

Responsible management of a bank could, of course, implement controls to curb excessive speculation by its foreign exchange department and to ensure that careful analysis of borrowers was undertaken. Three types of controls were especially valuable: first, the establishment of clear limits on the bank's position in various foreign currencies; second, internal controls to ensure that such limits were respected; finally, a system of credit analysis to ensure that borrowers could repay their foreign exchange loans. (It should be emphasized that this required somewhat more sophisticated credit analysis than that used in purely domestic lending, given the volatility of exchange rates, the greater difficulties of obtaining credit checks, and the possibility that clients were borrowing funds in foreign currencies simply in order to speculate.)

Although these controls would seem simple to design in theory, in practice they proved difficult for some banks to carry out. For one thing, bank managers were under constant pressure from account officers to increase their foreign exchange limits in order to meet the demands of clients, especially multinational corporations that needed access to large amounts of foreign currency; for another, during the early 1970s the internal accounting and operating systems of many banks were incapable of giving managers "real-time" data on the institution's foreign exchange position. Furthermore, since lending in volatile foreign currencies was a new game for many banks, they inevitably made errors in credit judgment, leading to losses. Finally, banks, like other organizations, found it difficult to shield themselves from fraudulent attempts by some account officers and traders to profit from the bank's foreign exchange book.

All these difficulties became apparent to bank supervisors in June 1974, only a year after exchange rates had begun to float. In the late afternoon of June 26, Bankhaus I. D. Herstatt of Cologne was closed by German authorities. The bank had suffered huge losses in its foreign exchange department, which it had covered up with fraudulent bookkeeping. In particular, the bank had speculated wildly in currency markets, borrowing in different currencies from banks around the world, and it had lost the gamble.[21]

The losses that other banks suffered as a result of the Herstatt failure, however, were compounded by the actions of the German authorities. The late afternoon closure of the bank was noted above for a reason. By the time the bank was closed, it was 10:00 A.M. in New York, and 3:00 P.M. in London. Funds had already been credited to Herstatt's accounts by its global correspondents that same day (not to mention in the days before), and foreign exchange trading had only begun for the day in the United

States. When news of the Herstatt failure came burning across the wires, trading stopped.

As Herstatt's creditors contemplated their next move, bank managers decided to provide only the highest-rated institutions with foreign exchange; all others would be shut out. In a classic example of market imperfection, thousands of smaller banks worldwide were simply unable to meet the foreign exchange demands of their customers through their traditional correspondent banking networks, tying up international trade.[22] Furthermore, the crisis immediately spilled over into the interbank lending markets as a whole, and small banks that were able to borrow were forced to pay substantially more for funds. According to an International Monetary Fund report, these banks faced a premium of up to 2 percent, making it impossible for them to compete with larger banks on a price basis in the market for commercial loans.[23] Indeed, a Bank of England study found that some banks "were virtually excluded from the market, suggesting some degree of quantity rationing also."[24] One student of the affair, J. F. Lepetit, went further, arguing that "the U.S. clearing system nearly collapsed with Herstatt."[25]

The German regulatory authorities suffered harsh criticism in the wake of the Herstatt closure, criticism that they initially protested. Many bankers said that the Deutsche Bundesbank should have honored Herstatt's debts and should have intervened in the foreign exchange markets in order to support the smaller banks, which had been shut out. The Germans justified their actions by suggesting that they "wanted to teach speculators, as well as banks dealing with speculators, a lesson."[26] But in spite of the initial German claim that their actions (or inactions) had been appropriate, subsequent changes in regulatory policy reflected some self-criticism on the part of the supervisory authorities. In particular, the Germans would go on to develop a new set of regulations governing foreign exchange trading, giving the Federal Banking Supervisory Office in Berlin additional powers.

Although it had international ramifications, the Herstatt failure was handled very much as a German internal matter. The bank lacked a far-flung branch network, and its problems were centered in the head office. Accordingly, outstanding issues between the German authorities and Herstatt's creditor banks were dealt with bilaterally, either at the official level (that is, between the central bankers of Germany and other countries) or at transnational levels (that is, between the banks and authorities directly). Nonetheless, the Herstatt crisis did force banking supervisors in different countries to begin speaking with one another on a regular basis and sharing information, and soon that process would become formalized by the Group of Ten central bank governors.

While German banking authorities were coping with the Herstatt mess, a second banking crisis was occupying the attention of American officials. On October 8, 1974, the twentieth-largest bank in the United States, the Franklin National Bank of New York, was declared insolvent and acquired (ironically) by the German-controlled European-American Bank. Unlike the Herstatt failure, there was nothing sudden about the demise of Franklin National. Its problems had initially been detected by federal authorities five months earlier. Franklin had what might be termed a "managed collapse."[27]

The Franklin National, like the Continental Illinois Bank, which would fail a decade later, provides a case study of an overly aggressive bank. In its thirst to expand, the bank made high-risk loans to a wide variety of customers—some less wholesome than others—and it funded these loans with bought funds on the international money market. These aggressive management techniques inevitably found their way to the trading floor, where Franklin bankers became avid speculators in currency markets. As the bank piled up losses in its various markets, Franklin's managers grew desperate and conspired to cook the books. By the spring of 1973, the word was out on the street that Franklin National was no longer a good credit risk, and the bank began to lose access to the financial markets.

Fearing that the failure of the nation's twentieth-largest bank could lead to a nationwide depositor stampede, and possibly to a global banking crisis, Federal Reserve authorities acted to prop up the ailing institution. One student of the affair, Richard Dale, has said that the "Fed" adopted a four-fold policy: first, as lender of last resort it provided the bank with more than $1.7 billion in funds; second, it took over the bank's foreign exchange operations, basically providing a guarantee that Franklin National would not, like Herstatt, leave its foreign creditors unpaid; third, the Federal Reserve gave support to the bank's London branch, extending the lender-of-last-resort provision overseas; finally, along with the Federal

Deposit Insurance Corporation (FDIC), it found a buyer for the bank's assets.[28]

In designing a policy response, the Federal Reserve worked closely with other central banks, particularly the Bank of England, which had some supervisory responsibilities for Franklin National's London branch. According to Joan Spero, this permitted the London branch to be closed without a separate liquidation process, which might have been timely and litigious. Furthermore, and no less important, the Federal Reserve's action stemmed any Euromarket fears concerning contagion beyond the Franklin National.[29]

Yet the Reserve Bank's action to save the London branch also had some chilling consequences for other central bank governors. Franklin National's London office primarily made Euroloans—loans to multinational corporations and foreign governments that were funded and booked in London rather than the United States. By bailing out this operation, the Federal Reserve said implicitly that it would act as lender of last resort for the Eurodollar operations of American banks. This was not a claim that all central bankers wished to make about the Eurobranches of their domestic banks, since it would encourage the booking of business offshore.

In July 1974, the Group of Ten central bankers met for one of their regular meetings at the Bank for International Settlements (BIS) in Basle. These meetings, it should be emphasized, did not yet include bank regulators, despite the recent failures and the growing interdependence of financial markets. The atmosphere was understandably grim. Financial markets were reeling under the strain of the oil price shock (described in the following chapter), the Herstatt crisis, and the Franklin National's collapse; and in Britain a number of "fringe" or small regional banks had gotten into trouble, requiring a lifeboat operation organized by the Bank of England. Financial intermediation in the Euromarkets was grinding to a halt, as banks sought to lower their risk profiles.

The position of the United States was that a firm and explicit commitment must be given to the marketplace that central banks would provide lender-of-last-resort assistance to banks operating in the Euromarkets. The Germans, however, refused to make an explicit statement, for three reasons. First, in its enabling legislation the Deutsche Bundesbank lacked formal lender-of-last-resort powers; and in 1974, as one response to Herstatt, it was in the process of establishing, along with members of the German banking industry, a Liquidity Consortium Bank which would serve this function in the event bank failures were deemed to cause liquidity crises.[30] Second, it did not wish to be committed to providing liquidity to banks that had failed owing to illegal or highly risky activities. Finally, for reasons of "moral hazard" the Bundesbank thought it was a bad idea for central bankers to make explicit commitments.[31]

The inability of the Federal Reserve and the Bundesbank to reach an agreement spread through the financial markets, making it difficult for a variety of banks (for example, smaller banks and consortium banks without a clearly defined home base) to access funds in the interbank markets. Pressured by domestic banking actors for a stronger statement, the central bank governors had no choice but to make a formal announcement following their September meeting of their market intentions: "The governors had an exchange of views on the problem of lender of last resort in the Euromarket. They recognized that it would not be practical to lay down in advance detailed rules and procedures for the provision of temporary liquidity. But they were satisfied that means are available for that purpose and will be used if and when necessary."[32] This statement was vague enough to win support from all the G-10 central bankers, while providing the banks with sufficient confidence to resume their lending activities, especially to developing countries that faced mounting import bills in the wake of the oil crisis. As a Bank of England analyst has written, "this move did not guarantee automatic lender of last resort intervention but did indicate the willingness of central bankers to intervene in a crisis."[33]

Yet it is by no means clear that all the central bankers present had agreed to provide what their commercial bankers saw as lender-of-last-resort facilities. To be sure, central bankers, bank regulators, and commercial bankers had cooperated in meeting the foreign exchange and petrodollar crises (see Chapter 3), but the terms of that cooperation raised more questions than they answered. What the central bankers could agree upon, however, was that the crises of international finance had made their policy actions interdependent, and that purely national solutions to banking problems would no longer prove adequate.

The Basle Committee and the Origins
of International Banking Supervision

Despite these bonds of interdependence, some countries were more ex-posed than others to the domino-like structure of international banking. In particular, the United Kingdom was concerned about how to supervise the growing number of international banks on its soil. By the early 1970s there were over two hundred foreign banks with branches in London, and the Bank of England wanted to have confidence that these branches would be supported by the home country's central bank in the event of difficulties. The bank had already gotten a bitter taste of what might come with the "fringe banking crisis," in which a number of virtually unregu-lated regional institutions had borrowed "hot" money (short-term funds with floating interest rates) and loaned it long at fixed rates in support of various real estate projects. This was a sign that unregulated markets could bring chaos, and that Euromarket failures could have much greater consequences for the international financial system.

During the autumn of 1974, Bank of England governor Lord Richard-son met with his head of banking supervision, George Blunden. They dis-cussed the need for greater cooperation among bank supervisors, and es-pecially the Bank of England's requirement for more information from home country supervisors concerning the overall activities of foreign banks with branches and subsidiaries in London. At that time, banks did not present consolidated statements of their activities, making it difficult if not impossible for supervisors in any single country, including the home base, to assess the bank as a whole. Richardson decided to propose to his fellow central bank governors that they establish a committee of banking supervisors which could have as its chief function the exchange of such vital information.[34]

At their monthly meeting in December 1974, the G-10 central bank governors voted to support Richardson's idea, establishing the Standing Committee on Banking Regulations and Supervisory Practices, now known informally as the "Basle Committee."[35] Richardson offered to pro-vide a small staff for a secretariat, and the BIS provided an institutional home. Questions then arose concerning the committee's membership. Since it was being created by central bankers, obviously each central bank should appoint a representative.

The problem was that not every central bank had primary responsibility for banking supervision. The Deutsche Bundesbank shared regulatory duties with the Federal Banking Supervisory Office in Berlin, the Bank of France shared duties with the Commission Bancaire, and the Federal Reserve Board shared supervision with the Treasury's Office of the Comptroller of the Currency (OCC) and the Federal Deposit Insurance Corporation. Furthermore, since the major banking crises had arisen out of the foreign exchange markets, it seemed sensible to appoint members who knew something about this topic. It was finally decided that each country would have two representatives: one a central banker with responsibilities for foreign exchange, the other a banking supervisor from whichever agency the member country decided was most appropriate.[36]

The first meeting of the committee was held in February 1975, and George Blunden, who was appointed chairman, remembered it well.[37] He said that the supervisors sat around a table, quiet and suspicious of one another. The "ice was broken," he said, by the jocular Huib Muller of the Netherlands (who would go on in later years to serve as chairman for a few months before his untimely death in 1991), who put everyone at ease with some light conversation.

It is not surprising that the supervisors found their initial discussions difficult to get started. After all, until the moment the committee was formed, and despite the globalization of finance, "supervisory authorities [had] continued their isolation, acting as if banking systems were still compartmentalised."[38] The idea of international coordination of banking supervision was puzzling, since the structures of national financial systems were so different, as were the legal and accounting regimes.

Indeed, the central bank governors had made it clear that the committee's objective "should *not* [my emphasis] be to make far-fetched attempts to harmonise the twelve countries' individual systems of supervision, but should be to enable its members to learn from each other and to apply the knowledge so acquired to improving their own systems of supervision, so indirectly enhancing the likelihood of overall stability in the international banking system."[39] The committee was thus charged with the following tasks: first, general education about how banks were supervised within the member countries; second, information sharing, to include the passing of "sensitive information" on banks to supervisors who were hosts to its branches; third, the establishment of an "early warning system" to detect problems within international banks; fourth, conducting studies on topics in banking supervision; finally, policy coordination in supervising international and consortium banks. In sum, as George Blunden put it, "there is agreement that the basic aim of international co-operation in this field should be to ensure that no foreign banking establishment escapes supervision."[40] As we will see, the committee's brief has moved well beyond its early charter, and now it stands at the center of international financial regulation.

In supervising international banks, the regulators faced one of the classic problems of interdependence: simply, that banks crossed borders while they did not, bound as they were by state structures. The question was what if anything should be done to manage this state of affairs. A number of solutions were possible, and one must explain the road taken in the context of the other possibilities.

First, the supervisors could have sought to build a *supranational* organization, in which international banks were regulated by a new body with powers granted to it by its sovereign members. In this case, the regulatory body would have developed a common set of international rules for all banks that operated in two or more countries. Given the globalization of finance, it would not have been extraordinary for a proposal along these lines to have gone forward, yet it seems that no supervisor foresaw a truly supranational organization in 1975; and as late as the early 1990s few would bet on its development, even on a regional basis in the European Community, where a single central bank has been the topic of debate for many years.

Second, the supervisors could have focused on reaching *multilateral* agreements. Under these conditions, bank supervisors would retain their national identity, but they would attempt to coordinate policies with their colleagues and, in certain cases, act to promote policy convergence. In 1975, this approach seemed desirable, but it was uncertain how far along these lines the supervisors could proceed in practice. The national differences of banking, legal, and accounting systems seemed too great to overcome in any significant way, limiting the scope for international policy coordination.

Third, they could have pursued *bilateral* arrangements whereby the home *and* host countries shared the burden of banking supervision. Under this scenario, the home country would have looked to the host to supervise foreign branches and subsidiaries, and a process of information sharing among the supervisors would have led to an integrated picture of the bank as a whole. It should be noted here that *host country supervision* was never considered as an alternative on a stand-alone basis, given the reasons provided in Chapter 1.

The bilateral approach, however, had adherents in the Bank of England, given their belief in the bank's unique ability to supervise financial institutions. Since London played host to hundreds of foreign banks, some of which had home countries in the third world, or in smaller European countries, or in other countries with inadequate regulatory systems, it is not altogether surprising that the bank had a preference for a strong host country role in financial supervision, albeit a role that did not include unlimited provision of lender-of-last-resort facilities to foreign banks.

Finally, the officials considered staying on their present course, in which regulation was looked upon primarily as a domestic matter. The underlying principle here was *home country control,* in which the supervisors of a bank's headquarters assumed responsibility for regulating its overall operations, including foreign operations. As the United States demonstrated in the Franklin National case, home country control also implied extraterritorial provision of the lender-of-last-resort facility in order to prevent the spread of banking crises. Indeed, the lender-of-last-resort facility provides the ultimate justification for international regulations based on home country control.

All four approaches to supervision have been proposed at one time or another by members or observers of the Basle Committee, although the supranational concept has yet to be taken seriously. Over time, the regulators came to adopt the rather flexible formula of "international cooperation based on home country control."[41] Such cooperation has been pursued on both a bilateral and a multilateral basis, and in a variety of ways. At the outset, the terms of international cooperation were quite limited, concentrating mainly on information sharing and the exchange of policy ideas; but as we will see later in the book, this sort of cooperation has evolved significantly over the years.

The cornerstone of international banking supervision, however, has remained home country control. This is because states have demanded that, in a world of global finance, national central banks take responsibility for the operations of their domestic banking institutions. Indeed, as banks expanded internationally, host countries did not wish to assume lender-of-last-resort responsibility for both the domestic and foreign banks operating on their soil; this concern was sharpest in the British case, which was home to so many foreign banks. At the same time, banks have found that they still need states for lender-of-last-resort, regulatory, and diplomatic services. While states have reached bilateral and multilateral agreements on banking supervision, these agreements have all been based on the fundamental principle of home country control.[42]

The Basle Concordat

In its earliest efforts at supervisory cooperation, the Basle Committee looked upon banking regulation as a task that had to be shared between the home and host country. This is evident in the first product of the committee, the so-called Concordat, which was prepared in 1975, made public in 1981, revised in 1983 in the wake of the Banco Ambrosiano scandal, and revised again in 1991 in the wake of the BCCI collapse. With the Concordat, the supervisors demonstrated the promise of international cooperation; but ironically, they demonstrated its limits as well.

The initial version of the Concordat was the product of the Basle Committee's first four or five meetings.[43] During these meetings the committee focused its attention on "carving out first principles for international supervisory co-operation."[44] In the words of Peter Cooke, a Bank of England official who would become chairman of the Basle Committee in 1977, these principles "had to be built up from virtually nothing." The supervisors agreed that their immediate responsibility in the wake of the Herstatt and Franklin National crises was to "reach an understanding of the appropriate division of responsibility for the supervision of banks' foreign establishments with the object of ensuring that no foreign banking establishment escaped supervision." The Concordat, approved by the central bank governors in December 1975, represented the first fruits of this labor.[45]

The Concordat laid out the five following principles:

1. The supervision of foreign banking establishments should be the joint responsibility of host and parent authorities.
2. No foreign banking establishment should escape supervision, each country should ensure that foreign banking establishments are supervised, and supervision should be judged adequate by both host and parent authorities.

3. The supervision of liquidity should be the primary responsibility of host authorities, since foreign establishments generally have to conform to local practices for their liquidity management and must comply with local regulations.
4. The supervision of solvency of foreign branches should be essentially a matter for the parent authority. In the case of subsidiaries, while primary responsibility lies with the host authority, parent authorities should take account of the exposure of their domestic banks' foreign subsidiaries and joint ventures because of the parent banks' moral commitment in this regard.
5. Practical cooperation would be facilitated by transfers of information between host and parent authorities and by the granting of permission for inspections by or on behalf of parent authorities on the territory of the host authority. Every effort should be made to remove any legal restraints (particularly in the field of professional secrecy or national sovereignty) which might hinder these forms of cooperation.[46]

In many respects, this Concordat was a very British document. As the Bank of England had wanted, it gave the host authority an enlarged role over banking supervision, including the supervision of a foreign establishment's liquidity position. At the same time, the bank was given the assurance that the supervision of *solvency* for foreign branches would be the concern of the home country; subsidiaries, in contrast, which were separate operating entities, would be supervised by the host, with the expectation that the home country would maintain a "moral commitment" to the subsidiary.

The Concordat, however, failed to address a number of critical issues for international banking supervision. First, it left open the question of which if any central bank would support a commercial bank that had failed due to fraud; the Germans were consistent in their stated refusal to bail out such institutions. Second, the supervision of subsidiaries and agencies remained unclear. Was a "moral commitment" the same as providing lender-of-last-resort support? Indeed, third, and most important, the Concordat failed to discuss the lender of last resort, at least explicitly. In short, while the members of the Basle Committee found that the Concordat was useful as a conceptual framework, there were many questions about how (and if) it would work in practice.

One of the curious things about the Concordat concerns why it was not disseminated to the public until 1981. Indeed, the Basle Committee provided no public record whatsoever of its work until that year. This preference for secrecy is very much part of the central banker's operating procedure, but for bank supervisors it would appear unnecessary and even counterproductive.

The bank supervisors have provided two justifications for their secrecy, one theoretical, the other practical. From a theoretical perspective, regulators have preferred secrecy or a masking of intentions owing to the "moral hazard" problem they face—the problem that bank managers will become more reckless if they know the conditions under which they will be bailed out. The supervisors believe that managers will act more prudently if they are unsure about bailout procedures. From a practical standpoint, regulators, like most officials, do not want to have their hands tied in advance of a crisis. They would rather leave their response unstated, providing them with additional flexibility to meet immediate challenges. Indeed, to this day the committee produces little in the way of public documentation, and no record of its internal meetings—a fact that has caused some consternation in the U.S. Congress.[47]

Perhaps another reason for keeping the Concordat a secret was that it had no executive authority. The Basle Committee, it must be remembered, had and still has no legal power of its own; basically it arrives at "gentleman's agreements." These agreements achieve the force of law only when they are embodied in domestic legislation, and clearly no supervisor wanted to bring the Concordat before a parliamentary or congressional committee for hearings, since it would open up a wide-ranging public debate on the international responsibilities of national central banks. In general, central bankers prefer to work informally with the institutions they regulate, seeking legislative cures only as a last resort.

In sum, the Concordat marked a first, tentative step toward developing an internationally accepted approach to banking supervision. It emphasized the role of the home country's central bank in providing for the solvency needs of branches in trouble, while giving host country regulators added responsibility for supervision. But given its cautious wording, notable gaps, and lack of authority, it would prove a weak reed for managing international banking crises.

Indeed, soon after the committee accepted the Concordat, a notable loophole in its coverage became apparent. Simply stated, the parts of a bank might not add up to the whole. Home and host country supervisors might cooperate in painting an overall picture, but given different accounting rules and regulatory standards, and the large gaps in reporting within the banks themselves, the result could well be a partial view with important pieces obscured or missing.

The solution to this problem had already been discovered by the more sophisticated banks, which had developed *consolidated* reporting—that is, reporting that looked at the institution's balance sheet and income statement from the perspective of an integrated entity. Taking this approach as its starting point, the committee in 1978 recommended to the central bank governors that banking supervision be conducted on the basis of consolidated statements. According to Peter Cooke, "consolidation in effect provides a clearer picture of a bank's overall exposure to risk and enables parent supervisors to apply their own standards to the monitoring of their banks' business irrespective of where that business is conducted."[48]

The principle of consolidated accounting led to a further strengthening of home country control, and it reflected the preferences of those countries which already utilized this system—namely, the United States, Canada, and the Netherlands. The Japanese adopted a consolidated approach in 1978, with the British, Germans, Swiss, and Italians following suit over the ensuing years; but in the latter case, not before another major banking collapse, to be discussed below. For the Germans, consolidation could not be imposed upon the banks because the law gave the supervisors only limited access to information about the foreign activities of bank subsidiaries and agencies. Indeed, getting the necessary information would require a change in the banking law. Accordingly, in German regulatory fashion, the supervisors struck a gentleman's agreement with the banks, whereby the banks would endeavor to provide consolidated statements.[49]

The Basle Concordat and consolidated supervision had gone a long way toward tightening supervision of international banks, but by the mid-1970s some central bankers felt that greater regulation of the Euromarkets was desirable. In the United States, two Federal Reserve governors in particular, Robert Holland and Philip Coldwell, expressed fears that the Euromarkets were eroding central bank control over the money supply and fueling inflation.[50] Accordingly, in 1978 the United States began informal multilateral discussions with its allies regarding the economic and regulatory consequences of growing Euromarket activity.[51]

The issue was given to another Bank for International Settlements (BIS) committee for further study, but no firm agreement could ever be reached among the member states regarding what if any problems were being created for central bankers by these financial markets. Economists and regulators debated whether the Euromarkets were really a separate financial system, given that they had no independent mechanism for creating money, but they failed to reach any definitive conclusions. Differing ideas about how the Euromarkets worked and about their impact on domestic monetary policy were thus an important source of disagreement.

Yet James Hawley points to an additional reason further Euromarket regulation did not occur. To the extent that banking regulations reflect the outcome of negotiations between regulators and the regulated, each party must have firm ideas about what it wants to achieve. In the case at hand, such ideas were not in evidence. Within central banks—especially the Federal Reserve—differing opinions existed as to whether such regulations would really serve monetary policy objectives. Similarly, American banks seemed satisfied with the level of support to the Euromarkets already provided by central bankers in their declaratory statements. There was thus no overwhelming bureaucratic or special interest pressure in favor of further regulations.[52]

In short, after 1980 central banks no longer pursued the idea of placing reserve requirements on Eurobanks. There was no common interest among the G-10 member states in support of such a regulation, and even within its most ardent supporter—the United States—opinion was divided. Indeed, the ironic result of this episode in the United States would be the creation of International Banking Facilities (IBFs), which were in effect offshore Eurobranches that American banks were permitted to establish at home as a base for serving their foreign customers; in other words, they were branches of American banks, based in American cities, that could take Eurodeposits and make international loans. The Federal Reserve had decided that its best course of action was simply to bring the Euromarket home to the greatest extent possible.

Despite this failure to find a multilateral policy solution to the Euromarket problem, the Group of Ten countries had achieved important advances in the supervision of international banks with the Concordat and consolidation. Furthermore, the Basle Committee recognized that the power of these supervisory tools would be blunted if they remained solely in the hands of the Group of Ten countries. Accordingly, in 1979 the committee prompted the banking supervisors from the major offshore centers, which were largely in the Caribbean, to form their own organization and to adopt the supervisory principles already accepted in Basle. This "Offshore Group of Banking Supervisors" commenced work in October 1980, and by 1982 it had worked out an agreement with the Basle Committee which extended consolidated accounting to offshore branches and subsidiaries.[53]

In sum, during its first four years the Basle Committee created a forum in which bank supervisors could exchange information and reach agreement on basic supervisory principles, as well as a base upon which the influence of the G-10 could be expanded. These were not small achievements in themselves. But despite its collegiality and degree of common cause, the committee would still prove too weak to cope with the next crises that would come crashing down on the financial marketplace.

Banco Ambrosiano

On June 18, 1982, the chairman of Italy's Banco Ambrosiano was found hanging by his neck from Blackfriars Bridge in London. This estimable banker, Roberto Calvi, had been missing from Milan for ten days, and with news of his death depositors began to withdraw their funds. As Ambrosiano verged on a liquidity crisis, the Bank of Italy mounted a lifeboat operation with the support of the nation's largest commercial banks. Soon thereafter, however, news stories began to leak concerning the bank and its myriad legal and illegal activities and networks. Unable to control the loss of confidence, the Bank of Italy moved to close Banco Ambrosiano in August, but not before protecting all of the parent bank's depositors from loss.[54]

Yet the bank refused to provide the same treatment to Ambrosiano's overseas subsidiaries, particularly its Luxembourg office, which was the center of its Eurolending activities. Active in the interbank market as a source of funds, Ambrosiano owed various creditors $450 million, who were not given protection by the Bank of Italy. For their part, the Italian authorities claimed that they had no responsibility for the affairs of a foreign subsidiary, which they neither supervised nor served as lender of last resort. Unfortunately, Luxembourg also felt that it had no responsibility for the subsidiary, asserting that it did in fact fall under the supervisory umbrella of the Bank of Italy. In the end, Ambrosiano's Luxembourg subsidiary was "left to default on its loans and deposits," leaving creditors no choice but to fight their battle in the courts.[55]

The Ambrosiano crisis had a number of consequences. From the perspective of the interbank market, as with the Herstatt failure, smaller banks found themselves paying more for money than their larger, better-known competitors. According to an International Monetary Fund report, these banks had to pay upwards of .5 percent more than the going rate, seriously damaging their competitiveness.[56]

Bank supervisors would also draw lessons from the Ambrosiano affair. In Italy, the weakness of international banking supervision became a topic of widespread debate, leading, most prominently, to a change in the banking law which required that banks provide consolidated statements. Yet the Italians did *not* draw the lesson that they had to provide lender-of-last-resort support to subsidiary operations, especially in cases like Ambrosiano, where there was evidence of massive fraud. The chairman of the Basle Committee, Peter Cooke, supported the Bank of Italy in this regard, pointing out that the Concordat related "to *supervisory* responsibilities, not *lender of last resort* responsibilities."[57] The continuing ambiguity over which central bank *did* perform this function in international markets, however, would continue to dog the committee's work.

The failure of the Luxembourg authorities to act as lenders of last resort raised further questions about the role of host country supervisors. According to the Concordat, the host country assumed primary responsibility for regulating bank subsidiaries, but it is unclear whether Luxembourg had (or has) the capability to supervise and regulate a financial institution as complex as a multinational bank; the scandal in 1991 involving the Bank for Credit and Commerce International (BCCI), which was headquartered in Luxembourg, gives further evidence of that country's lack of effectiveness.

Nonetheless, the authorities in that country reformed their banking laws to some extent in the wake of Ambrosiano, easing bank secrecy in certain areas and requiring bank subsidiaries to provide the information needed in order for the parent to form consolidated statements. Furthermore, the Luxembourg authorities sought "comfort letters" from parent banks indicating their support for the subsidiaries which were based in that country.[58]

Overall, however, it is difficult to argue with Richard Dale's conclusion that "the Ambrosiano affair represented a serious breakdown in international supervisory co-operation. From the point of view of preventive regulation a glaring loophole in international supervisory arrangements had emerged."[59] Indeed, in the wake of Ambrosiano the Basle Committee would sit down to redraft its Concordat in an effort to close those very loopholes and reach a new understanding among its members.

The revised Concordat was released by the committee in 1983 under the title "Principles for the Supervision of Banks' Foreign Establishments." From the outset, the document made clear that its aims were quite limited: "The report deals exclusively with the responsibilities of banking supervisory authorities for monitoring the prudential conduct and soundness of the banks' foreign establishments. It does not address itself to lender-of-last-resort aspects of the role of central banks." Furthermore, it stressed that the principles formulated were not "laws"; instead, they represented what the committee called "best practices."

The Basle Committee, it must be remembered, has no authority for making laws; it can only make policy recommendations. In some cases, however, banking authorities have requested that domestic banking legislation be changed to incorporate the committee's suggestions. Indeed, the days of informal supervision in such countries as England are coming to an end, one victim of globalization. Today, even though a country may be home to only a handful of domestic banks which could be supervised by informal means, the same country may play host to hundreds of branches of banks from around the world. This makes an informal system of supervision impractical, and increases demand for formal regulations. Regulations substitute for informal supervision when the number of agents to be supervised becomes too large for public officials to handle.

Moreover, the bank failures of the 1970s and the Ambrosiano scandal called into question the ability of supervisors to do their job using traditional techniques. Elected officials, rating agencies, and depositors were demanding more precise measures of bank performance and strength. The Basle Committee, in revising the Concordat, was responding to these "consumer" demands.

The basic message of the new document was that home country supervision would be further strengthened through the continuing consolidation of bank statements and risk evaluations. The banks were to consolidate to the degree that supervisors could analyze the capital of the group, the quality of its worldwide assets, and its exposure to risk, especially in its foreign exchange position. In those cases where the bank was unable to consolidate adequate information about a foreign operation (owing to, for example, secrecy laws) and where it could not rely upon the host authorities, the home country supervisors "should be prepared to discourage the parent bank from continuing to operate the establishment in question."

Home country supervision of international banking was thus the fundamental principle that animated the Basle Committee. Despite a number of international banking failures in which home country supervision appeared less than adequate, the committee did not recommend a supranational response to regulation. In an age characterized by globalization, nation-states still classified banks as either "foreign" or "domestic." Indeed, the history of international cooperation in banking supervision is really one that demonstrates the extension of home country control over the affairs of allegedly global multinationals.

During the 1950s and 1960s, the world economy reemerged from the ashes of the Second World War. That reconstruction effort was aided by an international structure that maintained currency values at more or less fixed rates, and that fostered trade through the steady reduction of tariff and nontariff barriers. As trade and investment mushroomed, banks followed their corporate clients to distant shores. Multinational banking was largely a reflection of the spread of American-, European-, and ultimately Japanese-based corporations to new markets.

The macroshocks of the 1970s did not bring an end to global finance; on the contrary, they provided a fillip. With the wild fluctuations in foreign exchange values, corporations looked to banks for help in managing their currency exposure. The banks themselves saw speculation as a road to new profits, and foreign exchange trading floors expanded in all the major financial institutions. As we will see in the next chapter, with the oil crisis a new flood of money entered the Euromarkets, generating unprecedented opportunities for financial intermediation.

The end of the Bretton Woods structure of international finance in the early 1970s was kinder to some banks than to others. In Europe and America, banks failed as a result of reckless speculation and lending. The failures of even small banks, however, could not always be localized, given the tight bonds that brought firms together in the interbank market. This interdependence could not be denied or avoided by bank supervisors.

In 1974, the Basle Committee was formed under the auspices of the Group of Ten central bank governors. The objective of the committee was to develop a set of basic principles for supervising international financial institutions. These principles were duly articulated, and over time, as we will see, the committee would play a useful role in promoting regulatory convergence among its members. But the committee and its Concordat were of little help in dealing with scandals of the Banco Ambrosiano variety, much less in managing the grave crisis that awaited the international financial system in the early 1980s. That management task would fall not to multilateral committees, but to powerful states.

3 | The Politics of Petrodollar Recycling, 1973–1982

Smith's *Wealth of Nations* . . . specifically warned of the dangers of leaving the management of banking . . . entirely to the self-interest of bankers.

—PAUL VOLCKER AND TOYOO GYOHTEN

On October 6, 1973, Egypt and Syria launched a surprise attack against Israel. The war caught the Jewish state at an especially bad time, since reserve troops were at home for the high holiday of Yom Kippur. The first days of battle marked the greatest military success ever achieved by the Arab states in their struggle against Zionism.[1]

The Arabs took the offensive on the oil front as well. On October 7, Iraq nationalized U.S. oil company interests in the Basrah Petroleum Company. At the same time, military operations halted shipment of more than 1 million barrels of petroleum per day through various Middle East pipelines.

One week later, the war took a crucial turn. The Israelis had begun to win momentum and push the Arabs back, but their human and matériel losses were enormous. Now the Soviets demonstrated their willingness to prolong the conflict by increasing shipments of military supplies to Cairo and Damascus. The United States had no choice but to respond, and on October 14 President Richard Nixon ordered emergency arms shipments to Israel.

Two days later, ministers representing the Organization of Arab Petroleum Exporting Countries (OAPEC) met at Kuwait's Sheraton Hotel to plan a joint response. Their first action was to raise oil prices unilaterally, from $3.011 to $5.119 per barrel. The following day, the ministers agreed to a 5 percent production cutback from the September output level, and warned that similar cuts would occur monthly until Israel withdrew "from the whole Arab territories occupied in June 1967 and the legal rights of the Palestinian people [were] restored."[2] With that announcement, the oil crisis began, and it was a crisis that seemed to threaten the economic and political stability of a world hooked on cheap fuel from the Middle East.

On the financial side, the oil shocks caused, among other things, the biggest income transfers in history, as consumers from importing nations spent billions of additional dollars on petroleum products (almost all oil sales were made in U.S. dollars—a fact that, as we will see, is quite important). This flow of funds to oil producers created a challenge for Arab financiers and their Western advisers, as they sought appropriate domestic and foreign investments for their cash.

For consumers, in contrast, the oil crisis created an economic hardship, given their inelastic demand for petroleum products over the short run; that is, consumers had no choice but to spend more money on oil, and thus they had less money for other goods and services. The economic crunch was especially hard on the countries of the developing world, which had fueled their postwar economic development programs on cheap petroleum. Now, years of progress were about to be reversed by the combination of higher import bills for fuel and lower demand for their exports. For these countries, the oil crisis would cause a severe cash crunch.

And yet the immediate financial needs of the less developed countries (LDCs) were met, largely by banks, and this chapter examines the process by which that flow of funds took place. According to the common view, international banks which received Arab petrodollars as deposits "recycled" them to the have-not nations of the developing world, as if by an invisible hand. This miraculous outcome occurred as a marketplace response to the crisis of the moment.

I argue in this chapter that the received view of history needs to be supplemented by a fuller account of the role of powerful states in the recycling process. Petrodollar recycling indeed occurred, but it was lubricated by significant political intermediation, especially on the part of the United States government. Ironically, banks in 1974 were initially unwilling to lend funds to most of the developing countries for balance-of-payments support, in part because these countries had already accumulated large stocks of debt as a way of financing their economic development. More unconditional lending seemed to involve unacceptable risks.[3]

But the industrial countries, led by the United States, did not wish to gamble on the political and economic consequences of a moratorium on loans by the banks. The United States and its postwar allies had, during the postwar years, built an international economy characterized by relatively free flows of trade and investment. The developing countries had been gradually brought into this system, and some of them were now, to borrow Walt Rostow's famous phrase, in the midst of their economic "takeoff."[4] That takeoff had been made possible in large measure by imports of hard currency and cheap oil, and now the developing world faced the worrisome prospect of being denied both these critical inputs.

Such a denial, Western officials feared, would lead to economic instability and, eventually, to political discontent. Should the United States and other great powers fail to assist the developing countries, they would become prey to the contending forces then vying for influence in the third world, including Arab oil producers, nationalists of various stripes, and communists.[5] As the *Washington Post* editorialized at the time, Saudi King "Faisal did probably more damage to the West than any other single man since Adolf Hitler."[6]

And so governments provided their international banks with a number of incentives that helped maintain and indeed bolster lending to third-world countries. Years later, of course, a tragic combination of higher oil prices, rising interest rates on the sovereign loans, and a global recession that reduced demand for exports would cause these borrowers severe economic difficulties. By 1982 a new crisis—a debt crisis—would be under way.

The Petrodollar Problem

In the annals of the postwar international economy, the story of petrodollar recycling has achieved a mythical status. Following the oil shock of 1973, billions of dollars had to be transferred from oil-exporting to developing nations, in order to provide those countries with the means to keep paying their import bills. But development assistance was lacking on the part of nations belonging to OECD and OPEC (Organization of Petroleum

Exporting Countries), and the developing world was threatened with oil starvation. Incredibly, the Invisible Hand itself played the role of White Knight, solving the problem without any government intervention. Operating in the unregulated Euromarkets, banks automatically transferred funds from have to have-not nations.

Former Federal Reserve Board chairman Paul Volcker recounts the conventional wisdom in his 1992 book *Changing Fortunes*. Volcker writes that in the wake of the oil crisis, finance ministers in the industrial countries were gravely concerned by the prospect that funds would not be channeled to those countries most in need of balance-of-payments support. Unfortunately, given domestic economic pressures, little in the way of a governmental response could be expected from the industrial countries, especially in the form of aid.[7] He continues:

What happened was that international banking markets, *acting on their own* [emphasis added], seemed to be doing an effective job of recycling the surpluses of the oil countries, which soon came to be known as Petrodollars. The mechanism was simplicity itself. The major oil exporters found it convenient to place large parts of their dollar accumulations in the big, well-known international banks, particularly in the form of short-dated Eurodollars . . . The banks, now awash with liquidity, found willing borrowers for these huge sums in Latin America and elsewhere.[8]

A careful study of the historical record suggests the need for a more nuanced account. On the one hand, the notion that the banks acted "on their own" is simplistic. What does it mean for such highly regulated institutions to act autonomously? On the other hand, the transfer mechanism was not as straightforward as Volcker claims, and as the analysis in this chapter will amply demonstrate. Before looking at the statistics, however, a conceptual framework that relates oil prices to international financial markets must be established.

The immediate impact of higher oil prices on the world economy was to be found in the balance of payments. The oil crisis raised import costs for petroleum-consuming nations, leading to changes in the trade balance. In many cases, trade surpluses fell to trade deficits, which had to be financed. The industrial countries pursued a variety of strategies for righting their balance of payments, but common to all of them was a push for increased exports—exports that were financed in large measure with the help of government guarantees given to trade credits. Indeed, whereas in 1974 the seven largest industrial nations had a deficit on current account of almost $3 billion, by 1975 they enjoyed a surplus of nearly $25 billion.[9]

Higher oil prices also reverberated throughout the economy as a whole, and these were passed through by policy mechanisms that varied from one industrial country to another.[10] In some countries, like the United States, price controls were used to offset the direct impact of higher oil prices; this resulted in domestic shortages of refined petroleum products, especially heating oil and gasoline, and a slowdown in economic activity. In other countries, the price hikes were absorbed directly, leading to higher costs for capital and labor as wage demands were met. These higher costs, in the absence of related productivity gains, also tended to slow economic growth, which curbed demand for imports besides oil.

For the developing countries, the oil crisis meant that export markets contracted while import prices rose, precipitating a foreign exchange crunch. In theory, they could adjust to this problem by reducing imports, finding new export markets, or borrowing. In practice, many would find this last road to be the most appealing.[11]

A first-best solution to the oil crisis would have been found in the oil-producing nations themselves—that is, the income effects of the oil crisis would have been immediately offset by increased demand for investment and imports on the part of the oil-producing states. For example, developing countries which lost markets in the industrial countries could have shifted their sales to OPEC, maintaining foreign exchange earnings. But some OPEC countries—the "low absorbers," with small populations— were unable to make immediate use of all the funds they had collected following the price shocks, although both investments and imports did increase significantly after 1974; prominent low absorbers were Saudi Arabia, the United Arab Emirates, and Kuwait. Instead, they sought short-term solutions, such as purchasing treasury bills from the United States and other industrial countries, and parking funds with international banks as short-term deposits.

Here, too, the story of American power looms large. Following the oil shocks of 1974 and 1978, about 10 percent of OPEC money was invested in U.S. Treasury bills of one type or another. These purchases are not surprising in themselves, given the risk-averse nature of Arab investments.

But what is perplexing is that the astute Arabs continued to buy Treasury bills even as their paper investments were losing money, owing to pressures on the dollar. In a careful study of petrodollar recycling, political scientist David Spiro has shown that the United States government actively lobbied the Saudis and other oil producers to continue their purchases of Treasury bills, and to keep denominating oil sales in dollars. Thus, with the changing value of the dollar, oil prices in real terms had dropped significantly by 1976 from their 1974 peak, and Arab investments in U.S. Treasury bills therefore also declined in value. In short, a major beneficiary of petrodollar recycling was the United States itself.[12]

American power also emerges in the story of recycling to other parts of the world, especially the developing countries. The assertion that petrodollars were simply and autonomously recycled to these countries cannot be supported by the data on OPEC savings and investment behavior, or by statements of bankers at the time. During the three-year period following the first oil shock from 1974–76, OPEC revenues exceeded expenditures by approximately $140 billion. During that same period, the developing countries that lacked oil had deficits of nearly $78 billion, while the OECD countries as a whole had deficits of $62 billion (as noted above, the largest seven countries taken as a group were back in surplus by 1975).[13]

Of the approximately $125 billion in OPEC investments that can be traced from these years, the distribution of funds is revealing of the oil exporters' preferences. According to a report done by the U.S. Senate's Committee on Foreign Relations, "An estimated $48 billion was invested in government paper, portfolio and long-term direct investments in the industrial countries; another $9.75 billion was loaned to international organizations; and by far the largest amount, $49 billion, or 37 percent of the total, was deposited with private commercial banks, mostly in New York and London. Only $16 billion, or 12 percent of the total OPEC surpluses, went directly to the developing countries, mostly in the form of grants to Moslem countries."[14] Direct OPEC aid to the IMF and developing countries, therefore, accounted for only $26 billion in financing, leaving an additional $52 billion to be made up elsewhere.

It is this $52 billion which is the source of much of the conventional wisdom. These funds, according to most accounts, were allegedly moved by the Invisible Hand to the developing world. But once again, both quantitative and qualitative analyses fail to support the argument.

On the qualitative side, there were severe doubts following the oil crisis about the ability of developing countries to attract bank financing. As Brookings Institution analyst Edward Fried wrote in early 1974:

> Conventional standards of credit worthiness . . . will have to be altered since the oil-importing countries as a group will not be able to repay their obligations until the exporting countries are in a position to accept payment in the form of goods and services. In this respect, many developing countries face particularly difficult problems since doubts about their ultimate repayment capability severely detract from their present borrowing capacity. Taken together, these operating requirements suggest that *private commercial banks will not be willing, on their own, to handle a large portion of the financial load on a continuing basis* [emphasis added]. Therefore, the effectiveness of the financing network as a whole will depend on the extension or contingent availability of very large-scale intergovernmental credits; these credits could be provided bilaterally or through international financial institutions and would have to be offered on a quasi-automatic basis. *In effect, the complex of intergovernmental credits will have to serve internationally the lender-of-last resort function that central bank credits serve domestically* [emphasis added].[15]

Fried's analysis was remarkably perceptive, but many other similar sentiments can be found. Thus, an establishment think tank, the Committee on Economic Development (whose trustees included leading bankers and industrialists), wrote that "the banks that receive Eurocurrency deposits from OPEC prefer to lend them to governments and borrowers in countries with modest debt burdens and more favorable payments prospects. The problem therefore is to recycle OPEC funds among oil-consuming countries so that those in a weaker position are enabled to finance their essential . . . imports. To the extent that capital markets do not accomplish this . . . special government initiatives or new international facilities are required."[16]

Following the oil crisis, bank portfolios had a risk profile that was of growing concern to regulators throughout the industrial world. They were characterized by a maturity and interest rate mismatch, with short-term, floating-rate deposits funding long-term fixed loans; concentrated lending to the governments and state enterprises of a few developing countries (of these, Mexico, Brazil, and Argentina alone constituted more than one-third of the total); foreign exchange exposure; and declining capital ratios. With the failures of the Herstatt and Franklin National banks coming on the heels of the oil shock in 1974, and the tiering of interest rates in inter-bank markets that followed, supervisors became even more sensitive to the risks facing both individual banks and the payments system as a whole. As the Basle Committee's chairman, George Blunden, wrote, "These developments greatly magnified the risks involved in international banking . . . Furthermore, in these circumstances there began to be doubts about the ability of some countries, with less robust economies, to service their obligations in the international markets."[17]

Bankers were also becoming more cautious, given the volatility of the financial markets on the one hand, and the savings preferences of the oil producers on the other. This was not an environment that encouraged "autonomous" recycling, and indeed, according to David Spiro, bankers "wanted a political solution" to the petrodollar problem. Spiro correctly argues that bankers

> knew better than others that there was no inherent reason for recycling to take place automatically through international capital markets. On the liability side . . . banking officials feared the short-term nature of Arab deposits, and they saw no reason that those deposits would neces-sarily continue or stay in their banks. On the asset side, they feared reaching the prudent limits of credit exposure to any one borrower [and] they did not like lending for periods that were substantially longer than the maturity distribution of the deposit base.[18]

The world's most prominent banker, David Rockefeller of Chase Man-hattan, saw four impediments to recycling petrodollars. First, the mis-match of assets and liabilities, noted above; second, the credit exposure problem; third, the fact that Arab investors would ultimately seek alterna-tive investments to their short-term deposits in low-yielding accounts; and finally, the simple fact that most developing countries were not credit-worthy. In short, Rockefeller did not believe that markets would work without government assistance.[19]

Nor did the Central Intelligence Agency have confidence in the market mechanism. A CIA report, written in July 1974, stated that "financial markets . . . are not well suited to recycle surplus petrodollars. Many oil consumers will be unable to borrow enough on acceptable terms to finance their oil-related deficits."[20] The agency went on to suggest that the United States might have to play a more active role "in supporting lending to consuming countries."

Clearly, the banks were hesitant to place their funds in developing countries in the absence of government support for this undertaking, and ultimately they got the support they were looking for from the central bank governors of the Group of Ten Nations. It will be recalled that in September 1974, after the Bankhaus Herstatt and Franklin National crises, and in the face of the petrodollar problem, central bankers stated that "means are available . . . and will be used if and when necessary to help banks in the Eurocurrency system that get into trouble."[21] With this statement, the central bankers had provided the financial marketplace with the safety net that it needed before recycling could proceed. Indeed, upon hearing this statement, the Washington-based Committee on Economic Development, which counted such senior bankers as Ralph Leach of Morgan Guaranty and William Moore of Bankers Trust among its members, said that it "strongly" endorsed "the joint policy announced by the monetary authorities of the principal industrial countries."

Yet there was another element in the international financial system that gave the banks comfort as they proceeded to recycle petrodollars to the third world, and that was the presence of official loans through bilateral agreements and the international lending agencies, prominently the IMF and World Bank, in many of these same countries. In 1974, out of the $36 billion in net capital flows to developing countries, some $16 billion came from official sources. In 1975, when the developing world received $43 billion, $20 billion came as a result of bilateral or multilateral agreements. These loans were important to the commercial banks, because no country had defaulted on its official loans before, and it seemed impossible to default on the commercial banks while still hoping to receive official assistance. Thus, while the commercial banks may have become the largest providers of capital, official sources still made up 45 percent or more of all capital flows, making state and private sources intertwined in the developing world.[22]

Further, the IMF played a leading role in orchestrating the response to the recycling problem. According to Dankwart Rustow and John Mugno, "the first major initiative in this field was taken by H. Johannes Witteveen, managing director of the IMF, in January 1974, at a time when estimates of petrodollar surpluses were at their highest and fears of the deterioration of the world economy into a universal game of 'beggar thy neighbor' at their most acute."[23] Witteveen sought to establish an "oil facility" that would assist IMF members in meeting any "oil-induced deficits." By May 1974, Witteveen had received pledges from several oil-producing countries, including Saudi Arabia and Iran, and the following month the fund was established. Thus, petrodollars were recycled in this case with the explicit hand of the world's monetary policeman. And again, even though the size of the oil facility was relatively small in the context of the debt crisis ($6 billion), banks believed that with the IMF in the lending game they now had the equivalent of official support for their loans.

On the quantitative side, the story is also more complex than that indicated by the received wisdom. Indeed, within the Euromarkets, non-OPEC developing countries borrowed $25.5 billion in 1974–76, which amounted to less than one-third of those countries' overall current account deficit, and one-half of the requirement that remained after IMF and direct assistance.[24] Furthermore, 30 percent of the bank loans went to just two countries, Mexico and Brazil.[25] Thus, when we combine lending through the Euromarkets, and OPEC grants to the IMF and the developing countries, we have accounted for only $51 billion of the deficit.

The remainder of LDC borrowing took place not in some offshore financial center, but in the home offices of the European and American banks that also received deposits of oil money; in later years funds would also come from Japan, as its banks expanded internationally in the 1970s and early 1980s. But recycling these petrodollars to the developing world would also prove troublesome. In most of the industrial countries, including the United States, capital controls limited the outflow of funds from banks to international customers. "Autonomous" recycling had thus hit a roadblock.

The policy response was found in the lifting of such controls, and in January 1974 President Richard Nixon led the way. According to one account, "there was . . . an official desire to permit countries suffering large oil-induced trade deficits to seek compensating financing in the United States."[26] The World Bank would also raise over $2 billion during the years 1974–76 in the American marketplace. And in June 1974 the

United States led the International Monetary Fund in the creation of a special "oil facility" for developing countries, which ultimately made a further $6 billion of funds available.[27]

In short, "there were three major policy initiatives addressed to the problem of financial intermediation during the first half of 1974."[28] The relaxation of capital controls was of decisive importance, since it meant that those countries which were unable to raise funds directly from OPEC or via the Euromarkets could seek additional loans in the United States and western Europe. The IMF oil facility was important because it gave those countries in severe economic difficulties an emergency source of funds for import payments; the facility was largely financed by the oil exporters. Finally, the loans taken by the World Bank during this period were translated into developmental grants, largely in the energy field, for a number of developing countries.

In addition to these three financial policies, a fourth policy was adopted in the major industrial nations which further encouraged bank lending, and that was an increase in export guarantees. As Philip Wellons has shown, nothing less than a "trade credits war" erupted in the mid-1970s, as the industrial countries sought market share for their exports in the developing world. Export guarantees were a government insurance program, in which banks loaned money to the borrower (the developing country) so that it could buy imported goods from the home country. Principal and interest payments on these loans were guaranteed in whole or in part by the export-import bank of the industrial country.[29]

David Spiro has pointed out that "competition among advanced industrialized nations to improve exports to OPEC began almost as soon as they had promised each other not to compete. By 1975 Germany had reached a trade surplus with half of the members of OPEC, and by 1977 it was in surplus with all of OPEC. Similarly, the United Kingdom, which had been in deficit to OPEC before the oil shock, reached a surplus by 1977."[30]

The importance of these trade credit and promotion programs is often overlooked in accounts of financial recycling after the oil crises. But the scale of such programs was immense. By the end of fiscal year 1981, Japan's Export-Import Bank had outstanding loans of $22.5 billion, Germany's counterpart institution had loans of $13.4 billion, and the U.S. Ex-Im Bank held loans of $15.8 billion.[31] By the early 1980s, Britain's Ex-Im Bank was providing guarantees for fully one-third of all British exports.[32]

Beyond the direct impact on bank lending to the developing world, these programs also had an indirect impact on bank management. By demonstrating that governments were interested in promoting exports to the third world, the banks had been given the equivalent of a "comfort letter." Again, it seemed unthinkable that the developing countries would treat their official and bank creditors differently, since reneging on the one would immediately spill over to the other.

Thus, in the aftermath of the first oil shock, a number of policy measures were implemented that effectively encouraged the continued flow of funds to the developing world. To be sure, the measures were often ad hoc, and in hindsight many of these policies have proved to be mistaken.[33] But at the time, public officials in the industrial world believed that they had no choice but to respond to the crisis at hand, for both political and economic reasons. For the United States in particular, whose banks still dominated the international payments system and whose currency provided the international system with its liquidity, there was no obvious alternative to serving as crisis manager and (implicit) lender of last resort. Reluctantly, the central bankers of other industrial nations followed America's lead, but with some anxiety about where that path would ultimately take them.

The Clash of Domestic and International Objectives

Nonetheless, it should be emphasized that in 1974 and 1975 the deficits of the developing countries were hardly at the center of financial debates in most countries, including the United States. Throughout the industrial world, leaders were primarily concerned with their own domestic economies. For the United States, however, which stood as leader of the international economic system, the economic policy calculation was more complex. As Harvard economist Benjamin Friedman has written, "a feature of American monetary policy . . . since World War II has been the degree of influence associated with international considerations."[34] The U.S. government had to strike a balance in macroeconomic policy that took into account the needs of both the domestic and international economies.[35]

Most accounts of U.S. macroeconomic policy following the oil crisis focus solely on domestic politics, and indeed one could make a strong case for that approach. After all, policy shifted course on several occasions between 1974 and 1979, apparently because the government was trying to calm political pressures. The immediate response of Federal Reserve chairman Arthur Burns to the oil price shock in 1974 was to tighten monetary policy as a way of curbing inflationary pressures. Monetary policy continued on its restrictive course throughout the year, but unemployment had risen to nearly 9 percent by the beginning of 1975. With threats of congressional intervention in monetary policy growing daily, Burns began to relax his policy, and the money supply was allowed to grow rapidly from 1975 until 1979, when Paul Volcker became the new Federal Reserve Board chairman.[36]

Despite the tightening, however, expected inflation fears allowed real interest rates to turn negative between 1974 and 1977, as revealed in Table 3.1. These negative real interest rates, in turn, proved a boon for borrowers and consumers, and a loss for the OPEC nations that maintained short-term liquid investments in the United States and Euromarkets.

The data suggest that developing countries responded to the negative real interest rate environment, as demonstrated by the enormous growth in their debt between 1974 and 1979; indeed, the stock of debt grew at more than 20 percent per annum. At the same time, an increasing share of these loans was made by private financial institutions. Confident in their central banks' role as lender of last resort, they allowed the most important developing countries to obtain larger and larger amounts through "syndication," whereby many banks would subscribe to the loan package. Table 3.2 reveals the growth of external debt either held or guaranteed by the public sector in the developing world. Of this debt, American banks held about one-third of the total; when loans to the private

Table 3.1.   U.S. inflation and interest rates, 1972–1978.

	1972	1973	1974	1975	1976	1977	1978
Inflation (in percent)	3.3	6.2	11.0	9.2	5.8	6.5	7.7
3-month certificate of deposit	5.6	9.2	8.5	5.2	4.7	6.8	10.9

Source: David Lomax and P. Gutmann, *The Euromarkets and International Financial Policies* (New York: John Wiley, 1981), pp. 21–22. Reprinted by permission of John Wiley and Sons, Inc.

Table 3.2. Non-OPEC developing countries: Public and publicly guaranteed long-term external debt, 1973–1979 (in billions of dollars).

	1973	1974	1975	1976	1977	1978	1979
Total outstanding	76	95	115	139	172	212	246
Private creditors (banks, suppliers)	27	36	45	58	77	100	119

Source: International Monetary Fund, *International Capital Markets* (Washington, D.C.: IMF, 1980), p. 8.

sector are combined with the public debt cited above, the debt owed to U.S. commercial banks amounted to some $82 billion by 1979. Of greater significance, the debt held by the major commercial banks constituted, on average, more than 165 percent of their capital base.[37]

The increase in debt would not, by itself, necessarily pose a problem to the international economy, so long as the interest payments could be sustained by export earnings. But the data show that the "debt service ratio"—that is, the ratio of debt service payments to export earnings—was rising sharply in most debtor countries throughout the 1970s; note, however, that Korea's ratio was consistently below that found in Latin America. The debt service ratio was among the most important measures used by banks in assessing the creditworthiness of developing countries. Table 3.3 provides the debt service ratios of the major debtor nations.

In studying the borrowing capacity of developing countries, bankers examined a number of political and economic variables, in addition to subscribing to numerous consulting services (for example, Frost and Sullivan)

Table 3.3. Debt service ratios, 1973–1978.

Country	1973	1974	1975	1976	1977	1978
Brazil	27.5	25.3	36.5	42.0	44.0	53.7
Mexico	30.3	21.9	34.5	65.0	67.8	74.1
Argentina	22.0	22.1	34.0	30.0	20.5	45.6
Chile	40.8	34.5	47.4	44.5	55.0	58.4
Korea	13.6	12.4	13.6	11.1	12.0	14.0

Source: Bela Balassa, "Adjusting to External Shocks: The Newly-Industrializing Developing Economies in 1974–1976 and 1979–1981," *World Bank Reprint Series* 355 (1985).

that claimed some expertise in "country risk analysis." Over time, bankers would attach particular importance to the debt service ratio, which "relates the fixed foreign exchange outflow obligation of debt service payments to what is generally the major foreign exchange inflow. A shortfall in export earnings will force the government to draw down exchange reserves or cut down imports in order to accommodate debt service payments. Increased capital imports might, of course, compensate for the export shortfall."[38]

The importance of the debt service ratio in lending decisions is revealed in the following quote from one of the leading economists in the banking world, David Lomax:

> A measure I find convenient to use in assessing the creditworthiness of countries is their debt service ratio. The ratio measures on the one hand the payments required to service medium- and long-term debt, which means interest payments plus amortisation. This amount is then compared with a country's export receipts from goods and services, to give a percentage ratio. In assessing the creditworthiness of a country it is desirable first of all that the ratio shows stability or falls, thus indicating that the situation is under control. It is also preferable that the ratio be relatively low, and my own view is that a ratio of 20–25 percent is quite high enough. In the mid-1970s the criterion which I would have applied would have been that a country's debt be under control, which would be measured by the debt service ratio being stable or falling, and by the ratio being expected to continue to behave like that in so far as one could project into the future. In fact, debt service ratios were doing just that. The debt service ratio of all developing countries increased from 14 percent in 1975 to 19 percent in 1979, and then fell back to 17 percent in 1980 before rising to 28 percent in 1982.[39]

Yet the largest borrowers had debt service ratios much higher than that of "all developing countries." In 1976, Brazil's debt service ratio was already 37.2 percent, rising to 63.3 percent in 1979. For Mexico, the ratios climbed from 48.6 percent to 69.1 percent over the same time period.[40] Thus, the largest borrowers also seemed to have the highest ratios, leaving us with a puzzle.

Indeed, even as bankers were examining these ratios, some economists were questioning their usefulness. In a now-classic paper on international debt, Richard Cooper and Jeffrey Sachs argued that "the conventional indicators of capacity to handle external debt, such as the debt-servicing capacity or the debt/GNP ratio, have little theoretical basis." Cooper and Sachs found too much variability across a large number of cases to have confidence in this ratio as a predictor of either economic comfort or impending trouble.[41]

Where were the regulators as this debt mountain was piling up? Paul Volcker's account leaves an ambivalent picture. On the one hand, he tells the story of Federal Reserve chairman Arthur Burns calling a meeting in 1976 of senior officials from the major money center banks. Burns allegedly warned them "about the risk of repeating in foreign lands their recent excesses in real estate lending." What Burns got for his trouble, according to Volcker, "was a response that they knew more about banking than he did." On the other hand, he admits that "recycling [of petrodollars] was proceeding with surprising ease through the private banking markets, accompanied by a certain amount of cheerleading by the United States government itself."[42]

But policymakers cannot dismiss themselves as sideline cheerleaders; they are players in the game itself. Thus, they cannot escape responsibility for their actions by claiming that "the market" was responsible for unpleasant outcomes. As the *Financial Times* has written, "The inflationary policies of industrial countries generated the negative real interest rates of the 1970s that made borrowing so attractive. The sudden *volte face* in US monetary policy under Paul Volcker [in 1979] then triggered the debt crisis."[43]

In short, a combination of macroeconomic and microeconomic policies was used in support of greater foreign lending by American and European banks in the wake of the first oil crisis. This is not surprising, in that these banks were expected to be the single largest source of liquidity for the international payments system. In the absence of commercial bank financing, the trade and payments system would be choked, lowering economic growth around the world. Given an international system which looked to the United States for leadership, it seemed that Washington had no choice but to ensure that liquidity was provided in adequate amounts.

The Second Oil Shock

By 1975, the industrial world could feel rather smug about its handling of the first oil crisis. Inflation in the United States was brought down from 9 percent in 1974 to 6 percent in 1975, and unemployment levels also fell. With low interest rates, there was a significant rise in investment; business investment grew at 7 percent per year from 1975 to 1979.[44] The OECD judged that by the summer of 1975 the industrial world as a whole was "poised for a moderate recovery," and growth was vigorous in Europe and Japan by early 1976.[45] With recovery in the industrial world, the export-oriented developing countries could also hope to increase revenues and gross national product. Indeed, the current account deficit of the non-oil developing countries fell from $30 billion in 1975 to $12 billion in 1977.[46]

Banks, too, reported higher earnings from their international operations. Indeed, Citicorp reported in 1977 that "Brazil was the only overseas country contributing more than 10 percent to consolidated operating earnings (13 percent in 1976 and 20 percent in 1977). Earnings from Brazilian operations were approximately $74 million in 1977 compared with $54 million in 1976."[47] It is often overlooked in discussions of the debt crisis that several of the money center banks earned healthy profits from their *domestic* operations in Latin America, even if they were concerned with the risks of their *cross-border* loans. For Citicorp, South America as a whole contributed 27 percent of the bank's operating earnings in 1977, making it the single most important contributor to earnings, surpassing even the United States! Table 3.4 provides the data on Citicorp.

The optimism would prove short-lived. During the summer of 1978, the contract between Iran's oil workers and the foreign consortium that managed the nation's petroleum industry expired, and the negotiations quickly stalled. As the differences between the parties grew over time, strikes became more frequent. In October, the great refinery at Abadan was closed by strike activity, creating turmoil in world oil markets. As the autumn wore on, the position of the shah became increasingly untenable. By February 1979, the Ayatollah Khomeini had returned to Tehran from his long exile in Paris, establishing a new Islamic republic.[48] With Khomeini's victory, a new threat to the West—Islamic fundamentalism—appeared on the world stage.

The closure of the Iranian oil industry during the revolution caused

Table 3.4.   Citicorp's operating earnings after taxes, 1975–1977 (in millions of U.S. dollars).

Region	1977	Percent	1976	Percent	1975	Percent
United States	68	18	112	28	102	30
Asia and the Pacific	28	7	42	10	56	17
Canada and the Caribbean	44	12	36	9	44	12
Europe	96	25	91	22	58	17
South America	104	27	81	20	44	12
Rest of the world	41	11	43	11	44	12

Source: Citicorp, *Annual Report, 1977.* Reprinted by permission of Citicorp.

panic in world markets. The "spot" price for a barrel of oil climbed past $14 per barrel, 20 percent above the OPEC price, and then kept rising. According to the former undersecretary of state for economic affairs, Richard N. Cooper, states were willing to "pay any price" to get secure supplies of oil.[49]

With the sudden rise in oil prices, the current account balance of importing countries again went reeling into the red. For the industrial countries as a whole, the balance shifted from a positive $31 billion in 1978 to a negative $11 billion in 1979 and a negative $51 billion in 1980. In the developing world, deficits rose to a negative $68 billion in 1980. Again, these deficits would have to be financed through the capital markets.[50]

For the international financial markets, the events of 1978–79 were in many respects a repeat performance. The oil-exporting countries once again experienced a huge jump in their current account surplus, and the oil-importing developing countries faced significant deficits. These new deficits, however, had to be viewed in light of the large stock of bank debt these countries had already accumulated since 1973. Between 1974 and 1978 "the number of countries with arrears on current payments or conducting or seeking multilateral debt renegotiations increased from three to eighteen."[51] Indeed, writing in the wake of the second oil crisis, one economist stated that "there is now little scope for much further expansion of bank lending."[52] It thus seemed doubtful that recycling could proceed as it had in the past. And yet the recycling did proceed, and debt stocks continued to rise, as Table 3.5 reveals.

Table 3.5.   External lending by banks to non-OPEC developing countries, 1978–1982 (in billions of dollars).

	1978	1979	1980	1981	1982
New loans	26	41	49	51	25
Total stock	196	237	286	337	362

Source: International Monetary Fund, *International Capital Markets*, various issues.

By the end of 1982, Mexico had accumulated $63 billion, Brazil $60 billion, Venezuela $27 billion, and Argentina $26 billion of debt.[53] The question, of course, is how could this happen? How could external debt continue to grow, and why did private commercial banks continue to provide the loans, in the face of evidence that the risk of not getting repaid had greatly increased? Again, is it sufficient to say that banks "autonomously" loaned the money?

Once more, Paul Volcker's analysis of the period is disingenuous. Before becoming Federal Reserve Board chairman in 1979, Volcker had been president of the Federal Reserve Bank in New York, which was at the hub of international banking activity. During the late 1970s, he recalls, there were efforts to "devise a much more sophisticated apparatus to guide our examiners and banks in the area of foreign lending." The idea was to develop a type of "warning system," and specifically the bank "began doing a lot of country analysis" in support of this effort. Volcker states that "I personally spent a long time working on the framework, but . . . we found it did little to slow the lending."[54]

With the oil shock of 1979, lending increased to accommodate balance-of-payments problems. But now the interest rate environment began to change. When Volcker became its chairman, the Federal Reserve Board focused its monetary policies on curbing inflation, "and the days of negative real interest rates were over."[55] This would clearly make it more difficult for borrowers to repay their loans, but again the lending continued. Volcker writes that "it wasn't hard to see the [debt] crisis coming," yet again he did nothing to halt the capital flows.

The reason simply is that nothing could be done at this point; the best policy was to muddle through. Volcker admits as much when he says that his policy in 1982 "was a matter of buying time," but this had been the unstated policy of the Federal Reserve since at least 1979 or 1980.[56] The

Economist goes even further, arguing that after 1979 "several central banks have been ready to twist arms, persuading the commercial banks to keep lending to Latin America."[57] A sudden slowdown in lending would have squeezed these countries, making it even harder for them to pay back the debt that had already accumulated. Ironically, more loans had to be provided if the old ones were to be serviced. Most individual banks, aware of the growing risks, would have been ready to halt LDC lending. But if each had taken this view, the lending as a whole would have stopped. This collective action problem was largely overcome by central banks. As the *Economist* reported, "though commercial banks dislike being bullied by their central banks, many admit it was necessary."[58]

Indeed, the United States government also changed important accounting rules that had previously limited commercial bank lending to sovereign borrowers. By the late 1970s, a major constraint on lending was being reached, and that was the rule that prevented banks from lending more than 10 percent of their capital to any single "person, copartnership, association, or corporation."[59] Bank examiners had traditionally treated a foreign government as a "person," meaning that obligations to various parts of the government, such as state enterprises, would all be combined for legal lending limit purposes. Once these limits were reached, lending to the foreign government in question would have to stop.

Facing these limits, in 1979 the comptroller of the currency, John Heimann, reached, in Volcker's words, "a Solomon-like judgment." It was determined that if a foreign borrower, even a government agency, had an independent financing operation—like Pemex, the state-owned oil company of Mexico—it would, for American accounting purposes, be considered a separate entity from its government or other public borrowers. Accordingly, foreign governments could now divide their bureaucracies into separate financial entities, allowing banks to lend without fear of hitting the overall 10 percent limit.[60]

It is important to note that Heimann's decision *went beyond the lobbying requests of the banks themselves*. According to Philip Wellons, Chase Manhattan Bank, for example, had proposed that the law should be relaxed to permit foreign governments to borrow up to 25 percent of capital. Heimann's decision, in contrast, would allow banks to loan many times their capital to a foreign government, so long as the borrowers had separate identities.

This change in the rules was not the product of haphazard decisionmaking. Instead, it reflected American strategy. The change "allowed indebted public-sector borrowers outside the United States to continue to borrow from U.S. banks."[61] Indeed, the Senate Committee on Foreign Relations would sharply criticize the Heimann decision, accurately predicting its effect on debt accumulation.

Yet while the Federal Reserve was watching over a substantial increase in third-world lending, it was simultaneously adopting policies at home that would make debt repayment more difficult to achieve, at least over the short run. As has often been the case, the United States acted to sever the domestic and foreign marketplaces, applying separate policies for each as it pursued its strategic goals. Obsessed with the domestic fight against inflation and with the depreciation of the dollar,[62] chairman Volcker applied the monetary brakes in 1979 and kept them on throughout 1980. Interest rates responded, rising quickly and increasing the floating-rate obligations of debtors. With increasing real interest rates, it was clear that borrowers would be forced to reschedule their loans. But a sudden announcement by the Federal Reserve in 1980 to the effect that lending must now cease would have sent financial markets into a panic. There was nothing to do but continue lending to developing countries in the meantime and muddle through until the crisis hit; with a little luck, perhaps the crisis would be altogether avoided.

This analysis, of course, is not provided to justify the behavior of the banks. As Benjamin Cohen has written, "Bankers are not indifferent to signals from the government sector, but ultimately bank managers must answer to their investors and shareholders."[63] This is undoubtedly true, but there is more to the story than that; after all, bankers and regulators are interdependent. When governments want something of banks, they are able to exercise substantial leverage over financial institutions. The ability to expand, to merge, or even to place a new ATM machine on the corner is contingent upon approval from banking authorities. Given the importance of these decisions to the bank as a whole, the acceptance of additional lending to a developing country may have been viewed as the price of doing business.

This is not to argue that bankers were simply coerced into lending by their governments. To the contrary, when it came to international lending, *the interests of bankers and officials were largely convergent during the years*

1974–79. Bankers sought profitable investments for their cash, and found them in the large, syndicated loans to sovereign states, with their generous fees and wide spreads. The loans seemed to be guaranteed; not only was it unlikely that sovereign borrowers would default, but the central banks of the industrial countries and the International Monetary Fund would have to play lender of last resort in the event of a crisis. As it turned out, the bankers were proved correct.

From the perspective of government officials, international bank lending also served important policy goals. The building of a liberal world economy had been a consistent American objective since the end of World War II, and that goal had been challenged by an oil cartel. If balance-of-payments financing were not provided, American leadership would be viewed as a failure. With insufficient funds available in official aid programs, however, the instruments of U.S. policy were largely in the private sector. Incentives therefore had to be provided to keep these actors in the game.

After 1979, the story becomes more complex for both states and firms. It is now clear that the conventional wisdom that asserts banks were throwing money at developing countries "autonomously" is incorrect. The historical record shows that there was ample discussion between the banks and their governments about further lending. But in the end, it seems that there was little scope for significant policy change. The debt stocks built up by 1979 would not dissolve of their own accord; the only hope was to await a return to global economic growth that would promote third-world export industries. The locomotive behind this growth had to be the United States. If high interest rates prompted developing countries to reschedule their loans, the Federal Reserve would have no choice but to deal with that crisis when and if it arose.

In no case study of international finance is there greater divergence between official words and official actions than in the story of petrodollar recycling. For a generation, central bankers have said (and observers have believed) that, following the oil shocks of 1973–74 and 1978–79, financial markets acted on their own to recycle Arab wealth to the developing world. As I have tried to show, this is largely a fiction.

In the aftermath of the first oil crisis, the leaders of the industrial world faced one of their greatest postwar challenges. The international cooperation that had been so carefully developed since World War II was on the verge of giving way to beggar-thy-neighbor trade policies and a mad scramble for oil supplies. For the developing world, the hope of sustained economic growth was about to be shattered by rising oil prices and indebtedness.

With the long view of history now granted us, it may seem that banks and governments sent excessive amounts of official and private funds to the developing world, or at least to some countries. Indeed, there is a powerful contrast between the economic performance of the East Asian "tigers" that adjusted to the oil shocks through outward-oriented policies, and the Latin American countries that delayed adjustment. Had the Korean and Taiwanese model been followed in other developing countries, perhaps the global debt crisis would have been avoided.

But under the pressure of time and the events then at hand, officials saw no choice but to encourage international lending to all those in need. The world economy rested on free trade and investment flows, and the developing world was only gradually becoming integrated into this international system. A failure to provide funds and maintain oil imports could have proved costly in both economic and political terms.

And so the money went south. For a brief period between the first and second oil shocks, it appeared that the financial strategy had worked and that stability would be regained. But after 1979, this hope could no longer be sustained. Having overcome the energy crises of the 1970s, the world's leaders would now have to confront the debt crisis of 1982.

4 | The Debt Crisis

The major difference between the 1930s and the 1980s appears to lie in the absence of a "hegemonic" power in the 1930s, a role that the United States fills in the 1980s.

—JEFFREY SACHS

The debt crisis that erupted during the summer of 1982 posed the greatest challenge to international economic stability that the world had faced since the Great Depression. At the time, many observers viewed the international financial system as a house of cards, ready to be blown down at any instant by Mexico or Brazil. The world's largest commercial banks held claims against the developing world that were a multiple of their shareholders' equity; thus, widespread debt repudiation would make the banks insolvent.

Yet within a decade, the debt problems of the developing world were already fading into history; by 1992 a headline in the *Economist* could read "The Debt Crisis: R.I.P."[1] In Latin America, political democratization and economic liberalization were combining to give the region new hope for sustained development. In East Asia, debt problems were generally a distant memory as the newly industrializing countries continued on their remarkable path of economic growth. In Africa, the record remained less optimistic, but even in that region some countries were beginning to remove the shackles of repressive state intervention in political and economic life. And in the industrial world, fears that the debt crisis would lead to the collapse of the banking system had largely evaporated.[2]

   This chapter focuses on the role of creditor governments, especially the United States, in managing the debt crisis. Indeed, one of the most important statements that can be made about the crisis is that it *was* managed by governments. During the early 1980s, bankers and public officials agreed that states must play a leadership role, since they both doubted that markets, acting on their own, could produce an outcome that was in anyone's interest.

   From a theoretical perspective, there were several good reasons to expect governments to take the lead in crisis management. First, everyone viewed the crisis as a systemic shock which could collapse the international financial system. Only states had the capacity to mobilize sufficient liquidity to keep the system running. Second, as economist Jeffrey Sachs has pointed out, "international loan agreements are difficult to enforce, so official pressures would be needed in order to keep countries from repudiating their debts."[3] Third, in the absence of the state's coercive power, individual banks would be tempted to withdraw from lending markets; if each bank followed its selfish interests, the system as a whole would grind to a halt.[4] Finally, creditor governments (often acting through international institutions) could impose conditionality on any new borrowing by the debtors.[5] None of these tasks could have been adequately carried out by the marketplace alone.

   However, the policies actually adopted by states during the crisis reflected not only a general public interest in maintaining a safe and sound international financial system, but the preferences of private banking interests as well. In the United States, the money center banks grew concerned that the government would overreact to the crisis by slapping them with burdensome new regulations. All things being equal, such regulations would place them at a disadvantage in the competitive world of international finance. The banks thus negotiated with public officials to ensure an outcome that addressed both state and private sector needs.[6]

   It should not be forgotten that one important group was largely excluded from the policymaking equation when the crisis erupted, and that group consisted of the poor in the debtor countries. There was nobody to give them a voice in the creditor governments, money center banks, or multilateral institutions, and one wonders how much they were heard even by their own governments. They would bear the brunt of the austerity measures that followed after 1982, guinea pigs to one economic theory after another. When we remember "The Debt Crisis: R.I.P.," we should remember, as well, those who suffered as a result of the policy choices made in industrial countries, international institutions, and the developing world during the 1980s.

Defining the Debt Crisis

Debt crises, of course, are nothing new in financial history. Indeed, as political scientist David Spiro argues, one of the best predictors of future debt crises is to examine from a historical perspective which countries have gotten into trouble in the past.[7] Repeatedly in the last century, investors have lost money in Mexico, Brazil, and other developing countries. Money lenders, it appears, have accepted the Hegelian dictum that "the only thing we learn from history is that we don't learn from history."

What, in fact, is a debt crisis? As economist Richard Kohl has observed, "discussions of LDC debt often suffer from a certain theoretical fuzziness."[8] In fact, some economists pose the question of whether a "debt crisis" should even be considered as a separate category for economic analysis. Paul Krugman, for example, distinguishes between what he calls a *currency* crisis and a *contagion* crisis. The former "involves a loss of confidence by speculators in a country's currency, provoking capital flight." The latter "involves not loss of confidence in a currency, but a loss of confidence in real assets." The debt crisis, for Krugman, was really a currency crisis; the stock market crash of 1987, which quickly became a global problem, is an example of a contagion crisis.[9]

In identifying debt and currency crises, Krugman points to an important issue: confidence. During the early 1980s the wealthy in many developing countries lost confidence in the ability of their governments to manage economic policy. Instead of investing in their homelands, people sent their money abroad, and capital flight became rampant, particularly in some Latin American countries. Thus, a vicious circle began to spin, because once domestic investors lost confidence, so did foreign investors. The currency of many countries—a proxy for confidence in the government—became virtually worthless. Table 4.1 provides some data on external debt and capital flight during the critical years 1974–82.

And yet Krugman's definition is somewhat too narrow for our purposes. It focuses our attention on the *economic* dimension of a debt crisis,

Table 4.1. External debt and capital flight for eight major debtor countries, 1974–1982 (in billions of dollars).

	Gross external debt[a]	Capital flight[b]
Argentina	43.6	15.3
Brazil	90.5	(0.2)
Chile	17.3	(1.9)
South Korea	37.1	0.6
Mexico	85.6	32.7
Peru	11.6	1.2
Philippines	23.3	n.a.
Venezuela	31.8	10.8

N.a. = not available.

a. Gross amount owed by the country at the end of 1982.

b. Net amount that flowed from the country during the eight-year period.

Source: Mohsin S. Khan and Nadeem Ul Haque, "Capital Flight from Developing Countries," *Finance and Development* 24 (March 1987): 4.

but not on its *political* dimension. What we seek is a definition that forces us to think about the interplay between economic and political forces.

In this regard, Richard Kohl's definition is useful. Kohl defines a debt crisis as "rescheduling under duress; the rescheduling of a country's contractual commitments with multilateral institutions, private lenders or both, because of an inability or unwillingness to meet its current obligations."[10] In addition to multilateral institutions and private borrowers, he might have mentioned "other governments," since much of the lending was done on a bilateral basis, often driven by export credit guarantees. (Indeed, these bilateral claims were negotiated in a separate forum, the "Paris Club," which consists of the major industrial countries.) Nonetheless, Kohl's definition clearly states that a country faces a debt crisis when it has no choice, for either internal or external reasons, but to go to its lenders and seek new terms. It requires us to ask about both the economic and political aspects of how the crisis developed, and how it was managed.

The question then arises: How *do* such crises come about? Three theories have competed for explanatory primacy: the *external shocks* theory, favored by bankers and many in the developing countries; the *overlending* theory, which places the onus on the banks; and the *adjustment policy* theory, which focuses on the policy failures of the developing countries themselves.[11]

Briefly, the external shocks theory focuses on the role of the oil crises of 1973–74 and 1978–79, the recession in the international economy, and the rise in world interest rates in 1979–80 as being the major causal factors in launching the debt crisis. In the absence of these external shocks, the debtor countries would have been able to continue servicing their debts. It was policy in the OPEC and OECD countries, and not in the LDCs themselves, that precipitated the debt crisis of 1982.

A major problem with this theory is that the developing countries responded differently to these external shocks, and some fared better than others. In particular, East Asian countries weathered the storms while maintaining low inflation and reasonable growth rates, whereas Latin American countries suffered. Given that the oil and interest rate shocks were exogenous to these countries, the divergence in performance can be explained only by differing policy responses.[12]

The overlending theory focuses on bank behavior following the oil shocks. Specifically, it regards the banks as essentially free agents in the recycling of petrodollars. In the words of one adherent of this theory, Robert Devlin, "unregulated private financial markets are prone to over-expansion and crisis." Moreover, Devlin asserts that "credit markets could aid and abet any domestic forces in the debtor country directed toward overborrowing."[13]

The weakness of this theory, as earlier chapters have demonstrated, is that banks and financial markets cannot be regarded as "unregulated" entities. On the contrary, they are among the most regulated economic sectors, and I have tried to show that much of their lending behavior was encouraged by governments. It is thus insufficient to argue that banks acted on their own in pushing money overseas.

Indeed, as we saw in Chapter 3, a major policy response by OECD governments to the oil shocks was to encourage developing countries to *accommodate* rather than *adjust* to the price increases by borrowing from banks. This point was made explicit by deputy secretary of state Elinor Constable in a 1983 review:

Our policy did not focus on the need to adjust. Rather, our primary concern was the encouragement of efficient "recycling" of the OPEC surplus—a euphemism for the assurance that countries would be able to borrow as much as they needed. The incentive to borrow rather than to adjust was strong. Interest rates were low or negative in relation to current and expected inflation; liquidity was abundant; and both borrowers and lenders expected that continued inflation would lead to ever-increasing export revenues and reduce the real burden of foreign debt.[14]

Official encouragement of LDC lending, however, does not necessarily explain bank policy unless the banks themselves had an interest in pursuing these new lending opportunities. When viewed through the lens of hindsight, perhaps most if not all banks would agree that they would not repeat the experiment of the 1970s and 1980s if given the chance.[15] Thus, there is an important grain of truth in the overlending hypothesis. To be sure, banks were encouraged to lend by their governments. But not all banks got into trouble, and some were less eager to lend than others. Bank managers, therefore, must accept their share of responsibility for the depositor and equity funds they invested in the developing world.

The final theory focuses on macro- and microeconomic policymaking in the developing countries themselves. Again, this theory arises out of a comparative analysis of different countries' experiences with debt in the late 1970s and early 1980s, especially those of East Asia and Latin America. On the one hand, this theory has enormous power. After all, governments are expected by their citizens to provide responsible economic management. There are many exogenous shocks of one type or another, and states exist to provide economic and military security to their citizens in a dangerous world.

But this theory also has limits. As we have seen, countries were encouraged to borrow not so much by banks but by OECD governments, which focused on accommodating the oil shocks rather than adjusting to them. Again, the story is more complicated than the adjustment policy theory suggests.

In the end, the three theories are best viewed as complementing one another. At the systemic level, there can be no doubt that countries were encouraged to borrow in the wake of the oil shocks, and that monetary policy shifts in the industrial world after 1979 (especially in the United States), coupled with a world recession, eventually made the debt burden unmanageable for many countries. With regard to banks, there is little question now that overlending occurred because they had every confidence in their lenders of last resort. And with respect to the debtors, the observer must be impressed by the variety of economic policies adopted in the wake of the crisis, and the ability of some states to withstand the external shocks better than others.

Managing the Crisis

On August 12, 1982, a startling piece of news flashed across the wires. Mexican finance minister Silva Herzog announced that his country would be unable to meet its upcoming interest payment obligations to foreign banks. The Mexican announcement was not entirely unexpected in Washington. For months the country had been relying on the discreet support of the Federal Reserve in maintaining its foreign exchange levels. But now it would have to take a more public approach to debt management.

The wider implications of the debt crisis were immediately appreciated by all concerned. As Benjamin Cohen has written, "Should the Mexican storm spread to other major Latin borrowers, such as Brazil or Argentina, there was no telling what might happen to the structure of international finance—or to the whole world economy for that matter."[16] But at the time, it was unclear how the crisis would be managed, and whether the United States, just coming out of a prolonged recession, would be willing to lead.

Mexico's cash crunch posed significant policy challenges to all of the actors involved, including the banks, the governments of creditor states, multinational investors, the relevant international institutions, and, most poignantly, the debtors themselves. Essentially, the crisis threatened the international payments system in two ways. First, it threatened to stifle trade, investment, and financial flows between the industrial and developing countries, choking the world economy. Second, it threatened the solvency of the banks, which did not have sufficient capital to absorb the losses from unpaid debts. If their depositors became aware of this shortfall, a run on the banks would begin, and only massive government intervention would be able to stem it.

From the perspective of each individual bank, the debt crisis was analogous to a prisoner's dilemma. As Clive Crook of the *Economist* pointed out, "It was in the interest of every individual bank to avoid new lending. But if every bank put that view into effect, the debtors' shortage of capital would have been so severe that it would have left them with literally no choice but to default—and that would have turned the banks' risk into a banking catastrophe."[17]

Yet it appeared at first that the prisoner's dilemma might play itself out. Whereas in 1981 total bank claims on Latin America had increased by $25 billion, and despite the fact that in 1982 another $23 billion was provided,[18] in the eighteen months following the Mexican announcement "there was absolutely no spontaneous new lending to the region at all."[19] In the absence of even short-term credits, the international trade and payments systems would grind to a halt.

But the world economy did not collapse as a result of the debt crisis, although suffering in the developing world reached new depths during the 1980s; indeed, according to the World Bank, "in twenty-one out of thirty-five low-income developing countries, the daily calorie supply per capita was lower in 1985 than in 1965."[20] But in contrast to the situation in the 1930s, when the leading industrial powers refused to cooperate in meeting a systemic crisis, after the debt shock the United States provided decisive hegemonic leadership.[21] The United States led the central banks of the richest nations in providing nothing less than lender-of-last-resort support to ailing Mexico, injecting the liquidity needed to keep the international financial system in operation.

The most immediate problem in August 1982 was to get more cash to Mexico—on top of the $700 million that had quietly been provided since the beginning of the year by the United States government. Mexico's crisis was caused not only by its inability to generate enough revenue to pay interest to the banks, but also by massive "capital flight": hard currency was leaving the country as soon as it entered. Wealthy Mexicans had lost confidence in their country; now the confidence would have to be provided by the U.S. Federal Reserve. In effect, the Federal Reserve would have to take the place of the Central Bank of Mexico.

Over the weekend that followed Herzog's debt moratorium announcement, American officials, led by Paul Volcker and Treasury secretary Donald Regan, scrambled to put together a massive bailout package that linked several U.S. government agencies and the Group of Ten industrial countries. The Department of Energy purchased oil from Mexico, the Department of Agriculture advanced food aid and credits, and the Federal Reserve and its fellow central banks put together a $1.85 billion loan; in total, Mexico enjoyed a $3.5 billion weekend. Nonetheless, the country would still be forced to reschedule its debt payments with the commercial banks.[22]

During the early stages of the debt crisis, a fundamental element of government strategy was to tighten the bonds of interdependence between central and commercial banks and the international institutions in the creditor nations; the debtors would therefore face a united front. This strategy was apparent at the outset. During the week following the Mexican bailout, a meeting was held in New York between the Federal Reserve, the government of Mexico, and commercial bank representatives. The banks were told that not only must the existing debt to Mexico be restructured, but additional loans must be made. At the same time, the creditor governments would provide Mexico with an emergency injection of liquidity.

Many of the banks, especially smaller, regional institutions, wanted to get out at this point and take their losses. But the Federal Reserve, through a mixture of persuasion and coercion, did its job of keeping the banks together; after all, commercial banks that were members of the Federal Reserve system could not even open a new branch or install an ATM down the street without Volcker's approval.[23] Indeed, one of the Federal Reserve's most important functions during the debt crisis was to keep the commercial banks in the lending game.[24]

During the summer and autumn of 1982, Volcker and Treasury secretary Donald Regan fashioned a two-pronged strategy for dealing with the debt problem. The broad purpose of this strategy, which consisted of "short-term crisis management and longer-term stabilization,"[25] was nothing less than to maintain the international payments system (see figure on page 90). In effect, the short-term solution was to inject enough liquidity into the payments system to ensure its uninterrupted operation. The longer-term plan was to strengthen the international banks that were threatened by the crisis and restore the economies of the debtor countries so they would ultimately be able to reenter the international economy on "spontaneous" terms.[26] Both strategies required massive government support.

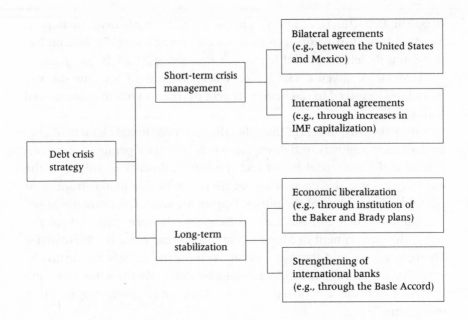

The question arises as to why the central banks of western Europe and Japan joined in the bailout if the United States was indeed the "hegemonic" leader. As they have done in so many other issue-areas (such as defense), why didn't the allies simply act as "free riders," and let the entire burden rest on the Federal Reserve? Paul Volcker has called the support of his central bank colleagues "a remarkable example of international financial cooperation." What does "cooperation" mean in this context?[27]

The parsimonious explanation is that they, too, were worried about the effect of a Mexican collapse on their national banking systems. The United States argued that it could not put together a rescue package that would win domestic political acceptance without the support of the other major central banks. Each central banker then had to decide whether or not to call the Federal Reserve's hand. The risk of having the package fall through was too great for the central bankers to accept.[28] After all, Japanese and British banks also had substantial exposure to Mexico, as did Canadian, French, and German banks. Rather than view the bailout as a loan to Mexico, a central bank would view it instead as an advance to its own nationally based financial institutions. In this context, each central bank was acting as lender of last resort for its own banks, affirming the principle of home country control.

Mexico, of course, would be only the first of many countries that rescheduled their debt in 1982 and the years thereafter.[29] Argentina and Brazil would soon follow, each receiving emergency aid from the world's central banks, additional lending from the commercial banks, and IMF support. Indeed, in 1983 some twenty countries signed rescheduling agreements with the IMF and the banks.[30]

It should be emphasized that a critical element of the creditor strategy was to work out each crisis on a case-by-case basis. Each debtor was treated individually, and as a result the divided debtor countries faced a united front of creditor banks, governments, and international institutions. This worked against those countries, such as Peru, that sought (with vociferous Cuban support) to establish a "debtor's cartel."

To be sure, this sounds unfairly sinister. As Citicorp banker William Rhodes has pointed out, "a look at the distinctive varieties of . . . plan employed . . . in Mexico, Venezuela, Argentina, Brazil, the Philippines and Uruguay shows how ill-suited a generic response would have been."[31] Nonetheless, at the outset of the crisis a number of academic solutions all called for a global as opposed to a case-by-case response.

Yet another major element of creditor strategy was to place substantial responsibility for crisis management on international institutions, especially the IMF. Ironically, in its first years of office, the IMF was subject to heated criticism by the Reagan administration, and there were even intimations that Washington would withdraw from active participation in the organization. With the emergence of the crisis, the utility of the IMF became readily apparent. It could help depoliticize crisis management and lead to greater burden sharing by the IMF's member states. In short, even the Reagan administration recognized that it needed the help of international organizations.

But in order to play a significant role, the IMF would need greatly enhanced resources—a prospect that in 1982 seemed unlikely, given the history of hostility by the Reagan administration toward its operations. Furthermore, in order for it to obtain these resources the Reagan administration would have to go to Congress, which was scarcely a hotbed of support for either the IMF or the money center banks. Given this background, it is not surprising that one U.S. Treasury official found the mood of the September 1982 meeting of the IMF and World Bank to be "almost universally morose. Fear was widespread that the world's banking system would collapse, bringing an implosion of credit, then trade, and ultimately an inevitable worldwide depression."[32] Yet following the Toronto meeting, the administration would indeed seek additional funds for the IMF (as part of an overall increase in the IMF quota), and with that request the debt crisis would become fully enmeshed with domestic politics.

The Domestic Politics of the Debt Crisis

In early 1983, the Reagan administration went to Congress to seek $8.4 billion for America's share of an IMF funding increase. The request was not greeted warmly. As Jake Garn of the Senate Banking Committee responded, "There will be legislation . . . The price of $8.4 billion in the Congress is going to be legislation . . . so we can go home and say we didn't bail out the big banks."[33]

Congress demanded that the three bank supervisors—Paul Volcker of the Federal Reserve Board, C. T. Conover of the Office of the Comptroller of the Currency (OCC), and William Isaac of the Federal Deposit Insurance Corporation (FDIC)—report back to them with a new package of banking regulations. This demand, it should be noted, was made at a time when the country was undergoing massive banking deregulation, especially in the savings and loan industry. In the event, the three supervisors returned to Congress on April 7, 1983, with a joint "Program for Improved Supervision and Regulation of International Lending."

The program contained five key elements: (1) the existing program of examination and evaluation of country risk should be strengthened; (2) banks should provide greater information regarding their country exposure; (3) special reserves against losses, called allocated transfer risk reserves (ATRRs), should be created; (4) supervisory rules for accounting for fees associated with loan transactions should be established; (5) international cooperation among foreign banking regulators and through the IMF should be increased. The goal of such cooperation, according to the supervisors, would be "to help achieve the objectives of risk diversification and strengthened financial conditions that we have set for ourselves."[34]

Overall, the regulators had presented Congress with a general set of guidelines rather than any new body of rules. This suggests that, despite claims by some observers that bank lending to the developing world had been "excessive" for nearly a decade, public officials believed they had sufficient instruments at their disposal to provide adequate supervision of these institutions. The regulators preferred to deal with the banks in an informal and flexible manner rather than be tied to a new set of laws mandated by Congress.

Of the five proposals, only the third—to create special reserves—could have resulted in some modification of bank behavior. But even here there were so many loopholes that almost every bank was able to avoid its implications. The purpose of this provision was to force banks to establish a new set of reserves—apart from the "loan loss reserves" that every bank had, in order to absorb credit losses in the portfolio—against foreign debt. Unlike loan loss reserves, these provisions would be deducted from current earnings and would not be included as part of bank capital. Obviously, no bank wanted to keep such costly reserves on its books.

But in reality there were only a few cases in which they would be required to do so. The regulators said that such reserves were unnecessary in those cases "where the terms of any restructuring of debt were being met, where interest payments were being made and where the borrowing country is complying with the terms of an IMF-approved stabilization program."[35] In the event, there were not many countries in these categories, and banks were prepared to write off such loans from their books, counting them as partial or total losses; this mitigated the need for any special reserves.

One additional issue raised by the supervisors would prove to be the most important of all, and that had to do with capital adequacy. The authorities stated in their memorandum that "federal banking regulators will . . . analyze a bank's capital adequacy in relation to the level of diversification of the bank's international portfolio. Those institutions with relatively large concentrations will be expected to maintain generally higher overall capital ratios." But no minimum capital standards were as yet applied to the money center banks, even though their smaller brethren had been required to meet a minimum standard since 1981; Congress, however, would demand that minimum capital levels be placed on large commercial banks as well.

In the hearings that followed, the U.S. banks warned that any new unilateral regulations could result in decreased domestic and international lending, as well as a loss in relative competitiveness with regard both to foreign banks and to nonbank financial institutions. The banks argued that further pressure to raise capital levels—pressure that they had been experiencing since the late 1970s—would place them at a competitive disadvantage with respect to banks from such countries as Japan and France, which faced lower capital requirements. Whatever its merits, this analysis resonated on Capitol Hill. As Representative Charles Schumer of New York, a regular target of bank lobbying, stated, "We cannot put our banks at a competitive disadvantage to German, Japanese, or other banks."[36]

The bankers' pleas created a dilemma for Congress. The congressmen wanted stiffer regulations, if only to help them sell the IMF package to their domestic constituents. But they did not want American banks to suffer competitively as a result. A Solomonic decision was thus made in the process of reconciling the House and Senate versions of the banking bill; interviews I have conducted with public officials suggest that the breakthrough ideas were proposed on the Senate side—a result that echoes Nelson Polsby's finding that the Senate is indeed a "great incubator of policy innovation."[37]

The senators felt strongly that bank capital should be raised, for two reasons: first, bank capital generated positive externalities, in that its social benefits were greater than its private benefits to bank shareholders; if each bank went out and raised more capital, it would help restore confidence in the international financial system as a whole. Second, the imposition of tougher capital standards would demonstrate that the American taxpayer alone would not have to recapitalize the entire financial system, but that bank shareholders would also bear some responsibility.

Tougher standards for U.S. banks, however, might permit highly leveraged foreign firms to gain market share at American expense. The system would be no stronger as a result, and American jobs would be lost. Congressmen were concerned about the safety and soundness of the international financial system, but they were also paid to worry about competitiveness and jobs. The obvious solution to this dilemma was to promote international convergence in banking regulations, especially in the area of capital adequacy. This topic is treated in detail in the following chapter.

The IMF quota increase, the new regulatory package, and the banks' concerns about competitiveness were synthesized in the subsequent IMF-related legislation known as the International Lending Supervision Act (ILSA) of 1983. In addition to legislating the five points put forward by the supervisors, Congress also demanded that minimum levels of capital adequacy be determined for all banks. However, such a move would not be done solely at the domestic level. Indeed, ILSA called upon "governments, central banks, and regulatory authorities of other major banking countries to work toward . . . strengthening the capital bases of banking institutions involved in international lending." If the banks were going to be forced to raise capital, at least it would be done on a multilateral rather than a unilateral basis. In the best Washington tradition, ILSA was officially passed in the spring of 1983 as Title IX of a large housing bill.

ILSA exemplifies the interplay of public and private interests in the shaping of regulatory policy toward commercial banks. The state and the banks had a convergent interest in managing the debt crisis in such a way as to maintain the stability of the financial system. For their part, the banks wanted to escape paying any financial penalty for the actions they had taken in lending excessively overseas; indeed, with sufficient government support, the banks might even avoid taking a hit in the stock market. But state actors, forced to advance state interests in such a way as to maintain their positional power and legitimacy in the system, could not ask the taxpayer to foot the entire bill for the debt crisis. Instead, a formula had to be devised which made banks pay a share of the costs without placing them at a competitive disadvantage in the international marketplace. As we will see in Chapter 5, U.S. officials would push for international convergence of capital adequacy regulations as the centerpiece of a new regime for international finance.

Muddling Through

There can be no doubt that the U.S. government's overriding objective at the outset of the debt crisis was to maintain the stability of the international payments system and, by extension, the safety and soundness of the commercial banks. As Harvard economist Jeffrey Sachs has pointed out, "Although it is sometimes asserted that official creditors and bank creditors have been treated equally in the management of the debt crisis, in the past five years the commercial banks have received large net transfers from the debtor countries, while the official creditors, including the creditor governments and the multilateral institutions, have made large net transfers to the debtor countries. Operationally, it can be argued that the official creditors are indeed 'bailing out the banks.'"[38]

Yet over the long term, officials believed that the only remedy for the debt crisis was economic growth in both the industrial and developing worlds. By 1983, the industrial world seemed to be doing its part, as the painful recession of the early 1980s was being left behind in the wake of more expansionary economic policies. Many developing countries, however, seemed unable to capitalize on the resurgence of growth. Heavily regulated economies and repressive regimes were preventing markets from flourishing. Thus, economic reform in the debtor countries became the other focal point of U.S. policy. But the management of this reform process would not be undertaken on a bilateral basis; instead, Washington looked to the International Monetary Fund to play a leadership role in this regard.

As a debtor country's lender of last resort, the IMF tied its loans to acceptance of an "adjustment" program. These programs, of course, varied somewhat from country to country, but in most cases they involved cutting state spending, raising taxes, and reducing the money supply; in a word, they focused on austerity. Over the short term, at least, these austerity programs caused acute suffering in many countries, causing the "IMF" to become a dirty word, on a par with "Yankee," especially throughout Latin America. While objective analysis would recognize that local governments often capitalized on hatred of the IMF in cynical fashion, putting off needed reforms, the fund also made its share of mistakes in planning these programs.

Jacques de Larosière, the chairman of the IMF during most of the 1980s (he would go on to become the president of the Bank of France and, in 1993, of the European Bank for Reconstruction and Development), also devised a unique way of dealing with the commercial bank creditors. He tied IMF funding to fresh commercial bank lending, refusing to provide official aid until the bankers had also contributed additional loans. Again, the knots of interdependence were tied between the banks and official lenders. In this way, adequate funds would be provided to meet the liquidity needs of the debtors, and lending decisions would be fashioned between bankers, central bankers, and the international institutions.[39]

But this approach could do nothing to overcome the significant reduction in new lending that occurred after 1982. Indeed, in 1982, with the debt crisis impending, the commercial banks had supplied Latin America with $23 billion of fresh loans; the following year the number dropped to $2 billion.[40] By 1985, the debtor countries were making large net transfers of funds to the banks; whereas new net flows from commercial banks to the seventeen largest debtor nations totaled $3.7 billion in 1985, the banks received almost $22 billion in interest payments that same year![41] In short, insufficient funds were entering the developing world to back the IMF economic reform programs.

A new approach to the debt crisis was thus required by the mid-1980s. Economic growth had returned to the industrial countries, but Latin America was still suffering. Per capita levels of gross national product had declined significantly, and calls were heard for the formation of a "debtor's cartel." Peru had elected a socialist leader, Alan Garcia, who moved to repudiate his country's debt burden, and the Reagan administration was worried about the further spread of communism in the region under the influence of the Cuban and Sandinista regimes. At the same time, American banks, under pressure from regulators, Wall Street, and foreign competition, were shrinking their asset base, making it unlikely that they could play a major role in any economic renewal strategy.

With this as background, Treasury secretary James Baker launched a new initiative in October 1985, at the annual World Bank/IMF meetings held in Seoul, Korea.[42] Baker said that the key to managing the debt crisis was economic growth in the developing world, and to that end he proposed a reform package that tied substantial new loans from the commercial banks and international institutions to domestic programs that focused on structural adjustment, deregulation, and export promotion. The essential word was "growth." Baker's speech signaled a rejection of the IMF's austerity measures and a new approach that focused on the development of market forces. The specifics of this new approach, however, were left out of Baker's remarks, leaving one observer to remark that "it was more than a speech, but not a policy."[43]

The success of the Baker initiative rested on four key variables: first, whether the commercial banks would agree to provide fresh loans; second, whether the new monies would be used with greater efficiency than in the past; third, whether countries would really adopt adjustment programs at home; and finally, whether world economic growth would be sustained.[44] As it turned out, the Baker plan stumbled on the very first variable; but ironically, the bank's refusal to play along with new lending would, in turn, help pave the way for the realization of true economic reform.

Baker was perhaps also unduly optimistic about the reception his plan would get on Capitol Hill. Five years after the debt crisis had begun, many voices were expressing dissatisfaction with the "muddle through" strategy. Senator Bill Bradley of New Jersey, influenced by the writings of Jeffrey Sachs, had become a particularly strong advocate for debt relief. The Baker announcement, therefore, unleashed a lengthy debate over debt management strategies in Congress.

But the real linchpin of the program was winning a commitment from the banks, and it is curious that Baker did not provide any new set of incentives for the banks to comply with his program. To be sure, regulators had indicated a willingness to back off on enforcing stiffer capital adequacy standards, but banks had been raising capital levels in any event.[45] Indeed, the banks were placing themselves in a position where they would no longer be forced to stay in the lending game at all. They had been given time by American policymakers since 1982 to get their balance sheets in order, and had used it to their advantage.

Bank strategies were also being influenced by developments in the marketplace. By the mid-1980s, a "secondary market" for third-world debt had developed. This meant that banks could sell their loans for a fraction of their face value to investors. These investors would either use the debt paper to make investments in the third-world country, or hold the paper in the hope of making a profit later in time.

The creation of this market had a powerful impact on the banks. Significantly, it meant that their developing-country loans, which were still being carried on the books at 100 cents to the dollar, were valued by the market as being worth far less. In the fall of 1986, for example, Brazilian government debt was valued at 75 cents on the dollar, for a 25 percent discount. As equity investors began to calculate the actual value of the bank loans, the stock price would accordingly be adjusted downward.[46]

Banks could always seek relief from governments; but when left to operate without interference, market pressures can become inexorable. The widespread realization that the banks were carrying assets that had far less value than once presumed could lead to a wholesale run on the institutions, precipitating a financial collapse. Governments in this instance would have no choice but to pump money into the system as the lender of last resort.

As market forces surrounded them, the bankers thus had to develop an appropriate response. Their policy choice was significantly narrowed in February 1987, when the largest debtor of all, Brazil, announced that it was suspending its interest payments. The banks could have put up new money to support Brasilia, but with Brazilian debt trading at a large discount they would have been quite literally throwing good money after bad. The time had come for a radically new approach.

In May 1987, Citicorp, the largest commercial bank in the United States, declared that it was adding $3 billion to its loan loss reserves. The next day, Citicorp shares rallied on the New York Stock Exchange. By adding to its reserves, the bank had said in effect that it was prepared to write off a substantial portion of its third-world debt, and in so doing it had turned the tables on the debtor nations, which had ironically used the threat of default to obtain fresh loans.[47]

The Citicorp announcement, however, created a dilemma for public officials. On the one hand, this action would serve as a powerful message about the need for developing countries to enact economic reforms at home before obtaining further credits. On the other, it would keep the banks out of the lending game, since they no longer had to lend money in order to maintain the fiction of carrying existing loans at full value.

Indeed, with the Citicorp announcement, which was quickly followed by similar actions on the part of all the major commercial banks, a fundamental piece of the Baker Plan had eroded. Baker had called for $20 billion of new lending by the banks over the three-year period 1986–88, but according to Citicorp only $13 billion had been raised.[48] Furthermore, many banks were now out of the lending game altogether, having sold their loans on the secondary market, and the creditors had thus become more concentrated. Given these changes, the U.S. government would now have to develop another debt strategy, but that would await both a new administration and new Treasury secretary.

To the Brady Plan

At the same time, the financial markets continued to devise new instruments for rearranging the debt mountain, and even reducing it slightly. Debt equity swaps, exchanges of bank loans for bonds, and other financial instruments contributed to a small nibbling away of the problem. But the other side of the equation—economic growth in the developing countries—was still failing to make the strain of interest payments any easier to accept.

The increase in loan loss provisions by commercial banks, coupled with these continuing economic difficulties, made it almost inevitable that debt reduction would become a key element in U.S. debt strategy. On March 10, 1990, in a speech before the Bretton Woods Committee, Treasury secretary Nicholas Brady launched yet another American initiative. He acknowledged that previous programs had failed to meet their objectives, and recognized that economic growth had been insufficient to put the debt crisis to rest. Toward the end of his speech, he made the critical statement: "The path towards greater creditworthiness and a return to the markets for many debtor countries needs to involve debt reduction."[49]

In point of fact, the bankers had already accepted the need for a debt reduction strategy. A unique arrangement between Morgan Guaranty and Mexico, which involved a swap of loans for bonds with an implicit U.S. Treasury guarantee, had been structured in late 1987 and involved a small reduction in Mexico's debt to Morgan. One year later, a panel of leading bankers stated before a United Nations–sponsored meeting that "debt service reduction" could play a role in "aiding economic recovery" in the developing countries.[50] The Brady announcement was thus a lagging indicator, but nonetheless critical given the U.S. government's continuing—indeed, leading—role in structuring debt packages.

The acceptance of debt reduction was one thing in theory, another in practice. The key question was: How much reduction? This would be at the core of negotiations between Mexico and the banks as a new round of debt-rescheduling talks opened in 1990, under the shadow of the Brady Plan.

For their part, the Mexicans came to New York with a proposed reduction of $4.2 billion per year over the next six years, an amount equal to somewhat less than one-half of Mexico's interest payments. This was way out of line with the banks' expectations. In response, Mexico was offered debt service relief of about $1 billion per year. Clearly, the two sides were not going to bridge their differences without outside intervention.[51]

That role was played by the United States government. It not only hosted the meetings, but cajoled both Mexico and the banks. The government's leverage over the commercial banks had, however, been greatly reduced by their provisioning for loan losses. To be sure, it could attempt to change regulatory and accounting policies, but this would inevitably involve Congress, and the outcomes were not certain to favor Treasury. In the event, Treasury wanted above all for the two sides to reach some agreement; numerous different scenarios were quite acceptable within that framework.

At the end, the agreement that Mexico got looked a lot like the one first proposed by the banks. It would result in debt service reductions of about $1 billion per year, a number far closer to the one offered by the banks than to the one offered by Mexico. At the same time, however, at least one bank demonstrated its confidence in the new economic policies of President Carlos Salinas by increasing its exposure to the country: Citicorp, the only American bank with domestic branches in Mexico. (The American business community's confidence in Mexico's future was also heightened in the early 1990s as a North American Free Trade Agreement, or NAFTA, between the United States, Mexico, and Canada became more likely; indeed, in November 1993 the U.S. Congress would pass the legislation needed to make NAFTA a reality.)[52] But little in the way of new monies was offered to Mexico by the other commercial banks, leaving the first Brady Plan restructuring as a mixed bag for the debtor.

Since Mexico's Brady Plan agreement, a number of other countries have negotiated debt reduction deals with their creditors, including the Philippines, Costa Rica, Venezuela, and Uruguay. The very different agreements struck between the banks and each debtor exemplify the case-by-case management approach. Some countries have used debt buy-backs as the focus of their reduction schemes, while others have issued discount bonds. The one generalization that can be made, however, is that the amount of relief actually provided has been small.[53] It appears that most of the debtor countries have come around to the view that they must adopt the kind of economic policies at home that eventually will allow them to return to the financial markets abroad as voluntary borrowers. Even so, it will be many years before these countries obtain loans on as favorable terms as they found in the 1980s.[54]

The debt crisis provided the international financial system with its greatest test in fifty years. In responding to the crisis, the United States exercised a leadership role, providing emergency liquidity to Mexico and bolstering its subscription in the International Monetary Fund. These actions, and the regulatory initiatives taken alongside them, served to maintain confidence in the payments network.

As the crisis wore on, however, market forces were allowed to introduce new products to the debt world, and these would also drive bank and debtor decisionmaking. Specifically, the development of a secondary market for debt would put an end to the myth that the loans were worth 100 cents on the dollar, forcing the commercial banks to build up their capital and loan loss reserves.

By 1987, the banks had largely recovered from the debt crisis. This meant that they were less interested in throwing new money at the problem, and it became increasingly difficult to involve them in debt packages. Indeed, official lending would largely supplant commercial funds by the mid-1980s.

In the end, however, the solution to the debt crisis would have to be found in the debtors themselves. The experience of such East Asian debtors as South Korea, and such Latin American countries as Chile, had demonstrated that high levels of debt were not incompatible with economic reform and growth. During the late 1980s, the gospel of economic liberalism and privatization had spread throughout the developing world, creating new optimism about the economic future.

By 1992, it appeared that the crisis was over. As the *Financial Times* reported, the creditor solution had passed "the test of time."[55] Latin American countries were again attracting investors, and economic reform programs were showing some impressive results, especially in Mexico and Chile.

Yet questions remain about the lessons learned from the decade of the 1980s. In an age when unprecedented amounts of capital are needed around the world, especially in Eastern Europe and the former Soviet Union, one wonders whether governments will (or should) place limits on this new cycle of borrowing and indebtedness, or whether fears of economic and political instability will again override questions of financial prudence, as they did in the 1970s. To be sure, the financial markets have changed enormously since the 1970s, and international organizations have become increasingly prominent as economic watchdogs.[56] Still, it does not take enormous amounts of imagination to foresee that a new debt crisis could be upon us as we reach the millennium.

5 | International Cooperation: The Basle Accord

In the English language, "capital" is a word with many uses.

—WILLIAM ISAAC

The debt crisis brought the international financial system to the brink of collapse. As we saw in the last chapter, central bankers formulated both short-term and long-term management strategies to meet the crisis. In the short term, liquidity had to be provided to the developing countries so that they could maintain interest payments to their creditors. In the long term, the banks would have to be strengthened and recapitalized in order to restore public confidence in the international payments system.

As the debt crisis wore on, different countries adopted somewhat different approaches to rebuilding their banks; the banks themselves, of course, also developed a variety of internal strategies in response to their individual predicaments. In the United States, the regulators focused on capital adequacy, balance sheet transparency, and new accounting rules; in Japan, the tax code was changed so as to allow banks to deduct a portion of their loan losses. In western Europe, a number of new regulations were coming into play, some in response to the debt crisis, others in response to the need for some common standards as European integration proceeded. These are discussed in greater detail in Chapter 6.[1]

Overall, the new regulations and standards developed during

the 1980s reflected a shift in the focus of banking regulators from crisis management to crisis prevention. That is, they were putting into place a set of regulations that would protect deposit insurance funds from the effects of excessive risk taking by imprudent bank managers, and shareholders in turn were being asked to bear greater risks. With the collapse of the savings and loan system in the United States during the late 1980s and early 1990s, a collapse that would cost the American taxpayer untold billions of dollars, this emphasis on crisis prevention only increased.

Traditionally, there would have been absolutely no reason for either banks or bank supervisors to object to this national approach to regulation; indeed, it reflected the basic supervisory concept of home country control. But the problem of regulating the banks had become more complicated by the 1980s, as the pressure of international competition among financial institutions increased. Differences in national regulations could have important international implications, for these translated into differing costs for the banks and, in turn, differing prices for their customers. In a business where deals were often won or lost on the narrowest of margins, any cost advantage was disturbing to those banks which viewed themselves as being in a disadvantageous regulatory position.

Thus, by the mid-1980s, debates over regulation and competition became inextricably linked. This made life complicated for central bankers and bank supervisors whose primary concern was to maintain the safety and soundness of the financial system, not to enhance its competitiveness; now, pressured by the bankers, they had to worry about both at the same time.

It was this combination of concerns that brought the G-10 central bankers together in Basle in 1984 to discuss bank capital adequacy standards. Specifically, Paul Volcker had been encouraged by Congress to seek convergence in these. But the other G-10 central bankers viewed this as an impossible quest; laws and accounting systems were simply too different to push for convergence in this issue-area. Thus, it appeared unlikely that the central bankers would be successful in striking a balance between their regulatory and competitive concerns; to paraphrase a well-known song, something would have to give.

Despite these unpromising background conditions, on July 15, 1988, central bankers from the G-10 countries announced they had reached an agreement that would result in "international convergence of supervisory regulations governing the capital adequacy of international banks."[2] Bankers, bank supervisors, and observers of the negotiations leading to this agreement—known as the "Basle Accord," after the site of the Bank for International Settlements (BIS), where the discussions were held— have hailed it for two prominent reasons. First, although many central bankers had expressed concern over the erosion of capital levels in commercial banks, they entered the multilateral negotiations with conflicting definitions of what actually constituted bank capital, and how much capital banks should be required to hold. Second, national differences in capital adequacy requirements were being exploited by banks as a source of competitive advantage in the financial marketplace; all other things being equal, banks with relatively low capital requirements could charge less for their services and still give shareholders a satisfactory return. The Basle Accord reduces the scope for this type of "regulatory arbitrage" and helps level the playing field on which international banks must compete.[3]

Yet many legitimate criticisms of the Basle Accord have been raised, and they are also discussed in this chapter. Protestations of central bankers notwithstanding, the accord provides commercial bankers with incentives to reallocate assets within bank portfolios, to the detriment of lending activity; this reallocation away from lending allegedly exacerbated the "credit crunch" of 1991–92 in the United States.[4] The accord also raises important political questions, such as whether there is a loss of democratic control over the regulatory process when state actors pursue international agreements; political scientists have labeled this concern the "democratic deficit."

The purpose of this chapter is to explain how and why the Basle Accord was reached, and to provide a provisional assessment of its effect on commercial banks, bank supervision, and international financial regulation more broadly. In short, the story of the accord is ultimately about the process by which states make international rules. As we will see, a multilateral agreement on capital adequacy did not represent a self-evident response to the problems that faced international banking in the 1970s and 1980s; indeed most of the G-10 central bank governors were less than enthusiastic about entering discussions on convergence of capital standards when the issue was first raised by Federal Reserve Board chairman Paul Volcker in 1984.

I shall argue that the demand for regulatory convergence grew out of domestic politics in the United States, as public officials fashioned a response to the international debt crisis that took into account the views of both regulators and bankers. In Chapter 4, I stated that public officials were concerned with maintaining the safety and soundness of the financial system, especially after 1982, but they were concerned with the competitiveness of American banks as well. The challenge was therefore to adopt policies that satisfied both sets of concerns.

Having established a policy of pursuing an international capital adequacy agreement, the United States had to devise a strategy for placing the issue high on other states' agendas. A bilateral agreement on capital standards, reached by the Federal Reserve System and the Bank of England in 1987, served this purpose nicely, for it threatened to create a "zone of exclusion" disadvantageous to the international banks of other countries. Faced with the possibility that further expansion in the financial markets of the United States and Great Britain would be curtailed, commercial and central bankers in Paris, Frankfurt, and Tokyo recognized that an international agreement on capital adequacy had become a fait accompli. The story of the Basle Accord thus illustrates the enduring strength of the United States in shaping and advancing policies in international economic relations.

The use of state power by the United States (and Great Britain) to reach an international agreement does not imply that the objectives of the accord were illegitimate; in fact, all central bankers would now agree that the standards adopted at Basle provide a useful starting point for assessing the ability of international banks to withstand loan losses. Furthermore, having reached a capital adequacy standard, bank supervisors are currently pursuing other areas for cooperation, such as a single measure of bank liquidity. Indeed, it appears that the exercise of American power at Basle has catalyzed an international regulatory process that is spreading beyond bank supervisors and now includes the regulators of securities markets as well. The story of the Basle Accord may therefore shed light not just on financial regulation, but more broadly on the politics of rule creation in the international economy.

The Domestic Politics of Bank Capital

Bank capital has long been a vexing issue for bank supervisors, and regulations regarding minimum standards have changed frequently over time. In the United States, for example, the earliest capital regulations are found in the National Banking Act of 1864 and the Federal Reserve Act of 1913, both of which based capital adequacy on the population of the town in which the bank was situated! During the 1930s, banks were expected to hold one dollar of capital for every ten dollars of total deposits. During the 1940s, federal regulators again shifted course, now focusing on a capital-to-assets (instead of capital-to-deposits) ratio.

These ratios were suspended during World War II, to encourage banks to increase their purchases of U.S. government bills and notes, and to make loans to the defense industry. Following the war, federal regulators indicated that they favored adopting a capital-to-assets ratio that included a "risk weighting" (that is, the amount of capital that the bank had to hold would be a function of the riskiness of its asset portfolio), but this would not be formally adopted until 1988.[5] Indeed, during the period from 1950 to 1980, different federal and state regulators used somewhat different capital adequacy standards, and the three major regulators (the Federal Reserve Board, the Federal Deposit Insurance Corporation, and the Office of the Comptroller of the Currency) could not agree on a common standard until 1981.

As we saw in Chapter 4, bank capital reemerged as an issue for Congress in 1983 as it debated what to do about increasing the International Monetary Fund's quota. Members of Congress did not wish to be seen as bailing out the banks, but neither were they prepared to weaken the banks vis-à-vis their international competitors. The solution to their dilemma was to promote international convergence in banking regulations, particularly in the area of capital adequacy.

The IMF quota increase and regulatory concerns over capital levels were synthesized in the subsequent piece of IMF-related legislation, the International Lending Supervision Act (ILSA) of 1983.[6] This act was a distinctly American piece of legislation, in that it exemplified American politics both domestically and internationally. On the domestic level, the act synthesized the concerns of competing groups, particularly regulators and bankers. Internationally, it foisted American concerns and preferences on other states' agendas.

This does not mean that the ends ILSA sought to attain were inappropriate. After all, the international payments system *was* threatened by the debt crisis, and higher levels of bank capital could help restore public confidence. To the extent that the payments system had the character of a public good, it was reasonable to ask every state to contribute to its maintenance. In this light, ILSA and the congressional endorsement of international regulatory convergence can be viewed as part of the burden-sharing exercise that developed during the debt crisis.

With the passage of ILSA, the issue of bank capital became an ongoing agenda item for the U.S. Congress. The Federal Reserve Board and the U.S. Treasury Department were called upon to issue a progress report on international negotiations within one year of the act's passage, and Congress, at the request of House Banking Committee chairman Ferdinand Saint-Germain, also asked the General Accounting Office to present its own report on the activities of the Basle Committee. Saint-Germain further demanded that the FDIC be given a seat on the Basle Committee, in order to check the growing power of the secretive Federal Reserve in regulatory affairs.

Following the ILSA requirement, Paul Volcker dutifully presented Congress's request for more convergent capital standards to his fellow central bank governors at a meeting in Basle in March 1984. In the words of one Federal Reserve Board staff member who was present, his remarks were "greeted with a yawn."[7] Although the Basle Committee had issued a paper expressing concern over the erosion of capital levels in international banks and had urged in 1982 that no further deterioration be allowed, it seemed to the central bankers that policy convergence was too much to ask, given the vast differences in national banking systems. As Volcker and Treasury Secretary Donald Regan put it in a May 1984 report to Congress, "the difficulties involved : . . were recognized as substantial."[8]

Nonetheless, the Basle Committee did make progress during 1984 with regard to cross-national comparisons of capital levels. Recognizing the different definitions of capital and the varying methods for calculating capital-to-asset ratios, the committee devised a "framework" that enabled central bankers to compare their national methodologies and statistics. By providing a single framework, the sharp differences in standards and capital levels became readily apparent (see Table 5.1).[9]

Shortly after Volcker's presentation to the Basle Committee, bank capital once again emerged as a domestic political issue in the United States. In May 1984, the eighth-largest bank in the United States, Continental Illinois, required a $6 billion infusion of Federal Reserve funds to meet its immediate financial obligations. The story of Continental Illinois offered a textbook case of a bank that had combined high leverage with a risky

Table 5.1. Capital-to-asset ratios of major banks in five countries, 1979–1984.

	1979	1980	1981	1982	1983	1984
France	2.6	2.4	2.2	2.1	2.0	1.9
Germany	3.3	3.3	3.3	3.3	3.3	3.4
Japan	5.1	5.3	5.3	5.0	5.2	5.2
United Kingdom	7.2	6.9	6.5	6.4	6.7	6.3
United States	4.5	4.5	4.6	4.9	5.4	6.2

Note: Ratios are not strictly comparable owing to somewhat different definitions of capital in each country.

Source: International Monetary Fund, *International Capital Markets* (April 1989).

portfolio in its reckless pursuit of market share. Bank management had failed utterly in its job of asset and liability management, and by early 1984 rumors about asset quality were leading institutional investors to withdraw their deposits. Despite the emergency infusion of Federal Reserve cash, the bank collapsed, and a federal bailout followed. In the aftermath of ILSA and the Continental Illinois debacle, bank regulators found themselves under renewed pressure from Congress to bolster the supervisory process.[10]

The Continental Illinois case required regulators to contemplate more stringent regulations for two reasons: first, Congress was losing confidence in their supervisory abilities, given their recent track record, and would demand new regulations; second, an undesirable message might otherwise be sent throughout the banking community. The regulators didn't want to leave bankers with the impression that the Federal Reserve, having saved the eighth-largest bank, would save any large institution, no matter how poor its management quality and "no matter how substandard its loan portfolio might happen to be."[11] Furthermore, they didn't want observers to conclude that the U.S. government was now willing to bail the banks out of their third-world debts without any serious adjustment on the banks' part. This, of course, posed the moral hazard problem *writ large*.

Indeed, the Federal Reserve wanted the banks to make every effort to strengthen their balance sheets through the financial markets before any more of them had to turn to the federal government for assistance. Of greatest concern, the bank supervisors wanted to maintain the integrity of the deposit insurance fund, which would come under tremendous pressure if any other large banks failed. This involved actions on both the asset and liability sides. On the asset side, the Federal Reserve would place greater emphasis on loan quality in the banks that it examined; on the liability side, new capital adequacy standards would be established and capital levels increased in banks where the regulators felt this was necessary. The more capital available to absorb loan losses, the greater the protection for the insurance fund.

In search of a new capital adequacy system, a small group of supervisors at the Federal Reserve Board in Washington and the Federal Reserve Bank of New York began to explore the regulations that were in place in other countries, particularly within western Europe; the supervisors were assisted in this effort by a staff report of the Basle Committee which compared capital requirements across the Group of Ten countries. At this time, the Federal Reserve System and other bank supervisors (the Office of the Comptroller of the Currency and the Federal Deposit Insurance Corporation) were using a fixed capital-to-asset ratio. Banks had to hold $5.50 of capital (defined as shareholders' equity and the loan loss reserve) for every $100 of assets, no matter how good or bad the asset quality. The same fixed standard held whether a bank had all its assets in U.S. Treasury bonds, "blue-chip" loans (that is, loans to major corporations), or third-world debt. Moreover, the fixed ratio did not take into account the off-balance-sheet items that had accumulated in large banks; these had been one source of Continental Illinois' problems.

In contrast, several G-10 countries, notably Belgium, France, and Great Britain, had developed and put into use sophisticated "risk-weighted" capital adequacy standards that required banks to have more capital as the perceived riskiness of the portfolio increased. Thus, banks would be "rewarded" for holding liquid assets by having lower capital requirements, and "penalized" for holding high-risk loans by being forced to take on more capital. In these countries, banking supervisors determined appropriate capital adequacy standards for each of the financial institutions they supervised in informal meetings with the bank's managers.

Interestingly, these risk-weighted systems had been developed long before the outbreak of the debt crisis. Indeed, the Bank of England had formulated its capital adequacy system not in response to the debt crisis, but rather following the "secondary" or "fringe" banking crisis that had threatened Britain's domestic financial system in the mid-1970s; the Bank of England issued new regulations on bank capital in 1980.[12] Traditionally, capital had not been a focal point of British regulation, but with the col-lapse of a number of poorly capitalized institutions that had overextended themselves in real estate (akin to the savings and loan crisis that would later ravage the United States), the bank began to develop new standards.

Ironically, as it studied various national approaches to capital adequacy following the fringe crisis, it looked to the experience of the Federal Reserve Board, which had a considerable history of regulating bank capital. Rather than use a fixed capital-to-asset measure, however, the bank opted for the European risk-weighted system, though one that differed in sev-eral respects from those found on the continent.[13] Thus, as a result of do-mestic crises, the capital adequacy regulations of the United States and Great Britain were beginning to converge.

Initially, U.S. regulators other than the Federal Reserve were not keen on adopting new capital adequacy standards, for both political and techni-cal reasons. They did not want to engage in a battle with their banking constituents, and they believed the British standards were too complicated to implement. After all, the United States had more than 10,000 commer-cial banks, whereas Britain had only a handful. But after further study of the risk-weighted system, FDIC chairman William Seidman changed his mind. In remarks at a banking conference held in Britain, Seidman thanked the Bank of England "for providing us with the results of their analysis on off-balance-sheet risk." He also stated that "an international standard for capital would be most welcome, since it is difficult to make valid comparisons when every country counts it differently."[14] With Seidman's support for a risk-weighted capital standard, the American reg-ulators could move forward with a single voice.

The International Politics of Bank Capital Adequacy

The Federal Reserve System's Proposal

In January 1986, the Federal Reserve Board released for public comment its "supplementary" capital measurement proposal based on the risk-weighted system. In addition to the fixed capital-to-asset standard of $5.50 in capital for every $100 of assets, the board would now analyze capital adequacy in terms of the riskiness of the portfolios of international banks. Different "weights" were assigned to different categories of assets and to the off-balance-sheet items. The dollar amounts held in each category were then multiplied by the assigned risk weight, with the total giving the measure of risk-weighted assets. Thus, cash was assigned a zero weight, meaning it would not be counted at all in the asset measure; U.S. government securities were given a 30 percent weight; and all loans and off-balance-sheet items were assigned a 100 percent weight.[15]

The board provided three reasons in support of its new proposal: first, the need to address the growth in off-balance-sheet exposure; second, the need to reward conservatively managed banks that held relatively high cash balances; finally, the need to bring the United States in line with those industrial countries that had already introduced the risk-weighted standard. The board further asserted that stronger capital regulations were necessary in light of the growing risks associated with international banking.

As expected, the bankers protested this unilateral measure. The American Bankers Association (ABA), in its formal comments to the board, stated that the proposal would exacerbate the competitive inequities that existed between U.S. commercial banks and their foreign peers and also between commercial and investment banks, which were not subject to the new capital regulations. In sum, the ABA stated that the proposal would undermine "the ability of U.S. banks to compete."[16]

As in the ILSA hearings of 1984, the bankers' concerns about competitiveness were taken seriously and confirmed the need for continued international negotiations to promote convergence of capital adequacy standards; the domestic politics of bank capital had come full circle. But how should such negotiations proceed? Given the existence of the Basle Committee and the nature of its earlier work in this area, the Federal Reserve Board might have been expected to relaunch multilateral talks there. Furthermore, the board was aware that the members of the European Community (EC) were holding talks on harmonization of capital standards as part of the EC's 1992 project; it would have been natural to seek harmonization of standards between Brussels and Basle, since most G-10 members were also part of the EC.

But earlier efforts in Basle to promote capital adequacy had failed to make much progress, and there was a feeling at the Federal Reserve Board that the Basle Committee was not pursuing the issue as aggressively as it might, perhaps because of doubts about the feasibility of the task on the part of the committee's chairman, Peter Cooke of the Bank of England. Moreover, central bankers continued to defend their national standards as appropriate to their particular banking structures. The Germans, for example, had argued that their "universal banks" were unlike the commercial banks found in the United States and thus had different capital requirements. There was no separation in Germany, for example, between banks and industrial enterprises, or between banks and securities firms. It made no sense to seek one single capital adequacy standard, given these structural differences.

At this point, the Federal Reserve Board had three options: it could continue to negotiate in Basle; it could adopt its new standard domestically; or it could seek a piecemeal extension of the new standard to countries that had already adopted similar risk-weighted capital adequacy measures. In that regard, a joint effort with the Bank of England was tempting, since the board had already drawn upon the bank's capital adequacy standard in developing its own policies. The possibility of striking a bilateral agreement with the Bank of England was made even more attractive by the fact that a single standard in "both New York and London, two of the most powerful financial markets in the world, would represent a major step toward convergence on the issue of capital standards."[17]

The Accord between the United States and the United Kingdom

In July 1986, Paul Volcker suggested to Bank of England governor Robin Leigh-Pemberton that the United States and the United Kingdom should consider a joint agreement on bank capital adequacy. According to one American official involved in the talks, Volcker was "surprised" by "the speed with which they [the British] jumped on it."[18] For the British, a joint approach with the United States would be a powerful means of countering the emerging standard in the European Community, to which the Bank of England had objected. Now the British and the Americans, joined as allies, were in a powerful position to advance their preferences.

In January 1987, the Federal Reserve System and the Bank of England officially announced that they had reached agreement on common standards for evaluating capital adequacy. This banking accord was immediately hailed as a "landmark in financial regulation."[19] Specifically, the agreement provided for (1) a common definition of capital, which comprised shareholders' equity, retained earnings, minority interests in subsidiaries, and perpetual debt; (2) adoption of a risk-weighted system for evaluating capital adequacy; and (3) the inclusion of all off-balance-sheet commitments in capital adequacy determinations. But no minimum level of required capital was proposed in the agreement.

Paul Volcker vigorously defended the accord in hearings before Congress. It was designed, he said, to meet "several partly conflicting objectives." These included the need to address the rapid growth of off-balance-sheet commitments, the creation of a measurement system that would not lead to government determination of resource allocation decisions, the desire to promote regulatory convergence, and the effort to level the competitive playing field. Volcker stressed this last point. "I cannot emphasize strongly enough," he said, "our interest in the competitiveness of U.S. banks."[20]

This statement is of particular interest when contrasted with comments made in 1990 by the secretary of the Basle Committee, Peter Hayward, who claimed that the Basle Accord was "created not to ensure fair play, but to ensure the safety and soundness of national banking systems and to protect the interests of depositors."[21] Perhaps he made this comment in response to criticism that the accord had not done enough to level the playing field, but in truth the capital adequacy standards were designed both to strengthen the international payments system *and* to ensure fair play, and these objectives were seen as mutually reenforcing.

The banks, however, again expressed their dissatisfaction with the Federal Reserve Board. Ira Stepanian, president of the Bank of Boston, told the board that he had "serious concerns with the . . . Proposal as it related to competitive equity, not only between US banks and those overseas, but also between US banks and non-bank financial institutions." He noted that "a major segment of worldwide banking had been left out—including Japan, which now has seven of the top ten banks in the world."[22]

The Basle Accord

American and British supervisors recognized from the outset the problems inherent in their bilateral strategy. On the one hand, it could harm relations between Britain and the European Community; indeed, European

Commission president Jacques Delors had complained to the chairman of the Basle Committee, Peter Cooke, that the U.S.-U.K. agreement was not *"communitaire."*[23] On the other hand, the United States was concerned about the general feeling of ill-will that might be created among other G-10 central bank governors. Nonetheless, the United States and Great Britain wanted to ensure the extension of their standard, and they adopted a two-track route in 1987.

The Bank of England and the Federal Reserve pursued direct talks with bank supervisors in Japan and the major western European countries on one track, while reopening discussions in Basle on the other. In January, the president of the Federal Reserve Bank of New York, Gerald Corrigan, traveled to Tokyo, where he told officials that "the most important reform" the country could undertake in the financial area would be "a better alignment of Japanese capital requirements with those of other leading industrial countries."[24] Meanwhile, the head of banking supervision at the Bank of England, Brian Quinn, traveled to several European capitals in an effort to sell the capital accord.

At the same time, pressure was placed directly on the Basle Committee to respond quickly to the joint accord. A series of special meetings were held, in which criticism of the bilateral agreement was aired. Although these discussions were "tough," it was already clear to the participants that some agreement would ultimately be reached.[25] The fact that the United States and Great Britain would apply the new standards to international banks operating in their markets, as well as the threat that they would not approve banking applications from international banks that did not adopt more rigorous capital adequacy measures, made a committee proposal inevitable.

Yet the U.S.-U.K. agreement was not simply forced upon the other G-10 countries. In their negotiations with individual countries and the Basle Committee more broadly, the United States and Great Britain took account of the differing national systems that made a straightforward extension of their agreement difficult to accept. It was obviously in the interest of the Bank of England and the Federal Reserve to shape a standard which every G-10 member could agree upon and, just as important, live up to by domestic enforcement.

For the Japanese, the major concern was accounting for the hidden reserves held by banks, including real estate and corporate equities. The

Ministry of Finance and the Bank of Japan asserted that hidden reserves should be "marked to market" (that is, equities and real estate should be assigned their market value rather than their historical value) and the resulting capital gain added to base capital. The British and Americans objected, stating that existing regulatory and accounting rules prevented their banks from valuing similar holdings at market levels. Negotiations on this and other matters continued throughout the summer of 1987, and by September the United States, Britain, and Japan "had come to terms on the broad outline of an international agreement."[26]

The trilateral accord permitted the Japanese to count up to 45 percent of the unrealized gain on securities and other equities as part of base capital. It was also agreed that the risk-weighted system would be phased in over a five-year period, and that international banks would be evaluated according to the new system at the end of their 1992 fiscal year. That year, of course, coincided with the deadline for implementation of the Single European Act adopted by the European Community. Since the EC itself was having ongoing discussions regarding harmonization of banking regulations as part of the 1992 program, it was important that the new capital adequacy standard meet the concerns of the European members of the G-10.

For the Japanese, the trilateral agreement was not difficult to accept *at the time.* The Tokyo Stock Exchange was booming in late 1987, making an increase in bank capital relatively painless, especially in light of the provision regarding valuation of hidden reserves. Indeed, critics claimed that U.S. negotiators had done nothing to restore the competitive balance and to level the playing field, which the authorities had claimed was one of their objectives. Yet the point was not to make it easy or hard for banks to reach the new standard; it was simply to establish one standard which every bank must achieve. If Japanese banks *were* well capitalized, so much the better. Of course, Japan would regret its decision to tie bank capital to stock market valuations: in the summer of 1990, the market began its dramatic decline with the Iraqi invasion of Kuwait, choking capital levels and with them the ability of banks to lend.

The talks in Basle went at a slower pace than the trilateral discussions, but news of the agreement among the United States, Britain, and Japan led to an acceleration of the process; with Tokyo on board, it was clear to any remaining recalcitrants that they had to strike a bargain. Discussions in Basle focused on the definition of capital and how much of it banks must hold; the risk-weighted system itself was no longer a point of debate.

During the autumn the committee made breakthroughs on both fronts. First, a two-tier capital framework was established, which elegantly provided a common standard while respecting national differences. *Tier One* capital was confined to shareholders' equity; *Tier Two* capital included loan loss reserves, up to 45 percent of the unrealized gain on marketable securities, and hybrid debt-capital instruments. Second, a minimum risk-adjusted capital adequacy standard of 8 percent was agreed upon, half of which (4 percent) had to be in the form of Tier One capital. These levels were to be attained by the end of each bank's 1992 fiscal year, as had already been agreed by the trilateral group.

In addition, the Basle Committee assigned risk weights to the various asset categories, differing in some instances from those used in the U.S.-U.K. accord and its subsequent extension to Japan. Cash was assigned a zero weight, so that no capital would have to be held to support currency, coin, or balances on deposit at the central bank. Short-term government securities were also assigned a zero weight, while long-term securities, municipal bonds, and securities issued by countries outside the OECD were given weights ranging from 10 to 100 percent. Loans of all types (with the exception of those collateralized by cash) were given a 100 percent weight, as were residential mortgages on rental property; this would subsequently become a cause of controversy between regulators and domestic interest groups in the United States and elsewhere. Off-balance-sheet items were assigned an "asset equivalent" and given the appropriate weight; in most cases they would be considered in the same way as loans.[27]

On December 10, 1987, the Basle Committee announced that its members had reached agreement on a proposal for "international convergence of capital measurements and capital standards." The achievement of a capital adequacy accord, the committee stated, was a "desirable objective in order to remove an important source of competitive inequity for banks operating internationally."[28] Again, it is curious that the committee's secretary, Peter Hayward, would back away from the competitiveness issue in his post-Basle commentary.[29] In the event, with the issuance of the preliminary Basle Accord, a new, risk-weighted, international capital adequacy standard had emerged out of the bilateral U.S.-U.K agreement in less than one year.

During the six-month comment period which followed the December announcement, bank supervisors in the G-10 countries received a number of suggestions concerning changes that might be made in the final version of the accord. First, American and British bankers sought to include perpetual preferred stock as Tier One capital. Second, bankers and real estate interests were determined to see that all residential mortgages, including those on rental property, be treated as "collateralized" loans and therefore given a lower risk weighting. Third, commercial bankers expressed the view that it was inappropriate to assign the securities of all non-OECD countries a 100 percent weight, which would not only penalize those countries that were good credit risks but would also make it more difficult for banks operating in non-OECD countries to access interbank markets. Finally, banks suggested a number of changes regarding the treatment of off-balance-sheet items.[30]

In response to the comments collected from commercial banks and other interested parties, the Basle Committee members met again in July 1988 to discuss revisions of the preliminary accord. A number of major changes were made, including the inclusion of perpetual debt as Tier One capital, and the lowered risk weighting on rental properties. Claims on the banks of non-OECD countries were also awarded a lower risk weight, as were several off-balance-sheet items. The committee released its final version of the Basle Accord on July 15, 1988, under the title "International Convergence of Capital Measurement and Capital Standards." Table 5.2 provides an overview of the Basle agreement.

The Basle Accord represents the most significant step taken to date by bank supervisors in advancing policy convergence and creating an international banking regime, with formal principles, norms, rules, and decisionmaking procedures. To be sure, supervisors had already accepted the general principle that no international bank should escape supervision, and that banking regulation should rest on home country control. Rules had also been adopted in the past, particularly with respect to the need for consolidated accounts. But the Basle Accord went beyond these prior agreements in demanding complete convergence with respect to one of the most crucial areas of banking supervision: capital adequacy. With

Table 5.2. The Basle Accord: Weighting the assets (in millions of U.S. dollars).

Asset type	Asset amount	Risk weight	Risk-adjusted assets
Cash	100	0	0
Government paper	100	10[a]	10
Loans	90	100	90
Total	290		100

Capital type
   Tier One (common stock): capital amount = 4
   Tier Two (securities):[a] capital amount = 4
   Tier One / risk-adjusted asset ratio: 4%
   Capital (Tier One + Tier Two) / Risk-adjusted asset ratio: 8%

a. National discretion applies.

the Basle Accord, central bankers had demonstrated their ability to structure agreements that met the demands of safety and soundness, as well as international competitiveness. As we shall see, however, the effectiveness of this agreement ultimately rests upon the home country that is responsible for enforcement.

Evaluating the Basle Accord

The Basle Accord provoked a substantial amount of controversy from the outset. Critics claimed, as they had with the bilateral U.S.-U.K. agreement, that it represented nothing more than a central bankers' conspiracy to allocate resources, providing the banks with powerful incentives (in the form of lower risk weights) to purchase government securities. Others argued that the accord would lead to perverse outcomes, since banks would be tempted to make riskier, high-yielding loans in order to compensate for the cost of holding more capital against all loans. Still others proclaimed, in contrast, that the accord would lead to a "credit crunch," by curbing lending activity on the part of major banks. Finally, the various criticisms that had already been aired about competitiveness were circulated once again. Let us now look at some of the implications of the accord for bank safety and soundness on the one hand, and bank competitiveness on the other.

Safety and Soundness

The primary task of bank supervisors is to ensure the safety and soundness of the banking system, and it is in this light that the Basle Accord must first be evaluated. According to the secretary of the Basle Committee, Peter Hayward, "the purpose of the capital agreement was to strengthen the capital base of the banking system."[31] The presumption behind this remark is that highly capitalized banks are less likely to fail, since they have more resources available for absorbing unexpected losses.

Indeed, since the announcement of the Basle Accord, it is fair to say that "capital" has become the most important word in the bank regulators' lexicon. The failed 1990 U.S. Treasury proposal for banking reform, for example, was largely based on the foundation of capital adequacy. Highly capitalized banks would be permitted to engage in a number of new activities (for example, underwriting securities) that would remain closed to those with low capital levels.[32] Recapitalization of the banking system has been the primary objective of central bankers and other regulators, and in attaining this they have been successful.

Although economists have found no meaningful correlation between bank capital levels and bank failures, it is difficult to argue with the general proposition that higher capital levels increase safety and soundness.[33] First, bank capital provides assurance to depositors, who may feed a run on an unsafe bank by withdrawing their funds, even in the presence of deposit insurance. Second, capital serves to absorb unexpected losses; if the levels of capital are greater than the historical levels of unexpected losses, then the bank can be expected to weather downturns in particular sectors or the effects of occasional bad lending decisions. Since capital comes at a cost, the important question concerns precisely how much banks need to hold, and no theory to date has provided supervisors with a single, definitive answer.

In the context of the developing-world debt crisis, the arguments for increased capital levels would appear somewhat trivial. After all, bank exposure to third-world debt was a large multiple of bank capital, and doubling or even tripling capital levels would have done nothing to prevent insolvency in the face of massive repudiation. But the strategies adopted in 1982 and 1983 for dealing with the debt crisis, including the capital adequacy standard, have indeed bailed out the banks, in that they have managed to keep the international payments system working. By providing liquidity to the debtors, and thus making sure that banks would continue to receive some interest on their loans, governments made it possible for banks to raise fresh equity; indeed, by establishing stiffer capital adequacy standards, they required banks to do so. After 1985, banks were strengthened to the point that large loan loss reserves could be established, aided by changes in tax and accounting laws.[34]

This development, in turn, has encouraged the debtors to adopt many of the economic reforms advocated in the Baker and Brady plans and by the IMF and the World Bank, since they recognize that commercial banks are no longer obliged to keep lending them money in order to preserve the myth of solvency, as was the case in the early 1980s. In short, the Basle Accord must be judged in terms of the larger policy project of managing the debt crisis and maintaining the international payments system.

The response of the financial marketplace to the Basle Accord was surprisingly swift. Banks quickly began to raise capital and/or shed assets, and they advertised their strength in terms of the Basle standard in their annual reports, publicity, and publications. Most of the international banks at which the agreement was targeted proclaimed that they had met the 1992 capital levels before the actual date of implementation.

Ultimately, however, bank strength is a function of profitability, and here the outlook for banks remains unclear. International business for the banks has been sluggish, and the Japanese in particular have retreated to focus on the domestic marketplace, mired as they are in real estate problems. American banks emerged from the debt storm only to face a massive real estate crisis and the potential for severe losses in their leveraged-buyout portfolios; at the same time, their traditional lending business continued its long-term decline.

Furthermore, the solution to these problems, encouraged in large measure by the Basle Accord, has been for banks to hold an increasing percentage of their assets in the form of treasury securities, exposing them to interest rate risk.[35] According to one study, bank holdings of government securities have increased by 54 percent since 1988, while commercial and industrial loans have fallen by 24 percent; as of 1993, banks held more government securities as assets than they did commercial and industrial loans.[36] A sharp move in interest rates will thus cause significant changes in the value of the banks' asset portfolios. Given these continuing risks to the commercial banking system, it is not surprising to find that the supervisors who meet at Basle are now focusing on the development of new supervisory measures that capture market risk. Higher capital levels may restore public confidence in the ability of banks to withstand losses, but they will do little on their own to make banking a more profitable industry.

Competitive Effects

I have argued here that the Basle Accord seeks to strengthen the banks' capital positions in a manner consistent with a level financial playing field. As with its effects on safety and soundness, an analysis of its competitive effects must also be two-handed. On the one hand, bank supervisors have now made it clear that high leverage is not an acceptable basis for gaining market share, and as a consequence there must be some leveling of the playing field to the extent that capital levels converge. On the other hand, to the extent that national regulators are free to strengthen bank capital levels and standards beyond those agreed upon at Basle, there remains the possibility that regulatory discretion at the domestic level will disadvantage certain commercial banks. It should be noted here that differing capital levels are hardly the sole basis for international competition in financial markets, so the Basle Accord does little to make all financial institutions equal.

The accord has three parts, each of which is subject to national discretion, meaning that regulatory authorities have the right to interpret the agreement so long as the *minimum* capital adequacy standards are met or exceeded. These three parts are: the definition of capital, the application of risk weights to specific asset categories, and the treatment of off-balance-sheet activities. Discretion is particularly marked with respect to the first two parts, and a continuing issue for the Basle Committee will be whether or not national interpretations are in fact consistent with the spirit if not the letter of the multilateral agreement.

The potential for conflict among national regulators and between banks and their supervisors should not be dismissed. The concern of observers with implementation arises from one fundamental assumption: that a country's banks will be placed at a relative disadvantage, at least in the short run, if national regulators interpret the accord in a comparatively stringent manner. Such countries' banks will be forced either to raise more capital or to shed assets to meet target ratios. Banks that do not do either could be prevented from opening new branches or expanding into new geographic or product markets. Hence, banks will face a painful period of adjustment in the tougher countries.

Conflicts could arise in interpretations of both the asset and liability sides. On the liability side, the accord divides capital into Tier One and Tier Two capital. The overall capital level (which had to be achieved by the close of fiscal year 1992) is 8 percent, of which 4 percent must be Tier One. While there is no discretion regarding the definition of Tier One (it must be shareholders' equity), national regulators are given considerable leeway in determining what constitutes Tier Two. The greater the diversity of items allowed by a country's regulators into Tier Two, the easier it will be for their banks to meet the Basle standard.

On the asset side, the underlying theory of the accord is that the amount of required capital should depend on the credit risk associated with the bank's asset portfolio, including its off-balance-sheet activities. Risk weights are thus assigned to all assets, meaning that different levels of capital are required to support different types of assets. The possibility of a face-off between commercial bankers and their supervisors is made apparent by a simple example. Supervisors in the United States and Japan, for example, place a zero weight on banks' holdings of claims on all OECD governments; no capital is required to support these assets (fueling the criticism that the purpose of the accord is to finance government deficits). The Bank of England, in contrast, places a 10 percent weight on some government securities and a 20 percent weight on others. All things being equal, British banks would have to raise more capital to hold the same collections of assets, a fact that has led British bankers to cry foul.

Yet another area for national discretion is the applicability of the regulations to the various classes of financial institutions. The accord applies to "international banks," with no further attempt at definition. The Japanese have interpreted this to mean banks with "significant international banking activities," namely those with branches or subsidiaries overseas. Thus, a Japanese bank which maintains only agencies or representative offices in the United States would not be subject to the Basle requirements. The Federal Reserve Board, in contrast, has elected to apply the risk-based capital regulations to all banks and bank holding companies that it regulates. Since the FDIC and the OCC have also agreed to apply the accord to the institutions they supervise, coverage of U.S. commercial banking will be nearly complete. The Bank of England is also applying its regulatory regime across the board. Again, differing interpretations could become a source of tension if Japanese representative offices appear to take competitive advantage of their exemption from the accord's provisions.

Implementation Issues

The Basle Accord leaves many commercial banks with no choice but to raise equity and/or shed assets. Both of these strategies face hurdles. Securitization of assets may provide a partial solution, as it can be used to eliminate from bank balance sheets those assets that are fully weighted. But not all assets can be securitized, and if too many banks try to sell those assets that can be packaged and sold, the prices of the assets will drop. Moreover, to the degree that securitized loans are bought by the same institutional investors who could have bought bank shares instead, it denies the banks a potential source of equity.[37]

Securitization has also become a political issue in those countries, like Japan, which previously prevented commercial banks from selling their assets on the marketplace. For securitization to occur, Japanese laws must be changed, and the question of who may be allowed to deal in such securities must be resolved. The outcome of the debate in Japan could have far-reaching implications for the country's financial structure, since Japan has on its books American-type laws that separate commercial and investment banking; these laws, of course, are an artifact of the postwar occupation.[38]

Raising equity may be no easier than shedding assets. As a *Wall Street Journal* headline announced, "Banks Find Their Sources of Capital Are Drying Up."[39] The recession in the United States, the explosion in problem loans, and the continued loss of markets to other providers of financial services have all conspired to discount the long-term value of bank shares. In response, many banks were cutting dividends and shedding workers in a belated effort to control costs; although these were important steps, they did nothing to improve the long-term outlook for bank profitability. To be sure, bank shares had risen from their depths of the mid-1980s, but a decade later most of them remained far from their historical highs.

The global stock market decline and the rise in the value of the dollar that followed Iraq's invasion of Kuwait in August 1990 compounded the banks' difficulties, especially outside the United States. Japanese banks had counted on the revaluation of their equity holdings to make up a large part of Tier Two capital, but between January and October 1990, the value of the Tokyo Stock Exchange dropped by more than 40 percent. But American banks were not immune either. The global stock market decline made it more difficult to raise Tier One capital, and the banks' continuing problems caused the shares of such money center banks as Citicorp and Chase Manhattan to decline by more than 50 percent between the summer and autumn of 1990. Since that time, share prices have rebounded, fueled by low interest rates and high spreads. But bank portfolios, for the first time in recent history, are holding treasury securities as the bulk of their assets, just as critics of the Basle Accord had predicted and feared.

The capital adequacy agreement poses yet a different set of concerns for bank customers. "Middle-market" firms (companies with annual sales of $25 million to $100 million) are particularly worried, because the risk-weighting system favors bank asset allocation toward cash and government securities and away from loans. Given the new capital requirements, banks would have to earn a healthy spread on middle-market loans to make them profitable, and they have not done so in recent years because of intense competition for this market segment. Unfortunately, these middle-market firms—unlike large, Fortune 500 corporations—are relatively dependent on banks for their financing, and a credit crunch would hurt them disproportionately. Since small and medium-sized firms make substantial contributions to new investment and job generation, the implications of reduced financing for these companies are worrisome.

A provisional assessment of the accord, then, suggests that its promise to increase safety and soundness in a manner consistent with a level playing field will be met, but not completely or without costs to the banks themselves and their customers. While it is certain that central bankers will disagree over national interpretations of the agreement, these disagreements will in all likelihood be peacefully resolved in the Basle Committee; indeed, a major activity of the committee is to iron out any disagreements over interpretation and implementation. By the end of fiscal year 1992, depositors, bank analysts, and regulatory officials will have at their disposal a single standard by which bank capital can be evaluated.

It would be misleading, however, to assess the Basle Accord without examining the larger context in which it was negotiated. Fundamentally, the accord represented an effort by states with very different banking systems to set common rules for a greatly altered international payments system. While there is legitimate room for debate over the means employed to advance the Basle Accord (basically, threats of market closure by the United States and Great Britain), there is little argument over the importance of the end—namely, the creation of a supervisory framework for global banking. A smoothly running international payments system has something of the quality of a public good, and each country which enjoys its use also has a responsibility to contribute to its maintenance. To the extent that higher capital levels bolster confidence in international banking, the Basle Accord must be viewed as a welcome development.

The competitive advantages and disadvantages associated with the Basle Accord's provisions will never become an issue if the capital requirements are not enforced. But enforcing a multilateral agreement will prove challenging. The credibility of the regulators' main enforcement weapons, such as cease and desist orders and civil penalties, remains in doubt, and it is unclear how stringently they will be applied to banks that fail the Basle test in the United States and abroad.

Assisting the committee in its work, however, is the marketplace. If nothing else, the Basle Accord has established a capital adequacy *standard*, and financial analysts are assessing banks in terms of that standard. As the Basle supervisors wrote in a 1990 report, "The market itself has imposed its own discipline. Banks have found a distinct advantage in being able to satisfy the rating agencies and the market generally that their capital was adequate in terms of the final Basle standard."[40] To the extent that market and regulatory forces are reinforcing, positive incentives will exist for banks to meet the Basle requirements as quickly as possible.

One frequently mentioned criticism of the accord concerns its applicability. It is said that, since the capital adequacy standards must be met only by banks based in G-10 countries (and the European Community, which has more or less incorporated the Basle capital requirements in its recent banking directives), they will be disadvantaged in competition with offshore international banks, such as those of Australia, Hong Kong, Singapore, Korea, and the Middle East. Sensitive to this allegation, the Basle Committee has carried out intensive discussions with bank supervisors in these and other countries to ensure that they understand the purpose of the agreement and its implications. Indeed, many countries outside the G-10 have already signaled their acceptance of the Basle standard.[41]

Yet a number of systemic political and economic forces lie beyond the committee's reach, and these could make it extremely difficult for banks to meet the accord's provisions. The overall decline in stock market values, and the decreasing value of money center bank shares in particular, are impeding banks that seek more Tier One capital. And asset shedding will also prove challenging in the prevailing economic climate.

Given the environment for commercial banks, it is not surprising to find executives suggesting radically new approaches to reshape the financial sector. The chairman of Citicorp, John Reed, sees as one possibility the creation of strategic alliances between major banks, or the ownership of commercial banks by industrial concerns, both of which could lead to higher capital ratios. "My guess is that the legal barriers between industry and banking in the United States will eventually dissolve," Reed has said. "Giant industrial companies have immense capital. They could absorb a bank and add essentially no capital."[42] Although current legislation in the United States prohibits commercial banks from implementing some strategies, Reed's comments suggest that the demand for bank capital could force significant legislative changes.

Peering into the future, we see that economic historians may very well view the Basle Accord as having heralded an era of banking consolidation and structural change, especially in the United States. Several major bank mergers have already been announced since the accord was promulgated, including that between two of New York's most important money center banks, Chemical Bank and Manufacturers Hanover Trust. In the words of a Federal Reserve Board official, "the plain fact is that in the current environment we need a leaner and more efficient banking system."[43] Higher capital levels can certainly contribute to the process of shrinking the over-banked American financial system.

At the same time, the restructuring of the banking system in general, and the making of international regulations in particular, raise profound questions of democratic control and domestic politics. It is well to remember the storm created in 1987 by the undersecretary of the Treasury, George Gould, when he stated his preference for an American financial system characterized by five or ten giant banks that could rival those of western Europe and Japan. Gould admitted that "any policy promoting the creation of very large financial institutions encounters deep-seated sentiments that date to the founding of the Republic."[44]

International regulations that promote structural change are also likely to antagonize "deep-seated sentiments." In western Europe, the question of a "democratic deficit" has already emerged, as an increasing number of important political and economic decisions are being made in Brussels. In response, public officials in Europe have promoted the idea of "subsidiarity," whereby political and economic decisions would be made at the lowest possible level of authority. The question of political accountability looms large as decisionmaking shifts from national legislative and executive bodies to international organizations.

These larger questions, however, still remain on the distant horizon when it comes to international finance. For the time being, the Basle Committee provides a useful forum for airing and resolving disputes among G-10 regulators and for seeking better methods of supervision in an increasingly complex international economic environment. But it is not a supranational organization, and it has no enforcement powers on its own; banking supervision remains the province of national authorities. The committee is only as effective as its member states want it to be.

Indeed, without the exercise of American power, a capital adequacy accord might not have been reached. To be sure, the Basle Committee had debated bank capital for some time, and it made progress with respect to information sharing and definitional issues that helped advance the ongoing multilateral discussions. But the gap between talk and action was bridged only when the United States provided the planks. This suggests that leadership by a great power will be vitally important if international policy coordination is to occur.

6 Regional Cooperation: Banking in the European Community

Willing and active cooperation between sovereign states is the best way to build a successful European community.

—MARGARET THATCHER

During the summer and autumn of 1992, and again in 1993, Europe was rocked by its worst currency crises since the breakdown of Bretton Woods. Owing to the sharp national differences in economic performance, interest rates and exchange rates diverged sharply across the continent, and states adopted a variety of strategies for regaining stability. Unable to defend the value of their currencies, Britain and Italy dropped out of the European Community's Exchange Rate Mechanism (ERM), which had kept exchange rates closely aligned even though an analysis of inflation and economic growth rates could hardly justify such a policy. France, in contrast, defended the value of its currency, aided by the steadfast support of the Deutsche Bundesbank. The currency explosion highlighted the severe impediments remaining in the path of a united Europe, and reminded observers of the influence that financial markets could exert over governments in a global economy.

This chapter focuses on Europe's efforts to create a common financial space and on how such a space would be regulated. Since the mid-1980s, the member states of the European Community (now called the European Union) have made significant progress toward the creation of a single market for goods, services, capital, and persons. While such a market promised impressive efficiency gains, it posed any number of challenges to European governments, which continued to be "sovereign" within their own borders.[1] Among the tasks of these governments, few were more important than the maintenance of a safe and sound financial system. In developing a response, the members of the European Community have taken the framework of international (or, in this case, regional) cooperation based on home country control to its extreme.

It seems paradoxical that European financial regulation would rest on a foundation of home country control. Home country control appears, at first glance, to be a rather inefficient means for advancing the goal of an integrated market. Given the continuing differences between the national banking structures of the twelve member states (contrast, for example, the competitive British and universal bank-dominated German systems), such a policy approach might produce a financial market that resembles a patchwork quilt rather than a single fabric.

Instead, one might have expected the European Community to create a Brussels-based bureaucracy to coordinate supervision and level the Community's financial playing field. Eventually, one would expect the European Central Bank, the "EuroFed," to assume supranational regulatory responsibilities. Indeed, as we will see, the EC *has* issued a number of directives that provide "minimum standards" and "essential regulations" for banks that all states must adopt. These standards and regulations, however, are passed into law by national legislatures, and enforcement of their provisions is the responsibility of national authorities.

Within the European Community, the concept of home country control has been taken far beyond that which animates the Basle Committee. In combination with the principle of mutual recognition of national rules, as well as the principle of a "single passport" which allows banks from one country to branch throughout the EC *without prior authorization,* the home state will assume near total responsibility for the activities of its national banks. Unlike the Basle model of international cooperation, which continues to permit the host country substantial scope for supervision and regulation of foreign banks, the Brussels model has greatly reduced the host's power. The differences between these two approaches could pose problems for bank supervisors in the years ahead, an issue which is developed in the concluding chapter.

Regulation based upon home country control points to a fundamental fact about Europe: community building is ultimately the work of sovereign states. States will not surrender national regulation of financial institutions so long as their central banks continue to provide the lender-of-last-resort function. Furthermore, as the number of foreign bank branches on domestic soil grows, states have sought to minimize their supervisory responsibilities for the banks of other member states and third countries. States wish to be "home" only to their domestic banks and "host" to all foreigners. Thus, in the European Community, bank supervision and regulation is still regarded as a *national* affair.

At the same time, as noted above, the European Community has adopted a number of sweeping "directives" that apply to all member states and are aimed at creating a single financial space. As a result, one finds in western Europe a heightened version of the classic tension of interdependence, the tension between state control over one's domestic financial market and transnational community building. I argue in this chapter that the European Community's approach to financial regulation must be understood as part of an ongoing effort to resolve that tension.[2]

The European experiment also has profound implications for third countries. Indeed, I will argue that the European Community has designed its approach to financial integration with the specific objective of promoting liberalization in the American and Japanese banking markets. The success of this gambit, however, will be a function of Europe's internal progress. To the extent that the EC succeeds in becoming a model of economic integration, its influence will naturally spread far beyond the boundaries of the twelve member states.

Toward the First Banking Directive

In principle, the legislation necessary for the creation of a common financial market was provided by the Treaty of Rome in 1957 and subsequent legal judgments by the European Court of Justice. Relevant articles of the treaty include provisions on the right of establishment, the freedom to provide services, and the right to move capital "to the extent necessary to ensure the proper functioning of the common market" (Article 67). To be sure, the drafters of the treaty recognized that time would be needed to realize this objective of a liberal financial market; specifically, Article 61 states that the freedom of banks and insurance companies to provide their services across borders is to be "established in step with the gradual liber-alization of capital movements."

The liberalization of capital flows was thus critical to banking integra-tion, and such liberalization remains an ongoing process after more than thirty years. In 1960 and 1962, the Council of Ministers adopted two di-rectives that aimed to lift capital restrictions. But true progress in this issue-area had to await a number of international and domestic factors which, by the early 1980s, had converged to accelerate the liberalization process. By the early 1990s, most states permitted capital movements throughout the EC with very few remaining controls.[3] In fact, the coun-tries that retightened capital controls during the summer of 1992, such as Ireland and Spain, were those that still had not fully adopted the EC's liberalization measures.[4]

The history of European financial integration efforts belies the claim made by some scholars in recent years that the EC '92 project to remove the remaining barriers to a single market represents a fundamental "disjunc-tion" or break with the past.[5] Instead, it appears to be an incremental pro-cess which has developed in fits and starts; the recent currency crisis, cou-pled with renewed "Europessimism," only serves to emphasize this point. Without gainsaying the remarkable efforts made by EC Commission pres-ident Jacques Delors, Internal Market commissioner Lord Cockfield, and the political leadership demonstrated by the troika of Thatcher, Mitter-rand, and Kohl in the 1980s, one must also do justice to the important work done by EC bureaucrats and national regulators during an earlier period of Europessimism in the 1970s. An exploration of that history— with its attendant successes and failures—will help us understand the path taken by the political leadership as expressed in the Single European Act of 1987 and subsequent legislation.

Concomitant with its early efforts aimed at liberalizing capital flows, the European Commission in the late 1960s began to examine ways to re-move roadblocks that stood in the way of a Community-wide financial sector. An obvious impediment was the existence in each member state of very different legal, accounting, and regulatory frameworks. In 1969, the commission established an ad hoc working party, made up of bank super-visors from the (then) six member states; the group was to direct its efforts at eliminating "the legislative and administrative disparities with regard to working rules for banks and other credit institutions and at harmonizing the control systems to which they are subject."[6]

This effort had several results of lasting significance. First, it led to the formation of an informal "club" which could provide a regular forum for discussion of common regulatory issues. This "Contact Group of EEC Bank Supervisory Authorities" (Groupe de Contact) first met in June 1972, providing an early model of cooperation in this issue-area; indeed, the Basle Committee has its roots in the European contact group. Since its founding, the contact group has served as a center of expertise for the commission's Banking and Financial Services Directorate, DG XV. The group, made up of national banking regulators, has played a critical role in shaping EC banking legislation and in coordinating European regulations with those developed in Basle.[7]

The second element of this early program had a lasting effect in that it established the fundamental principle behind financial integration: that of home country control. As early as 1972, the ad hoc working group had drafted a document that "envisaged the establishment of one comprehensive Community law which would enable banks to branch freely throughout the Community and to be supervised on equal terms with other EEC banks by the Member States in which they had their registered office."[8] That is, rather than create a market in which each member state was a host country for control purposes, the idea was that regulatory decisions would, for the most part, be consolidated in the home country. This is the cornerstone of the Community's approach to integration of financial markets, and, as we have already seen, it was adopted by the Basle Committee in the Concordat of 1975 as well as in a number of subsequent regulatory measures.

The question arises: Why home country control? Why didn't European officials pursue a different alternative at the outset? As I argued in Chapter 2, public officials, at least in theory, have a menu of options to choose from when it comes to supervising global financial markets—a menu including supranationalism, multilateralism, and bilateralism. The question of why one approach is chosen over another must loom large in any analysis of community building.

Even in its earliest and, perhaps, most idealistic days, the idea of creating a truly supranational European Community was quickly circumscribed. The European Coal and Steel Community (ECSC) treaty, for example, which envisaged an important transfer of state power to a supranational body, was quickly eroded by those who sought to protect the sovereign principle. Indeed, from the outset, there has been a tension in the EC between the member states and the single market that they are, in principle, committed to building.[9]

In the absence of a supranational community, the development of a single market has been left to a process of multilateral bargaining.[10] And multilateral bargaining, as we have seen throughout this book, is a Janus-faced process that looks both outward at other states and inward at domestic politics. Policy outcomes must be acceptable not only to the member states involved in the negotiations, but also to domestic polities; this, of course, was one of the powerful lessons of the 1992 debates in Europe over the Maastricht Treaty, which met with substantial public opposition.

As banking supervisors debated financial integration in the late 1960s and early 1970s, they could not get around the fundamental fact that each state was responsible for banking supervision and the lender-of-last-resort function. At a time when the creation of a single European Central Bank appeared to be a distant prospect, there was no existing regional structure that could supervise the member states' banks, short of the informal groups that had already been created. Certainly, regulators could meet to exchange information, as they were doing, but the ultimate supervisory responsibility had to remain with the authority willing to bail out a troubled financial institution. In all cases, this was the national central bank.

Yet the banking group could not end its work by simply reaffirming the centrality of national rules and regulations, since this would do nothing to advance the integration process. Even in a Community of sovereign member states, some fundamental principles had to be articulated in order to level the playing field for banks and to provide minimum standards that all banks should meet.

The decision was thus made in Brussels in the early 1970s to formulate a harmonized set of regulations, including the creation of a common deposit insurance scheme, the development of credit information exchanges, and numerous other rules concerning the supervision of bank liquidity and sovereignty. But this overambitious program of regulatory harmonization proved unacceptable to member states at the time, and it soon foundered.[11] Moreover, in 1974, when the Community admitted several new member states that had not been a party to the banking talks, notably Great Britain, the Commission recognized that it would have to return to the drafting table. Nonetheless, many of the core ideas presented in 1972 would be retained as EC integration proceeded.

This failed effort nonetheless had some important lasting effects on the member states of the Community. The 1972 draft banking legislation, for example, had called upon each member state to "authorize" the activities of bank branches from EC countries on the basis of home country control. But neither the United Kingdom nor Denmark, for example, had at this time any formal system for authorizing the establishment of banks, and indeed Britain had *no formal banking legislation at all!* The decision to enter the EC, coupled with the worst banking crisis in England in modern times, the "fringe" banking crisis of 1973–74, would lead Parliament to demand, and the Bank of England to propose, specific regulations which culminated in the Banking Act of 1979. Again, the interplay of external and internal pressures would result in specific policy responses.[12]

Rebuffed in its effort to draft comprehensive banking legislation, the commission returned to the council in 1973 with a more modest directive that simply reaffirmed the status quo. In this directive, the EC prescribed the freedom of establishment "in the sense that member states must abolish restrictions that formally discriminate against financial institutions from other countries with respect to the setting up of subsidiaries, branches or representative offices."

However, as the Banque de Bruxelles noted to its clients, "This freedom must not be exaggerated. It still rests within the power of a national authority to refuse the establishment of a subsidiary or branch for some general economic reason." The bank noted that France and Italy had long used "general economic reasons" to prevent the establishment of foreign banks, whereas Belgium and Luxembourg had quite liberal regimes in this respect, opening their markets to all comers in an effort to build dynamic financial centers.[13] (Indeed, Luxembourg would become a noted banking haven, known for its secrecy laws and lax regulations. Two important bank scandals with roots in Luxembourg's soil—the Banco Ambrosiano crisis of 1982 and the BCCI shutdown of 1991, would lead to a strengthening of European regulations.)

The various efforts to develop banking directives during the early 1970s also had another important and long-lasting effect, in that it got commercial banks and securities firms more involved in the affairs of the commission and in the community-building process. This was critical, for Europe's large banks became major proponents of an integrated market, in contrast with many small businesses that saw integration as a threat.[14]

The banks were asked to comment on draft directives, and this process led to more sophisticated efforts at lobbying. In short, the early work of the commission caused EC banks to take a greater interest in European integration and its consequences for their business.

According to the Banque de Bruxelles, this renewed interest was "as likely to promote banking cooperation" as any specific directive. Through correspondent relationships, and more formal alliances, European banks could develop closer transnational ties, even in the absence of a formal branching network. These ties would ultimately lead Europe toward a more closely integrated financial marketplace. Nonetheless, the banks themselves could not create an integrated market so long as state and other nonstate interests remained opposed to a single market.[15]

Humbled by its efforts to liberalize European banking through one sweeping directive, the European Commission undertook a fresh approach beginning in 1974. The core of the original proposal, namely financial integration on the basis of home country control, remained. But now the commission was to pursue a more gradual approach to harmonization of banking laws and regulations. According to a participant in this early work, "the idea was to start with a so-called 'umbrella' coordination directive, containing some of the essential features of the original draft and leaving other aspects to be tackled in separate initiatives in successive stages."[16] This approach led to the adoption of the First Banking Coordination Directive by the Council of Ministers in 1977.

The First Directive is the cornerstone of banking integration in the EC. From the start, the member states recognized that its impact on financial markets would be of a gradual nature. According to a report from the U.K. Treasury:

> The ultimate objective of the directive is that any bank with a branch office in one member state should be able to set up branches throughout the whole community and that the supervision of its operations should not be fragmented between different member states but rest with the competent authorities in the country of origin. This cannot be achieved overnight and that community recognizes that it will be a gradual process. *From a community standpoint therefore the importance of the present directive lies not so much in its immediate impact as in its implications*

for sustaining and shaping progress towards integration in the time ahead.[17] [italics added]

The directive had two central elements: first, it required the member states to set up a basic licensing procedure for all banks within the Community. This was important because, as noted above, some countries such as Britain and Denmark had no formal procedures for authorizing bank operations. Second, the directive looked, according to commissioner Christopher Tugendhat, "to the future, not in the sense that it prescribes specific tasks to be carried out at some future date in the coordination of banking legislation, but in that it attempts to create the machinery for the identification and implementation of such tasks."[18] That machinery, in turn, consisted of an Advisory Committee of bank supervisors and other specialists from the member states with a brief to assist the commission in preparing new directives that might be needed to accomplish the goal of financial integration; this committee would work in tandem with the contact group already established, which now focused its attention mainly on information sharing and the supervision of transnational European banks.

It should be emphasized that the underlying framework for integration is again provided by the concept of home country control. The First Directive states that "overall supervision of a credit institution operating in several Member States" is the responsibility of the "Member State where it has its head office, in consultation . . . with the competent authorities of the other Member States concerned."[19] This core idea has only been strengthened over time.

The First Directive, unlike the commission's earlier attempt at banking legislation, avoided the error of overregulation. In the words of Christopher Tugendhat, the member states had now adopted "a more pragmatic approach." It was "much better," he said, to adopt "a system of close cooperation between national supervisory authorities imposing a minimum number of legal requirements . . . than the lengthy and complex route of institutional harmonisation."[20]

The First Directive was thus self-consciously built as a cornerstone rather than a final structure. The commission and council had left to the Banking Advisory Committee the task of specifying the additional regulations that would be required to build the document into a durable framework. These included the specification of supervisory "observation ratios" that would be needed to monitor a bank's solvency and liquidity and its foreign exchange position; other authorization criteria; liquidation procedures; and harmonization of banks' published accounts, including balance sheets and income statements, so that banks from different member states could be compared.

The directive, however, also left three host country restrictions virtually untouched: first, banks that wished to establish a branch in another member state still required authorization from the host country concerned; second, host countries had wide scope for limiting the activities of foreign banks; finally, the initial capital required of branches in most member states was equivalent to that usually required for new banks. Furthermore, member states were given the opportunity to defer acceptance of the terms of the First Banking Directive upon application to the commission.[21]

The First Banking Coordination Directive, therefore, did not constitute the final word in financial integration. In effect, it provided the commission with a compass that would guide its future efforts in this issue-area. When it is seen in this light, we can appreciate that the Second Banking Coordination Directive, which grew out of the Single European Act, reflects both continuity and change. It built upon the earlier work of the EC, drawing on the major principles established during the 1970s. At the same time, it would make some decisively new contributions.

The Second Banking Coordination Directive

If financial integration was to become a reality for the continent, some set of minimal, community-wide standards and regulations would have to be articulated in order to create an operational framework and a level playing field. The first move in this direction was the adoption in 1983 of a directive on consolidated accounts which further strengthened home country control. Consolidated supervision is perhaps the single most important tool available to bank supervisors as they analyze the financial health of complex banking institutions. In the absence of consolidated accounts, it is impossible for regulators to get a complete picture of the bank, as became painfully clear in the BCCI story; more on this in the following chapter.

With the adoption of the consolidated accounts directive, it became apparent that the work of the EC and of the Basle Committee was converging, for in 1983 the Basle supervisors would also declare their intention to demand consolidated statements from banks. The supervisors, however, had apparently met with some resistance from their banks, for consolidated accounts would only become a reality over a period of several years. In fact, consolidation had been proposed to European banks as the basis for their accounting by Bank of England governor Gordon Richardson as early as 1979.[22]

The reason for the delay can be seen in the need to alter banking legislation or, in the cases where supervision remained informal, to alter working relationships between banks and their supervisors. In Germany, for example, the supervisors were severely limited in the type of foreign account data they could collect from banks. In Belgium and Luxembourg, secrecy laws prevented the publication of certain data. Furthermore, many banks lacked the internal accounting systems which would make consolidation possible.[23] Thus, it took several years to achieve this fundamental step in international bank supervision and, by extension, in financial integration.

The importance of consolidated supervision for bank supervisors can hardly be understated. With acceptance of this fundamental principle in Brussels and Basle, the authorities now demanded that banking groups be assessed as a whole, rather than by their constituent parts. It is no coincidence, of course, that the supervisors were finally able to demand consolidation in 1983, after the explosion of the debt crisis. Banks had booked their international loans out of different offices, making it difficult for supervisors to capture the exposure of the banking group as a whole. Although consolidation would not solve supervisory problems, it was a necessary step in gaining oversight of complex international institutions.

Three years later, the EC took another step toward harmonization with a directive on annual reports. Under the terms of this directive, credit and financial institutions were required at the end of each fiscal year to publish statements of their financial situation in a comparable format. The directive provides for harmonization of layout, contents, and terminology. With consolidation and harmonized accounts, EC banks were increasingly becoming comparable from a supervisory perspective.[24]

By the time this directive had passed (1986), efforts were already underway in the commission to hasten the integration process. In 1985

Jacques Delors, the former French finance minister, became president of the European Commission, and he appointed a new and impressive group of commissioners to work with him. Delors, who had previously engineered the "Big Bang" of French financial markets, winning passage of a dramatic banking liberalization bill with a *unanimous vote* in the National Assembly, was an adept politician and technocrat. Similarly, his Internal Market commissioner, Lord Arthur Cockfield, was a British industrialist known for his managerial talents.

The new team lost no time in building their "Europe 1992" project, supported by a favorable political environment in which the major players (Britain, France, and Germany) were all committed to liberalization of the European marketplace.[25] For Europe's best and brightest, Brussels became a more attractive place to work, and a capable team of these "Eurocrats" put together a White Paper which identified some three hundred pieces of legislation that would be needed in order to make the integrated market a reality.

In the White Paper, the "new" commission tried to avoid giving the impression that it was creating an overregulated Europe. On the contrary, the commission sought to prepare general directives that would provide working frameworks and minimal, "essential" regulations. Again, the lessons of financial integration, with its attendant successes and failures, weighed heavily on the EC as it formulated this new approach.[26]

Moreover, the White Paper reflected important strictures of the European Court of Justice in shaping the integration process. The commission adopted a regulatory approach based on *mutual recognition* of each member state's laws and regulations that had not been specifically harmonized at the EC level. In the path-breaking "Cassis de Dijon" case of 1979, the court found that Germany could not prevent the importation and sale of a French liqueur (commonly mixed with white wine to make a "kir") even though German law would not have allowed this beverage, with its low alcohol content, to be so labeled. The court ruled that since France recognized the drink as a liqueur and since the French were reasonable in so doing, the Germans would have to accept Cassis de Dijon as the French had labeled it, even though they would have called it something else.[27] Although the Cassis de Dijon case did not apply directly to services, later judgments by the European Court would do so, thus widening the applicability of the mutual recognition principle.[28]

Mutual recognition would seem a curious way to build a single market. The end result could be a hodgepodge of twelve countries with twelve different sets of laws all trying to make sense of one another. The European consumer in the grocery store might not know whether the bottle she was thinking of buying contained liqueur or syrup! Yet the commission believed that mutual recognition, coupled with a minimal set of essential regulations, must ultimately lead to policy convergence across the member states; it was simply the "lowest common denominator" way of getting there. If detailed legislation could not be imposed upon the member states from above, then the commission would adopt a "bubble-up" approach in which the member states would ultimately move toward common standards and regulations in order to avoid chaos. This was the thinking at the time, and historians may well find that it was a brilliant stroke.

With regard to financial services, the White Paper drew explicitly on the Cassis de Dijon case and subsequent European Court of Justice rulings that dealt specifically with the services sector.[29] Trade in financial products, it said, would be governed by "three major principles, i.e. minimum coordination of individual national rules, mutual recognition, and home country control." As we will see, in some areas the Second Banking Coordination Directive would even move beyond this framework.[30]

The White Paper's recommendations—with important changes in the decisionmaking procedures regarding European integration—were adopted into law as the Single European Act (SEA) of July 1, 1987. This act revised the Treaty of Rome, which had been approved thirty years earlier. With regard to implementation of most internal market issues, unanimity was replaced by majority decisionmaking. And although the leaders stopped short of committing themselves to monetary integration (a decision that would be made later, at the Maastricht summit of December 1991), the SEA does state that further cooperation would be warranted "to ensure the convergence of economic and monetary policies."

The banking manifestation of the SEA is the Second Banking Coordination Directive, which represents an evolutionary rather than revolutionary step in financial integration. It synthesizes the developments of the past twenty years, while providing some uniquely new solutions to market liberalization problems—solutions that could have widespread implications beyond western Europe.

Yet a historical approach to financial integration should also make us cautious about overselling the Europe 1992 project. To be sure, the Second Banking Directive is embedded within the framework of the Single European Act, and greater integration of financial markets should be expected as regulatory harmonization proceeds. It is unlikely, however, that banks and securities houses will, in the near future, come to view Europe as borderless, particularly on the retail side of their business. (Wholesale markets, in contrast, have existed outside national borders for many years, owing to the growth of the Euromarkets, although even in these markets European firms tend to borrow mainly from their national financial institutions.)[31] Ironically, many European financial institutions will no doubt continue for some time to find it easier to conduct business in New York and Hong Kong than in their neighboring capitals. Formal and informal barriers to financial trade remain in place and can be formidable. Specifically, to the degree that European banks maintain their national market share through extensive branch networks, a major barrier to entry exists. In some respects, the battle for European financial integration is just beginning. Table 6.1 provides some data on Europe's largest banks, and shows what a challenge it would be for foreign banks to penetrate the domestic markets of such behemoths as Crédit Agricole or Barclays.

The Second Banking Directive expresses the Single European Act's goals for the financial sector. Along with two technical, regulatory direc-

Table 6.1. Europe's ten largest banks, 1991 (assets in billions of dollars).

Bank	Home country	Assets
Crédit Agricole	France	242.0
BNP	France	231.5
Crédit Lyonnais	France	210.7
Barclays	U.K.	204.9
Deutsche Bank	Germany	198.3
National Westminster	U.K.	186.5
ABN-Amro	Netherlands	184.2
Société Générale	France	175.8
Dresdner	Germany	143.9
Paribas	France	138.7

Source: Euromoney (March 1991), p. S8. Reprinted by permission of *Euromoney*.

tives adopted in 1989—one covering bank capital (the Own Funds directive), and the other covering bank solvency (the Solvency Ratio directive)—"it provides for sufficient harmonisation to allow banks to operate throughout the Community under home country control."[32]

Formally, the directive applies only to European "credit institutions." Securities firms are not covered; they are the subject of other directives—the Investment Services and Capital Adequacy directives—that have proven extremely contentious. Nor are non-EC banks explicitly covered: in principle they must continue to seek authorization from each member state in which they wish to operate.

It should be stressed that the second directive, along with financial liberalization more generally, was made possible only by the continued relaxation of Europe's remaining capital controls. In 1988 a number of measures were adopted which in theory should result in the removal of all such controls from every member state by 1995, although the currency crises of 1992 and 1993 raise questions about this outcome. Indeed, liberalization of capital flows is perhaps the single most important development for consumers, since in principle it will enable them to establish accounts anywhere in Europe, undermining to some degree the importance that large branch networks now have for banks. But the freedom to move capital will also cause stresses in European economic policies, as is already evident.

At the heart of the Second Banking Directive is the concept of the "single banking license," or "passport," for financial institutions. According to the British Bankers Association:

Once authorized as such, a credit institution is endowed with a "passport" enabling it to conduct throughout the Community not only the business of a credit institution but also a wide range of banking and banking-related services . . . This is subject to the proviso that the institution is authorized to conduct the services at home. Thus the principle of home country control extends to controls over the range of services a bank may offer: if it is a "universal bank" in its own country, it can be a universal bank everywhere.[33]

Despite passports, home country control, and regulation based on mutual recognition, the second directive does leave the host country with some powers, and these may prove greater than commonly appreciated. According to the directive, a host member state may require an EC-based bank from another country to comply with "legal rules . . . adopted in the interest of the general good" (Article 21). This open-ended phrase could conceivably become a vehicle for protectionism, and it is likely that the European Court of Justice will have ample opportunities to establish the limits of what host states can and cannot do.[34]

At the same time that it seeks to liberalize, the EC is also seeking to harmonize those minimal regulations deemed necessary to ensure a safe and sound continent-wide banking system, and to level the regulatory playing field in those cases where regulations endow national banks with decided competitive advantages. The EC remains uncertain, however, about just what those essential regulations entail. Of course, they include capital adequacy (the Own Funds directive, based on the Basle Accord) and bank liquidity. It is also likely that harmonized rules will be written for deposit insurance, given the wide variety of insurance schemes that have existed on the continent. As financial integration proceeds, it is probable that an increasing number of essential regulations will be developed at the Community level; thus, the bottom-up approach will converge with the top-down approach after all.

Still, the second directive's philosophy of mutual recognition leaves open the process by which the member states' different regulatory regimes will converge. Will there be a "struggle to the top" or a "race to the bottom" as states compete to attract financial services?[35] In other words, will those countries with stringent regulatory frameworks pull the laggards upward, or will a deregulatory spiral prevail which leaves Europe with the classic problem of "competition in laxity"? Furthermore, which if any country will lead the regulatory effort, setting the pace and direction of convergence? Will it be the Germans, seeking to structure Europe along universal banking lines, or the British, who will push for a more open, Anglo-Saxon framework? Will a EuroFed also become a EuroRegulator and lender of last resort? As these questions suggest, the final form that regional governance of European finance will take has not yet become clear, and significant scope for policy debate and choice remains.

Nonetheless, some speculative comments about the future direction of European regulation can still be put forward. Specifically, it appears that the danger of a "race to the bottom" has been exaggerated by those who continue to view European politics as basically "beggar thy neighbor." Regulations, after all, reflect not just state interests, but the interests of bank and nonbank economic interests as well. Indeed, deregulation can go too far, as the City of London is now beginning to appreciate. According to a report published in 1992, some European corporations are contemplating moving their foreign exchange trading desks to other financial centers with *more stringent* regulatory environments. Apparently, "European corporate treasurers were concerned at the handling of the default of some local authorities on their swap obligations; the BCCI affair; and the number of large corporations running into difficulties."[36] A well-regulated environment probably has greater attractions for major financial players than a deregulated one, suggesting that competition in laxity will not go too far on the continent.

Moreover, substantial policy convergence has already occurred. The consolidated accounts, capital adequacy, and own funds directives have been accepted on a Community-wide basis, in addition to many other rules and regulations. Home country control could not become the basis for financial integration unless the member states had confidence in the ability of one another to regulate their national banking institutions. Should one or more states prove incapable of regulating the international activities of their banks, we would then predict a strengthening of host country controls; this, of course, would lead to a fundamental reassessment of the very foundations of the single market for financial services.

The Treatment of Non-EC Banks

How the EC regulates its own banks is one question; how it regulates third-country financial institutions is another, and a controversial one at that. Article 9 of the Second Directive, which addresses this issue, remains purposely vague. It specifies the conditions under which banks may be *excluded* from the internal market, stating that "whenever it appears to the Commission . . . that a third country is not granting Community credit institutions effective market access comparable to that granted by the Community . . . the Commission may submit proposals to the Council for the appropriate mandate for negotiation with a view to obtaining comparable competitive opportunities." The words "effective market access" have been at the core of disputation involving the United States, Japan, and western Europe.

But Article 9 goes on to speak of national treatment. It states that when Community credit institutions in a third country "do not receive national treatment," the Community may initiate negotiations to remedy the situation, and in addition may suspend requests for banking authorizations from third-country institutions. So here the focus is on national treatment rather than "market access comparable to that granted by the Community."

Mired in this Eurospeak is the Community's conception of "reciprocity," and there is no issue that has been of greater concern to third countries. In early drafts of the Second Directive, the EC made third-country access to the Community conditional on "reciprocity," but that term was left undefined. It seemed to mean simply "reciprocal treatment," with the Commission being given the power to determine whether such treatment was in fact provided. The United States responded strongly to this draft proposal, saying that "reciprocity in financial services is inconsistent with the principles of national treatment and non-discrimination . . . Reciprocity, by any standard, could easily result in discrimination and protectionism."[37] The draft wording was subsequently dropped, with the United Kingdom joining the United States in expressing displeasure. In subsequent revisions of the directive, the Community shifted "the emphasis away from blocking access . . . and towards negotiations with the offending third country."[38]

From the standpoint of international governance of financial markets, the Second Directive creates a new model which could have far-reaching implications across the industrial world, depending upon the progress of European integration in which it is embedded. The traditional path to global banking liberalization in the industrial world has been to accord foreign banks "national treatment" when operating in host country markets; that is, they are treated like domestic firms. This is the standard the United States uses when foreign banks enter its domestic market, and the standard that it demands for American banks overseas. National treatment means that Deutsche Bank, which operates as a universal bank in Germany, can operate only as a commercial bank in the United States.

The European Community's approach, in contrast, is to permit

Deutsche Bank to operate as a universal bank *throughout Europe, including those countries that do not allow their own domestic banks to offer universal banking services.* In such cases, Deutsche Bank would get *better than* national treatment. Supervision of Deutsche Bank and its branches would be the primary responsibility of German authorities, who would also be expected to provide lender-of-last-resort support to the bank's branches.

The combination of mutual recognition and the single banking license thus could act as a powerful force in reshaping not only Europe's financial markets, but those of Japan and the United States as well. There is no question that this is what the European Commission has intended. According to Sir Leon Brittan, the vice-president of the European Commission responsible for financial services and competition, one goal of the EC is to "persuade" the United States "that Glass Steagall and interstate banking restrictions should be liberalised."[39] The ability of the EC to negotiate liberalization in the United States, however, will be a function of how powerful a united Europe becomes in economic and political terms.

The United States government and much of the private sector share an underlying anxiety about the formation of a fortress Europe. The government has consistently criticized those proposals which could place American firms at a competitive disadvantage. But it has also done more. According to a State Department document, "the United States government will monitor developments closely and advise U.S. firms in the financial services sector concerning EC developments *as well as discuss specific business plans for individual companies vis-à-vis a strategy for dealing with the European single market*" (emphasis added).[40]

In defending the interests of American banks, the government has not flinched from using tacit threats. According to one U.S. government report, "the most fundamental argument" made by American officials in discussions with their European counterparts over reciprocity "has been the threat reciprocity poses for continued free trade among nations. [The U.S.] Treasury cautioned the Commission that using reciprocity as a tool to fight protectionism by other countries would only encourage a trade war among financial markets, affecting not just the individual countries involved, but the world's financial system."[41]

In responding to the EC's proposals, the U.S. government has worked closely with organized American economic interests. With regard to banking, the Treasury Department has requested the Bankers Association of

Foreign Trade (a leading trade organization for international banks) "to organize and to represent the views of U.S. international banks to the Community." These views were incorporated in government representations to Brussels.[42]

Ironically, it remains unclear how much power *Brussels* has with respect to reciprocity. As the British Bankers Association remarked, "The 'effective market access' test refers to access 'granted by the Community to credit institutions from the third country.' Strictly, the Community does not grant any access to third country banks; the authorisation of their branches and of their cross-border business . . . is left to each member state in accordance with the First Banking Directive."[43] In short, *it is the member states, not the commission,* that grant the authorization to conduct banking business.

Behind this legal language is a story of European politics, in which the principal actors are the member states, the commission, and the banks. With regard to market access, the commission has developed a tacit alliance with the major banks, which are represented in Brussels by the Banking Federation of the European Community. For their part, the bankers want greater market access overseas, especially in the United States and Japan, and recognize that the Community as a whole is a more powerful negotiator than any single state; witness the relatively growing power of the EC in negotiations over international trade. Indeed, the banks also pushed the EC to represent their views in the recently completed Uruguay Round of the GATT talks, which had market access for service industries as a focal point.[44]

But in this issue-area, the banks and the commission have gotten ahead of the member states, which still wish to reserve for themselves the authority to make decisions with respect to the opening of banks in domestic markets. After all, it is the states themselves and their central banks, not the commission, that must worry about the safety and soundness of national banking systems.[45] The granting of authorization to conduct banking business is a fundamental element of financial regulation, and it cannot be surrendered so long as the supervisory regime is based upon home country control.

In recent years, as a result of American fears of a fortress Europe, the EC has been careful to define reciprocity as "reciprocal national treatment," in which market access is defined in terms of foreign banks being treated like domestic banks, no matter what the prevailing domestic regime. But this is unlikely to end tensions between the EC and its trading partners. According to one student of the directive, the EC has created a banking regime "which is much more favorable to banks authorized within the EC than to those from outside."[46] Foreign banks wishing to branch in the EC basically have to capitalize new subsidiaries in one of the member states; they cannot rely on the capital of their home office. And if banks agree to do so, it raises questions about the lender of last resort. If Citicorp establishes a subsidiary in London to serve as its European headquarters, is its lender of last resort the Bank of England or the Federal Reserve? Clearly, the development of the European Community will create new challenges for the governance of international finance.

The Battle over Investment Services

If the Second Banking Directive demonstrates that community building is an incremental process, the story of the Investment Services Directive (ISD) shows just how competitive the member states continue to be among themselves. The Second Directive, as we noted above, refers to "credit institutions" in which such institutions are defined in terms of universal banks. A companion Investment Services Directive had been on Europe's table since 1988, which sought to provide the same single passport to securities houses. It proved much more difficult to accomplish.

The debate over the ISD was really about which type of financial firm will benefit from European integration; specifically, it pitted universal banks against merchant or investment banks. The major barrier to the ISD was not in the principles of mutual recognition, home country control, and the single passport; rather, it has been in the accompanying directive on capital adequacy. The question is, how much capital must an investment bank possess? Against what risks must it be adequately protected? As the *Economist* has written, "The debate matters, because the cost and deployment of capital will be a big element of firms' competitiveness."[47] In short, the Germans, with their universal banks, prefer heavy capital requirements; the British, with their lithe merchant banks, prefer looser requirements for investment firms than for commercial banks.

Complicating the capital adequacy issue is the fact that rules in this area have been under discussion for many years in three different forums: the

European Community, the International Organization of Securities Commissions (IOSCO), and the Basle Committee. Indeed, these forums have competed for primacy. The European Commission, angered by the Basle Committee's action with regard to capital adequacy for commercial banks, has been determined to shape its own approach to investment services.[48] For their part, IOSCO members have sought to avoid domination by central bankers and have tried to develop a capital adequacy standard of their own. And the Basle Committee, which is a central bankers group, plainly wishes to dominate the international regulatory process. It, too, has worked on the capital adequacy problem for investment services. Indeed, this reflects its interest in regulating not just commercial banks but also universal banks, which many central bankers view as the financial institutions of the future.

This tension became apparent in a letter written by Basle Committee chairman Gerald Corrigan (who was then president of the Federal Reserve Bank of New York) to EC commissioner Sir Leon Brittan in June 1992. At the time, the EC was on the verge of adopting a capital adequacy directive for securities firms. Corrigan wrote that his committee was "concerned that in the name of haste more fundamental objectives might be compromised. Specifically, the Committee is concerned that haste might produce a capital regime that does not meet reasonable prudential standards and, in the process, undercut efforts to achieve a reasonable degree of harmony within a broader scale of nations."[49] Again, the question underlying this debate is: Who rules?

Behind these technical discussions of capital adequacy lies a larger, political-economic issue: Which, if any, single financial structure will dominate European banking markets? The British have a "capital market system" in which equity capital is the main source of industrial finance. The Germans, in contrast, have a "bank-based system" in which the universal banks dominate capital markets.[50] The former system requires dynamic investment banks which are willing to channel funds to new and growing companies. The latter requires a tightly structured network of banks and industrial firms. Both countries like their own particular system. The question is, which of these financial models will dominate the new Europe? Or will Europe remain big enough to support a mix?

The capital adequacy issue is thus largely about state power and differing financial structures. But there are also technical issues at stake, and from this simpler perspective the world's securities regulators have found it more difficult to develop a Basle-like formula than their banking counterparts. The Basle Accord focuses on credit risk, and banks must hold risk-weighted capital as a function of the type of assets they choose to hold. Banks, of course, also face other types of risks, including interest rate and foreign exchange risk, and these, too, have been the topic of discussion in Basle. Universal banks, which combine commercial and investment banking, are exposed not only to credit risks but to the same type of market risks faced by securities firms.

Securities firms, however, do not take funds from depositors; they are in the business of profiting from investments which are risky by nature. Again, in the words of the *Economist:*

> The BIS ratios for banks reflect only credit risk (that a counterparty will fail to pay). In London's securities markets, low initial capital allows lots of firms, banks, and non-banks to compete, and additional requirements reflect position risk (that market prices, or interest or exchange rates, will move, reducing the value of the securities held). In West Germany, where all the participants are banks, high minimum capital limits the number of firms and no separate capital is required for position risk in securities dealing . . . The British and their allies believe that German rules kill competition. The Germans and theirs that Britain's would heap unnecessary burdens on their banks.[51]

Despite the technical and political problems, in the autumn of 1992 the European Commission finally adopted a compromise set of investment services and capital adequacy directives that met with the support of the member states. The Germans got what they wanted by winning agreement on similar capital standards for commercial and investment banks. But the British won a victory with an expanded definition of capital. In short, after years of debate, a negotiated settlement was finally reached which will enable the single market to proceed in investment services.[52]

Despite their difficulties in formulating an investment services and capital adequacy directive, it should be emphasized that the member states had already found common ground and have been proceeding with integration since 1985 in several important areas of investment services. The Council of Ministers has approved directives which liberalize the sale of mutual funds, provide investor protection, and require minimum disclosure requirements for prospectuses. But without an umbrella investment-services directive which liberalizes capital markets, opening them to competition and the sale of new financial products, the Europe 1992 project itself, with its vision of an economically dynamic continent, would have been endangered, for such markets provide the life blood of modern industrial states.

The story of investment services suggests that powerful national interests remain alive and well in the new Europe, and that the mediation of those interests has been evolutionary rather than revolutionary. It also shows how the European Commission has been in competition with groups outside the continent in shaping the regulatory environment—in this case with the Basle Committee (which largely reflects the preferences of American central bankers) and IOSCO (which largely reflects the preferences of American securities regulators). The need to have good relations with the Americans, and in turn to maintain access to the American financial marketplace, remains important to the member states that constitute the European Community; but at the same time, the commission has been determined to establish a unique economic space with its own rules and regulations.

The process of European integration has stimulated the imagination of people around the world. The promise of a new Europe in which ancient antagonisms give way to economic and political cooperation provides hope that humanity really can learn from past mistakes. And yet these hopes should not obscure clear-eyed analysis of the European reality.

This chapter has tried to show that financial integration has been a long and arduous process, and one that is far from complete. Since at least the early 1970s, when the member states began to make serious efforts toward financial integration in the interest of economic competitiveness, barriers to trade in financial services have only slowly been eroded. In the early 1990s, Europe remained far from being an ational financial space. On the contrary, as an analysis of the various directives shows, both home and host states will retain substantial power in setting the rules of the game.

Indeed, within Europe itself many observers are still expressing skepticism about whether a liberal, single marketplace will ever emerge. In the words of Jacques Thierry, a leading scholar of banking markets, "The implementation of the Second [Banking] Coordination Directive will probably result in an enormous regulatory tangle. Twelve sets of home-country controls with their corresponding versions of the single banking license will have to mesh in with the regulatory systems in force in the different host countries."[53] This is a vision of a Euronightmare.

Thierry suggests that even within the terms of the 1992 project many different outcomes for banking markets are conceivable. First, Europe could become dominated by a handful of core universal banks, forming something like a cartel structure. Second, national markets could remain sufficiently segmented, with distinct "national champions" dominating locally. Third, European banks could begin to engage in a feverish burst of merger and acquisitions activity, creating strategic alliances and cross-border networks. Finally, Europe could be invaded by more dynamic financial institutions from the United States and Japan, as has happened in other economic sectors.[54]

Yet another set of issues relates to the external influence of the EC on financial markets worldwide. As I have emphasized in this chapter, the European Commission has intentionally sought to use the Second Banking Directive as a liberalization lever against the United States and Japan. But Europe's ability to play this gambit will be a function of its internal success.

It is also doubtful that the European model of a "single passport" will be accepted as a principle of global financial regulation, even with strong home country control. The United States is unlikely to accept the single-passport principle, since it wishes to reserve the right to regulate foreign banks operating on American soil. Indeed, in recent years such regulations have tightened, especially in response to the BCCI scandal. In short, the United States remains a strong host country.

This raises the question of just how successful the United States (and Japan) want the new Europe to be. In official documents, American support for the single market has been unwavering, and remains, in the words of the State Department, "a cornerstone of our foreign policy. An open and vibrant Europe reinforces the common bond of democracy, strengthens the Atlantic Alliance, and can be a powerful engine for global economic growth."[55] And yet, as the U.S.-U.K. capital adequacy accord powerfully demonstrated, the United States has also shown its willingness to "divide and conquer" the EC when that has been in its interest.

The European Community remains an enigma, even to its closest observers. It is a unique experiment in international politics, and one that is not fully understood, perhaps even by Europe's leaders themselves. National policies continue to impede single-market integration, and there is no indication that these will be overcome anytime soon. Yet this fact should not obscure the tremendous, incremental progress that has been made to date; indeed, the chief puzzle is not why states are still strong, but why community building has gotten so far. The most likely outcome for Europe is that the process of integration will continue on its unique path. In the end, the Community will be something less than its most fervent adherents had hoped to achieve, but much more than the skeptics had ever imagined to be possible.

7 | BCCI and Beyond

You become lead regulator of an organization you believe you can regulate.

—BANK OF ENGLAND OFFICIAL BRIAN QUINN

On July 5, 1991, the worldwide offices of the Bank of Credit and Commerce International (BCCI) were closed in a coordinated shutdown initiated by the Bank of England. The official investigations undertaken in conjunction with that decision revealed a bank that was serving as the hub of an international crime network, involved in money laundering and illegal trafficking in drugs and weapons. In the words of one arms dealer who relied on the bank's extensive third-world branch network for shifting funds around, "BCCI was a full-service bank."[1]

BCCI was a regulator's nightmare, and its structure was expressly designed to escape consolidated supervision. The bank was headquartered in Luxembourg, operated out of London, and owned largely by Abu Dhabi. It spread globally like a virus, escaping the normal regulatory vaccines until an international effort was made to kill it.

The BCCI story would appear at first glance to undermine much of the argument of this book. How can one reconcile an argument that focuses on the role of the state in supervising international financial markets with the story of a bank that apparently outmaneuvered one government after another? Doesn't BCCI point to the primacy of globalization over the nation-state?

In this chapter, I argue that BCCI is the exception that proves the rule; indeed, history may ultimately show that it was not so much of an exception, as we learn more about the byzantine connections between the bank and various Middle Eastern and Western governments. It may be, for example, that the bank was allowed to operate in the West for as long as it did because it assisted intelligence services that were monitoring terrorist groups and drug dealers.[2] Two investigative reporters who spent years tracking the BCCI story have even claimed that "there are . . . indications that CIA officials were involved in the founding of BCCI."[3]

Leaving the melodrama and conjecture aside, BCCI reminds us that criminality is prevalent in international finance, and that it sometimes overwhelms state actors.[4] But the BCCI tale ultimately demonstrates that state power prevails over transnational forces if and when it is applied.[5] No enterprise, legal or illicit, can match the power of a mobilized state, or group of states. When public officials decided that they had had enough of BCCI, they acted conclusively to shut it down.

The BCCI story tells us much about state efforts to govern international finance, and how governance evolves in the aftermath of scandals and crises. Like other shocks before it, the major lesson that bank supervisors have learned from BCCI is that every international bank requires a national regulator and that the home country remains the focal point of regulation in a global economy.

But in a world comprised of nation-states, in which regulatory harmonization is absent, tensions between home and host countries will always remain—especially between those home states whose regulatory capability is relatively weak and those host states where it is strong—and international cooperation will prove incomplete. Indeed, it is suggestive of some bank regulators' lack of confidence in their foreign colleagues that the BCCI scandal has also led to a strengthening of *host country* supervision, especially in the United States and, by extension, in the Basle Committee. Whether the European Community reassesses its approach to banking regulation, with its unique emphasis on home country control, remains an open question. I will argue that eventually it must, although such a reassessment may have to await still another cross-border banking crisis.

The BCCI Story

BCCI was first incorporated in Luxembourg in 1972, the creation of a charismatic Pakistani banker named Agan Hasan Abedi.[6] In 1974, the structure of the bank changed to include a holding company based in Luxembourg and two main subsidiaries, one in the Cayman Islands and the other in Luxembourg. The choice of these headquarters sites was hardly a coincidence, since both were notable for their devotion to bank secrecy laws and lax or nonexistent regulatory regimes, regimes that had served to attract substantial financial investment. Over the next fifteen years, BCCI expanded to the point where it had branches in more than seventy countries and $20 billion in assets by the time of its closure in 1991. Its early backers included the ruler of Abu Dhabi, Sheikh Zayed, and Bank of America, which viewed BCCI as an opening to the rich Middle Eastern financial marketplace.

BCCI was designed to hinder effective regulation. It engaged two auditors to examine the separate books of its subsidiaries, and no consolidated accounts were made of the holding company. Although under the Basle Concordat principles the bank should have been regulated by the Luxembourg Monetary Institute (IML), the vast majority of its operations occurred outside that small country; indeed, the Luxembourg authorities admitted in later testimony that "it was impossible to exercise adequate consolidated supervision of a group 98 percent of whose activities fell outside its jurisdiction."[7]

Despite this peculiar structure, BCCI was able to expand not only into the third world, which provided much of its deposit base, but deep into the world's major financial capitals, including London and Hong Kong. Thwarted in 1976 and 1981 from establishing a direct presence in the United States, it clandestinely purchased banks in several parts of the country, including Georgia and Washington, D.C. By the early 1980s, BCCI had agency offices and separately incorporated banks in America, providing money-laundering services for international drug dealers. This expansion was made possible by the intervention of high-powered lobbyists and lawyers, including Bert Lance (President Jimmy Carter's old friend who served briefly as his director of the Office of Management and Budget) and the famous Washington legal team of Clark Clifford and Roger Altman.[8]

Perhaps most difficult to explain is the phase of BCCI's growth that occurred in England during the 1970s. Early on, Agan Abedi had targeted London and "the City" (London's financial district) to be his operational headquarters. As a U.S. Senate report explained, "At the time, London was a favored vacation and shopping destination for oil-rich Middle

Easterners, and BCCI needed to serve them."[9] London was also a major depository of petrodollars, which BCCI needed to capture in order to fuel its expansion. By 1977, BCCI had forty-five offices in the United Kingdom.

This expansion occurred despite consistent concerns expressed by the Bank of England about BCCI's structure, regulation, and management. Indeed, in 1979 the bank stopped BCCI from building any new branches, and the following year it rejected BCCI's application for status as a full-service commercial bank, limiting it to acting as a "licensed deposit-taker." Given these worries, the obvious question is why the Bank of England didn't stop its operations altogether, or make a greater effort as a host country to regulate the BCCI operations on British soil.

This question has been the subject of significant investigation by the U.S. Congress, the House of Commons, and an independent committee in Britain under Lord Justice Bingham.[10] But it is likely that only historians will be able to supply a complete answer, if and when the archives of the governments involved with the BCCI case should open. The Bank of England's main line of defense is simply that it was not the chief regulator of BCCI; that was the job of the IML. The Bank of England had the more limited task of supervising BCCI's branches, and this, it claims, it did. Allegations of criminality were investigated, and BCCI's auditors were questioned. In some cases, fraud was detected, but as the governor of the Bank of England remarked before the House of Commons, "If we close down a bank every time we find an individual act or two of fraud we would have rather fewer banks than we do at the moment."[11]

Yet the Bank of England's answer appears to be incomplete. For example, although in 1976 the New York State regulator of banking, John Heimann, prevented BCCI from purchasing a small New York City bank through an intermediary, owing to the absence of a lead regulator, BCCI was still expanding at this time in England. In 1985, Luxembourg's regulatory authorities pleaded with the Bank of England to force BCCI to incorporate in London, given that its operations were based there, but the bank refused, indicating that it did not want lead responsibility for the group. Furthermore, in 1988 bankers from BCCI's office in Tampa, Florida, were indicted by U.S. authorities on money-laundering charges, but the Bank of England was less than helpful in the American investigation; indeed, it would not launch an in-depth investigation of BCCI's London-based activities until 1990–91.

On the basis of the evidence currently available, therefore, one can only be puzzled by the Bank of England's relative inaction.[12] This leads the analyst to wonder whether the bank did not act more forcefully for fear of contagion in the banking system, or for "raisons d'état," such as support of ongoing intelligence activities that exploited BCCI's links to organized crime and terrorism, or out of concern over the repercussions of a BCCI closure in the Arab world. Lord Justice Bingham suggested that this latter reason may have played a role when he wrote in his report that the supervisors were less vigilant than they would otherwise have been owing to concerns that "the closure of 45 UK branches would cause substantial political and diplomatic problems."[13]

It is also disingenuous of the Bank of England to claim that it was concerned only with BCCI's domestic branches. This is true in a technical sense, but the bank was aware of BCCI's global activities and knew by the mid-1980s that its London office was at the hub of a criminal network. British officials also knew that Luxembourg was not up to the job of regulating such a complex institution, and indeed acted to assist the IML in building a complete picture.

On the suggestion of British and Luxembourg officials, the members of the Basle Committee took the extraordinary step of forming a "College of Regulators" in 1987, with the objective of trying to gain a larger view of BCCI's operations. The College gathered a substantial amount of information about BCCI's myriad activities, but again this was only slowly translated into action. As auditor Price Waterhouse remarked, "In our experience of dealing with the College each regulator tended to focus on its own domestic concerns rather than accepting full Collegiate responsibility."[14] Indeed, it was not until an ongoing American investigation of BCCI threatened to go public with several indictments that the College of Regulators and the Bank of England acted to close BCCI's worldwide branches.

Yet Britain is not the only country in which BCCI's expansion is troublesome. The other prominent case is the United States. Indeed, in some ways the American case is even more puzzling, since state and federal regulators denied the bank access to the marketplace on at least two occasions, in 1976 and 1979. Nonetheless, by the early 1980s BCCI would also be up and running in America, having acquired four banks that operated in seven states and Washington, D.C.[15]

The story of BCCI in the United States will provide grist for scholars, journalists, and novelists for many years to come. It combines the basic ingredients of a paperback thriller—money, power, sex, and drugs—with true heroism on the part of those undercover agents, prosecutors, and public officials who dug up the evidence needed to indict the bank. Yet, as is often the case in real life, it is a story whose plot, if fictionalized, would be dismissed by critics as unbelievable.

BCCI made its initial foray into the American market with an aborted attempt to buy a small bank in New York City, the Chelsea National. This was a state-chartered bank; therefore the acquisition would have to be approved by the New York State banking commissioner, John Heimann. In an early warning of what would become its standard operating procedure in America, BCCI sought to buy the bank through a nominee, hiding its direct connection. In this case the nominee was a young Pakistani national with few resources of his own, who said that BCCI was acting as his banker and adviser.

During his investigation, Heimann learned enough about BCCI to make him uncomfortable. It was clear that the bank had no central regulator and provided no consolidated reporting. Moreover, the Pakistani buyer lacked banking experience and sufficient assets of his own. Accordingly, the application was rejected.[16]

Shortly thereafter, Jimmy Carter was elected president of the United States. John Heimann would follow him to Washington, becoming comptroller of the currency, the supervisor of all national banks. Ironically, the election would give BCCI the entry to the American marketplace that it needed.

That opening was provided by Carter crony T. Bertram Lance, president of the National Bank of Georgia (NBG), who was appointed director of the Office of Management and Budget. Under government regulations, Lance was required to sell his shares in the bank as a condition of his appointment. At the time, however, NBG bank shares were depressed, and Lance would have taken a significant loss. On July 11, 1977, President Carter made a special request to Congress that the regulation be suspended. In the congressional hearings that followed, evidence of "unsafe and unsound" banking practices at NBG was uncovered, and Lance was deluged by bad press. Despite powerful legal representation on behalf of Lance by the team of Clark Clifford and Robert Altman, the director of the Office of

Management and Budget was forced to resign from government that September.

Lance's problems were now just beginning. The media's investigative reporting on the National Bank of Georgia had only served to lower the value of the bank's stock, driving Lance into deeper financial distress. Desperate for a buyer, Lance, through an intermediary, made the acquaintance of BCCI chairman Abedi. For Abedi, this meeting was truly heaven-sent, and for Lance, a crisis would soon become an opportunity.

With the National Bank of Georgia, Abedi had found his American beachhead. Exploiting the technique that had failed him in New York, he used a front man, this time working with his close associate, Saudi financier Ghaith Pharaon, in structuring the transaction. From the outside, Pharaon would appear as the sole buyer of Lance's NBG shares. In truth, however, Pharaon and BCCI would be working hand in glove.

Pharaon's application to purchase the National Bank of Georgia posed a dilemma for Heimann and the Office of the Comptroller of the Currency. Pharaon himself *was* an experienced financier and man of means, unlike the Pakistani national who had tried to buy Chelsea National. Furthermore, a rejection of the application would probably mean the collapse of the bank and a government bailout. Heimann's internal memorandums at the time indicate that he was clearly troubled by the back-door entrance of BCCI into the United States, but ultimately he chose it as the lesser of the two evils. In 1978, Ghaith Pharaon became the formal owner of the National Bank of Georgia.[17]

This was only the beginning. The National Bank of Georgia had been part of an interstate banking group called Financial General Bankshares (FGB), which was suffering significant divisions in its ownership and management ranks over the running of the company; several owners wanted to get out altogether. Lance arranged for Abedi and his associates to begin purchasing shares of the group, and in February 1978 he could announce at a meeting of Financial General's shareholders that BCCI now controlled 20 percent of the stock and wanted complete control of the group. The secretive accumulation of shares, with the intention of takeover, constituted clear violations of Securities and Exchange Commission regulations. A group of shareholders filed suit against Lance and BCCI for this violation, and soon they were joined by the commission itself.

BCCI, Lance, and their lawyers, Clark Clifford and Robert Altman, responded that BCCI was acting not as a group but only on behalf of several Middle Eastern investors. Each of these investors owned less than 5 percent of Financial General's shares; thus, they were not required to register their purchases with the Securities and Exchange Commission. (Indeed, Clifford and Altman have consistently defended their actions with regard to BCCI and Financial General, saying that there was never any evidence that the bank was simply using nominees as a way of entering the American marketplace.) In a consent decree, a federal judge enjoined Lance and several Middle Eastern investors from violating securities laws, and it sought assurances from BCCI that the bank was not behind the alleged purchases of Financial General shares.

This surprisingly light slap on the wrist did nothing to deter Abedi from pursuing his dream. Indeed, he had already been able to place some agency offices in the United States, with operations limited to serving foreign clients. But what he wanted was an American deposit base, and this is what had eluded him. Now, through a newly created, separate holding company known as Credit and Commerce Holdings (CCAH), he continued to amass shares of Financial General. In 1978, Credit and Commerce Holdings, represented by Clifford and Altman, applied under Maryland law to take over Financial General. Again, they denied that BCCI was behind the purchase. The State of Maryland nonetheless rejected the application, citing laws against hostile takeovers of banks; the Federal Reserve subsequently agreed with the state's decision.

Credit and Commerce Holdings then applied to take over Financial General through the Commonwealth of Virginia, the home state of another FGB bank. Virginia bank commissioner Sidney Bailey was sufficiently worried about the offshore CCAH group to seek information about it from the Central Intelligence Agency and the State Department; both denied having any information, although a Senate investigation subsequently learned that the Central Intelligence Agency was very familiar with several of CCAH's alleged principals, and that it had conducted business for many years with BCCI. Ultimately Bailey, too, rejected CCAH's application, but in 1981 yet another hearing was scheduled on the takeover by the Federal Reserve Board. Truly, there is no stronger testimony to the power of perseverance than Abedi's pursuit of Financial General Bankshares.

In his statement to the Federal Reserve, Bailey said that he had rejected

Credit and Commerce Holdings as a buyer of Financial General for three reasons: "First, the U.S. might not be able to insure that these foreign owners would abide by its laws. Second, it would be difficult to tell who really controlled the bank. Third, it was possible the bank's new Middle Eastern owners might strip the bank of its assets and move them else-where before anyone found out."[18] Furthermore, Bailey said he was sus-picious of any group that would pay such a high premium for the pur-chase of an ailing bank group. "What," he asked, "is the motive giving rise to this protracted, expensive campaign to buy Financial General?"

Responding on behalf of Credit and Commerce Holdings was the dean of the Washington establishment, Clark Clifford. In the company's de-fense, Clifford made passionate claims about American economic interests and American values. With regard to the first, he noted the staggering amount of money the United States had shipped to OPEC countries in recent years to pay for oil imports, and said that every effort should be made to get some of it back in the form of investment capital. The Middle Eastern investors assembled through Credit and Commerce Holdings were doing just that. Regarding American values, he suggested that Bailey had an anti-Arab bias and that this was an element in his rejection of the ap-plication. "I believe deeply in this country," Clifford said. "I believe deeply in its attitude of fairness . . . I do not believe in prejudice. I do not believe in bias. Our government does not."[19]

The Federal Reserve then listened to the statements of the major inves-tors in Credit and Commerce Holdings. All of them claimed that they were acting independently and were in no way serving as nominees for BCCI. Under questioning, though, they were asked whether it was just coinci-dence that BCCI had introduced them all to Financial General in the first place. "That is very possible," Sheikh Adham of Saudi Arabia replied. "Such things happen in our part of the world."

The Federal Reserve continued to probe the BCCI connection, asking if it was merely a coincidence that the names of the Bank of Credit and Commerce International and Credit and Commerce Holdings were so sim-ilar to each other. Clifford replied: "The term 'Credit' and the term 'Commerce' are terms that are used extensively in the Persian Gulf in financial affairs . . . Of course a number of banks used the term 'Commerce' . . . I know of no additional reasoning behind it."[20] Clifford was then explicitly asked whether BCCI had played any direct role in

CCAH's application to purchase Financial General. "None," he responded. On August 25, 1981, the Federal Reserve approved the application; two months earlier, it had agreed to Altman's request "to seal portions of the transcript of the hearing." To this day, therefore, only a portion of the historical record has been revealed to government investigators and private citizens know even less.

Over the next seven years—until its indictment in October 1988 on money-laundering charges—BCCI built up a substantial American network through its agency offices, the National Bank of Georgia, and Financial General Bankshares. This network, as a U.S. Customs undercover investigation, Operation C-Chase, would reveal, came to serve drug dealers and their money launderers, arms merchants, and those involved in capital flight from the third world.[21] During this period, Clark Clifford and Robert Altman would become increasingly enmeshed in the affairs of Financial General, ultimately becoming (respectively) chairman and president of the banking group; eventually, their banking careers would meet with a sordid end in front of various congressional and judicial investigating bodies, although they would be acquitted of any criminal activity.

Ironically, C-Chase stumbled upon BCCI as a by-product of its investigation of money laundering; the bank itself was not the original target. In 1986, the Customs Service decided to launch a major undercover investigation of drug-money laundering by American banks. An agent named Robert Mazur posed as a businessman who, among many other legal and illegal activities, assisted drug dealers in getting their street earnings out of the United States and beyond the long arm of the law. During the investigation, Mazur kept coming upon BCCI as the drug dealers' favorite bank. Indeed, he discovered that one of the bank's best clients was none other than American ally General Manuel Noriega of Panama.

Eventually, the bank itself became a target of the investigation. By 1988, Mazur had laundered approximately $14 million through BCCI's various offices. He learned in the process that many of the bank's top officials around the world were deeply implicated in all aspects of its criminal activities.[22]

In October 1988, under the guise of a party to celebrate the impending "wedding" of Mazur and his girlfriend, which had brought to Tampa (the location of a BCCI agency office, and allegedly Mazur's hometown) many of Mazur's newly acquired "friends" from the drug world and BCCI, the

American investigators launched their sting operation, arresting eleven bank officials and several drug dealers. At the same time, BCCI's offices throughout the United States were raided. In addition to those arrested, BCCI's holding company and bank subsidiary in Luxembourg were named in the indictment. The bank's final chapter was now being written, though it would take longer to close than one might have expected under these circumstances.

The Bank of England did not move against BCCI as a result of the Tampa indictment. As bank officials later explained in the Bingham Inquiry, they had "little knowledge" of "the truth of the US accusations," and the American indictments gave them no brief to move against the U.K. subsidiary. Indeed, even when the director of a small London bank with strong connections to the Arab world stated that the American indictments were certainly justified and that BCCI's criminality was widespread, the Bank of England refused to follow up on the allegations, or merely to discuss the issue with former BCCI officials who had expressed their willingness to come forward and share inside knowledge.[23]

Following the Tampa indictment, the Bank of England's primary fear was that public scrutiny of BCCI would provoke a run on the bank's U.K. branches, forcing it to accept responsibility for depositor accounts and inject liquidity into the system. Their objective was to "ring-fence" the British operation and safeguard its financial soundness. In so doing, they wanted to make sure that the bank's problems escaped public scrutiny to the extent possible. As a Price Waterhouse executive said, "Have you ever heard of a bank being qualified? You simply can't go around qualifying the accounts of a bank without creating all sorts of problems, without the whole thing collapsing."[24]

After 1988, the bank's strategy was to buy time, during which it attempted to get Abu Dhabi and other Middle Eastern investors to inject more capital into BCCI. In this the bank was only partly successful; new funds were provided, but these would prove insufficient to keep BCCI going in light of the continuing flood of information about its criminal activities that could no longer remain concealed or ring-fenced.

In 1991, the Bank of England finally launched a complete investigation of BCCI, under Section 41 of Britain's Banking Act, again relying on Price Waterhouse to provide a complete auditing of its operations. The Section 41 report concluded that "the scale of fraud is widespread, the culture of the bank is criminal."[25] Finally the Bank of England was forced to act, and in coordination with regulators around the world, it closed the offices of BCCI on July 5, 1991.

Lessons of BCCI

In the aftermath of the BCCI scandal, journalists, academics, and public officials filled Op-Ed pages in newspapers around the world with the "lessons learned." Common to these articles was the complaint that banking deregulation had gone too far in the industrial countries, and that international banking now needed a dose of reregulation.[26] As we have seen throughout this book, such calls have been heard after each financial crisis, and indeed states *have* responded. BCCI notwithstanding, states have increased their scrutiny of international banking operations over the past two decades, and have strengthened home country control.

The direction that banking regulation has taken after each crisis has remained remarkably consistent—namely, an increased emphasis on home country control. During the 1970s and early 1980s, home country control was enhanced through consolidated supervision and information sharing among regulators; in the late 1980s and early 1990s, regulations would be strengthened through the articulation of minimum regulatory standards in areas, such as capital adequacy, that each home country was expected to monitor. Following the collapse of BCCI, a bank which had escaped adequate supervision in its home country of Luxembourg, new rules for defining the home country would be implemented by the Basle Committee. In short, home country control has become increasingly formalized as the basis of international banking regulation.

Yet, as I will discuss in the following pages, the United States also drew from the BCCI scandal the need for greater *host country control* of foreign banks. Unlike the European Community, in which the relative power of the host has been declining with the acceptance of mutual recognition of banking laws and a single passport for banking services, the United States has rejected such an extreme view of home country control. If we go beyond BCCI, therefore, one place to look for tensions among states with respect to bank regulation concerns the division of home and host supervisory responsibility; I believe this will also be the case *within* the EC. This should not be surprising, for such conflicts have been inherent with the spread of transnational enterprises; indeed, they are inevitable under conditions of interdependence. As former IBM executive Jacques Maisonrouge has put it, the fundamental problem for multinational firms is "not so much a case of multinational corporations colliding with governments, as it is a case of governments colliding with governments."[27]

The United States

"Not all foreign bankers are crooks—but America's Congress wants to treat them as if they were, just in case." So wrote the London *Economist* following congressional passage of the major post-BCCI piece of banking legislation: the Foreign Bank Supervision Enhancement Act of 1991.[28] This legislation, which was written by the Federal Reserve Board at the request of the Senate Banking Committee, would prove divisive both within the U.S. government and between the U.S. and its allies.

The new law:

1. bars entry of any foreign bank into the U.S. unless it is subject to *consolidated home country supervision* [emphasis added] and agrees to permit supervisory access to any information regarding it that the regulators want;
2. applies to foreign banks the same financial, managerial, and operational standards governing U.S. banks;
3. grants specific authority to federal regulators to terminate the U.S. activities of any foreign bank that is engaging in illegal, unsafe, or unsound practices;
4. grants the Federal Reserve authority to examine any office of a foreign bank in the U.S.[29]

As the above suggests, one fallout of the BCCI crisis was to enhance the power of the Federal Reserve over other government agencies in banking regulation; the central bank had become *primus inter pares* on banking matters. This is somewhat surprising, since it was the Federal Reserve that let BCCI into the United States in the first place, after the bank's applications had been rejected in New York, Virginia, and Maryland. Nonetheless, there is a trend, evident throughout the Basle Committee, of central bank ascendance over regulatory matters.

Whether this should be viewed as a welcome development is questionable, for it may undermine the myth of central bank independence. Since the end of World War II, a growing number of countries have established central banks which have price stability as their transcendent interest, an interest that is to be pursued irrespective of the party in power. Central banks are supposed to pursue that interest despite the pleading of lobbyists, including bankers. But it is doubtful that the Federal Reserve, or any central bank, can regulate financial institutions without taking part in direct negotiations with those institutions themselves. The question thus arises: Can the central bank retain its so-called independence in the area of monetary policy when it is subject to lobbying pressure by banks in the area of regulatory policy? Can it keep the two areas separate?[30]

The rise of the Federal Reserve has, of course, met with opposition from the other major regulator of foreign banks: the U.S. Treasury, through its Office of the Comptroller of the Currency. This office had been responsible for supervising foreign banks that had incorporated their branches as national banks, but now that responsibility had to be shared. Furthermore, the Federal Reserve would not even rely on the Office of the Comptroller for on-site examinations of foreign branches; it would rely on its own examiners, and was given the authority to hire additional staff in this area. The upshot of the interagency controversy, which spilled into the public view during the hearings on the act, was to preserve for the Office of the Comptroller the right to grant banking licenses, but subject to ultimate Federal Reserve approval.[31]

With passage of the act, foreign banks faced substantial host country regulation by the United States; indeed, they faced not only Federal Reserve regulations, but also any additional regulations imposed by the Office of the Comptroller of the Currency or by state banking commissions. Not only could the United States block a foreign bank from entering the country altogether; it has also placed strict limits on the equity investments such banks can now make in American financial institutions without government approval. Previously, foreign banks could take an equity stake of up to 10 percent in an American bank without approval from the Federal Reserve; now the upper limit is 5 percent. Furthermore, and perhaps most important, any new foreign bank that wishes to obtain federal deposit insurance must establish a separately incorporated American subsidiary.

As the *Economist* has observed, "This last requirement is more than inconvenient red tape."[32] It means that new foreign banks wishing to enter the American market to lend will be effectively limited in their ability to do so, since under the Basle Accord lending is a function of capital adequacy. It should be noted that previously established foreign bank branches have been grandfathered under the law. Thus, new foreign banks will be placed at a disadvantage compared not only to American banks but also to foreign banks that were already operating in the United States. Under the previous regulations, branches could rely on the capital of the home bank; now the subsidiary itself must be entirely capitalized. The United States has, in effect, adopted a regulation for foreign banks that is similar to the one the Europeans have implemented with regard to third-country banks in the Second Banking Directive. Potential problems could arise with this approach to foreign banking regulation, however, as it raises questions about how much responsibility a host country should wish to assume over foreign banking operations. Again, the proper balance between home and host countries has probably not yet been found.

Despite these new regulations, there remain several weaknesses regarding foreign banks. The first is endemic in any system that rests fundamentally upon home country control, and it concerns the capabilities of foreign bank regulators. As noted above, the United States still looks to the home country to serve as primary regulator of its banks, but there is no indication that either Luxembourg or the Grand Caymans have altered their regulatory regimes in light of BCCI. Because of this weakness, a report by the U.S. Senate has called upon the Federal Reserve to "develop and publish criteria for measuring foreign regulators, and to establish a certification process that permits it to deny access for a foreign bank to engage in activities in the U.S. if it is based in a country that does not meet certain essential standards for banking regulation."[33]

Second, bank secrecy laws in foreign countries continue to prevent vital information sharing among national regulators. This was painfully evident during the BCCI crisis, as banking authorities, beginning with officials at the Bank of England, denied their colleagues around the world access to various reports at their disposal about BCCI's activities. Again, one can expect the United States to call for increased transparency *among* banking regulators in the Basle Committee and on a bilateral basis.

Finally, the BCCI case reveals the extent to which America's decentralized system of regulation provides financial criminals with a pleasing target. BCCI was able to enter the American market after being turned down by three different state regulators and twice by the Federal Reserve. Yet in a system with fifty state banking regulators and three federal regulators, perseverance by criminal groups may have its rewards. Although it is unlikely that the United States would centralize all banking regulation under the single roof of the Federal Reserve or some new authority (such a concentration of power runs deeply against the diversity of American economic and political interests), better coordination among regulators is clearly needed, and perhaps can be achieved through improvements to current interagency arrangements.

Thus, in the aftermath of BCCI, the United States acted to strengthen international banking supervision in two fundamental ways: first, it demanded consolidated home country supervision as the basis for foreign bank entry into the United States; second, as a powerful host country, it reserved for itself the right to grant banking licenses and to determine safe and sound banking practices. With the former, it continued a trend that had long been in evidence among supervisors—namely, the trend toward emphasizing home country control. But with the latter, it rejected European notions of a single passport and mutual recognition, instead developing a U.S. model that balanced home country control with host country supervision. Indeed, it would pursue this approach as a model of international governance in the Basle Committee.

The Basle Committee

BCCI had demanded the Basle Committee's attention at least since 1987, when the College of Regulators was established as a second-best solution to the absence of consolidated supervision. With the closure of the bank in July 1991, the committee reviewed its experience not only with the College concept but also with the Basle Concordat, which articulated the fundamental principles of international banking supervision. Both were found wanting.

The lesson that the committee has drawn from the College of Regulators is that it "is not a full substitute for a clearly designated lead supervisor who can effectively monitor the worldwide operations of a complex group. Much has been made of the opaque structure of BCCI as an impediment to effective supervision. From now on, supervisors will be increasingly wary of any major banking group which is structured in a way which makes consolidated supervision difficult to achieve."[34]

From the outset, the member states recognized the College as a second-best solution to regulating BCCI. As the Bank of England's Brian Quinn told a House of Commons committee, "It was not intended, and it was never intended in the minds of those participating, for the college to be a substitute for proper consolidated supervision with a lead supervisor."[35] Indeed, the failure of the College to act as a united body should give pause to those who view multilateralism as a model for international governance.

The College fell victim to the classic problem of collective action. As auditor Price Waterhouse said, "In our experience of dealing with the College each regulator tended to focus on its own domestic concerns rather than accepting full Collegiate responsibility."[36] This is reminiscent of Rousseau's "Stag Hunt," in which a group of hunters have pledged to act in unison to circle and capture a deer. Suddenly, a rabbit appears. One hunter breaks ranks and chases the prey, which is now in his sights. The circle is thus broken and the deer, finding the opening, escapes.[37]

Such are the problems that confront every multilateral organization in the absence of a clearly defined leader and enforcer of agreements. Indeed, BCCI would close its doors only when regulators followed the belated lead of the Bank of England in 1991, four years after the College had started to meet! Such lessons were not lost on the United States, which used the failure of the College as an opportunity to reexamine the Basle Concordat.

By 1991 the United States would be in an exceptionally strong position to share its views with other Basle Committee members, since Gerald Corrigan, president of the Federal Reserve Bank of New York, was elected the group's chairman following the untimely death of Huib Muller of the Netherlands. (In 1993, however, Corrigan would resign both posts and would be replaced by Tommaso Padoa-Schiappa of Italy.) In the same way the Federal Reserve had acted to place capital adequacy on the international agenda, Corrigan now did the same with American regulatory policies. It is thus no coincidence that the revisions made to the Basle Concordat were consistent with the regulations approved by Congress under the Foreign Bank Supervision Enhancement Act.

The "new" Concordat, released by the Basle Committee in June 1992, articulates the following principles of international banking supervision:

1. All international banking groups and international banks should be supervised by a home country authority that capably performs consolidated supervision.
2. The creation of a cross-border banking establishment should receive the prior consent of both the host country supervisory authority and the bank's, and, if these are different, from the banking group's home country supervisory authority.
3. Supervisory authorities should possess the right to gather information from the cross-border banking establishments of the banks or banking groups for which they are the home country supervisor.
4. If a host country authority determines that any of the foregoing minimum standards is not met to its satisfaction, that authority could impose restrictive measures necessary to satisfy its prudential concerns consistent with these minimum standards, including the prohibition of the creation of banking establishments.[38]

As I argued above, the revised Concordat clearly reflects American preferences, as articulated in U.S. legislation and declaratory statements. It reemphasizes home country control, but at the same time strengthens the role of host country supervisors. This approach to banking regulation could produce a fresh set of tensions between home and host states, and it is not clear how these tensions could be resolved within the structure provided by the new Concordat. Furthermore, the new Concordat suggests a growing divergence between American and European approaches to foreign banking supervision.

The European Community

Even though most Basle Committee member states are also part of the European Community, EC rules are clearly at odds with the revised Concordat; and according to some interpretations, standards (2) and (4) of the new Concordat do not apply to EC states at all, since they contradict the Second Banking Coordination Directive.[39] Nor have the Europeans shown any inclination to alter those rules in light of BCCI and the Basle

Committee's response. On the contrary, the lesson drawn in western Europe is that the Second Banking Directive provides a strong foundation for banking integration on the continent.

Like the United States and the Basle Committee, the European Community assessed the impact of BCCI on its internal banking regulations following the bank's shutdown on July 5, 1991. Under the leadership of Sir Leon Brittan, vice-president of the commission in charge of financial and competition policy, a study was carried out immediately in the wake of BCCI's closures, and the initial results were published as early as July 29, just three weeks after the Bank of England's action.[40]

The main conclusion of the EC report "is that the BCCI case strongly reinforces . . . the most important features contained in the Community's recent banking Directives, viz.: (1) the move to home country control for the authorization and supervision of multinational banking groups . . . (2) the principle of consolidated supervision by the home country supervisors . . . (3) the obligation of banking supervisors to cooperate and exchange information with each other."

Nowhere in its three points does the commission explicitly define a role for the *host country*. This fact was not lost on a House of Commons committee that reviewed the BCCI affair, and its questioning of Bank of England regulators focused on this issue, as revealed by the following exchange between John Watts of the House and Brian Quinn of the Bank:

> Mr. Watts: "Surprisingly, the European Commission has argued that the BCCI affair strengthens the case for the Second Banking Coordination Directive. Do you believe that the standards of supervision across the European Community are sufficient to ensure that the 'single passport' principle does not lead to the weaker regulation of branches?"
> Mr. Quinn: "That is a very important question, and one which has exercised not just us in this country, but supervisors from a number of countries as the program for the single market has gone forward . . . The proof of the pudding will be in the eating. It is quite right to ask oneself whether there are potential weaknesses."[41]

Interviews that I conducted in the European Community following the BCCI shutdown revealed significant discomfort with this exclusive focus on home country control, particularly in England, which remains the

Community's major host nation. Such discomfort might have been heightened by Luxembourg's response to BCCI, which ruled out adopting any additional regulations. Indeed, the prime minister of Luxembourg, Jacques Santer, proclaimed before his country's parliament that the bank regulators had "proved themselves" and were "in line with those existing in the most reputable financial centers."[42]

Clearly, European leaders did not believe that 1991 provided an opportune moment to revise directives that had been passed as part of the 1992 single-market project; such revisions might have set back the single-market process significantly. They have accordingly determined that it is necessary to go forward with the current legislation, adding to such legislation where necessary. The BCCI scandal, for example, gave impetus to an EC-wide proposal on deposit insurance, and a directive on this topic is under review; currently, the European member states have a wide variety of deposit insurance schemes.[43]

Yet despite little explicit recognition of a role for host countries, it does appear that those who seek a strengthened role for the host, such as the Bank of England, are beginning to make their influence felt. Thus, when questioned directly by the House of Commons about the role of the host country under EC directives, Sir Leon responded that "the host country supervisors may, in emergencies, take any precautionary measures necessary to protect the interests of depositors, investors, and others to whom services are provided . . . In other situations the host country supervisor may require the institution concerned to put an end to any irregular conduct . . . It is clear that situations such as the above require close bilateral cooperation between the supervisors on a case by case basis."[44] As noted in Chapter 6, the language of the Second Banking Coordination Directive remains vague enough to allow the host country continued supervisory powers; though when and if such powers are actually exercised, one might expect the home country to launch a challenge in the commission and the Court of Justice.

Nonetheless, unlike the United States and Basle Committee, the European Community has not explicitly revised its approach to banking regulation. Its philosophy remains wedded to home country control, the single passport, and mutual recognition. A more formal recognition of the host country's rights and responsibilities will probably occur only after the continent's next cross-border banking crisis.

The BCCI scandal reveals the ability of criminals to penetrate the international financial system and cause grievous damage before they are caught. It would thus seem to point toward the primacy of globalization over the nation-state. If firms of the BCCI variety can evade supervision year after year, doesn't that provide powerful evidence of the ineffectiveness of the state response to global finance?

I have tried to show in these pages that the answer to this question is no, albeit with some qualifications. To begin with, despite the heroic work done to date by journalists, congressional and parliamentary investigators, and various government agencies, the full story of BCCI has not been revealed publicly. When (and if) that happens, we may well learn that the bank was allowed to operate for as long as it did because of its contributions to Western intelligence operations.

Even in the absence of such a disclosure, the BCCI case points to the continuing primacy of the nation-state in the global economy. To be sure, the firm slipped through the regulatory nets for an extended period of time, and no agreement could be reached within the College of Regulators regarding which state was ultimately responsible for the bank's operations. Indeed, the BCCI case reveals the limits to home country control, although this principle was again emphasized in the wake of the bank's closure. But despite these important caveats, it must be emphasized that once the decision was made to shut down BCCI, its global operations were brought to a rapid close.

At the same time, as our two-level approach would suggest, domestic political considerations figured prominently with respect to BCCI and provide a critical piece of the story regarding its rise and fall. In Britain, BCCI had become an important local bank for the immigrant community, and the Bank of England was concerned about the implications of a shutdown for the domestic banking system. In the United States, BCCI had entered the market with the help, unwitting or otherwise, of one of Washington's most powerful gray eminences, Clark Clifford, and he was serving as chairman of the domestic bank it had purchased. Since closure of BCCI's international operations had important domestic political (and, to a lesser extent, economic) consequences for the world's two leading financial centers—the United States and Britain—this outcome was slower to develop than might otherwise have been the case.

In sum, the BCCI story encapsulates several of the larger themes of this book. I have argued that globalization has presented the nation-state with a new set of challenges, and that the state has responded to them. The nature of that response, however, is imperfect, since in a world of separate nation-states with different capabilities, harmony is unlikely to be found. This means that gaps in supervision will always exist and that they will be exploited before one or more states take action. Furthermore, the policy response to globalization also reflects domestic politics—in particular, the institutional linkages between regulators and the regulated. As I will show in the next chapter, this argument has important implications not only for the management of international finance but for rule setting in the global economy more generally.

8 | Assessing the Response to Globalization

The basic asymmetry between multinational enterprises and national governments may be tolerable up to a point, but beyond that point there is a need to reestablish balance.

—RAYMOND VERNON

Since the early 1970s, the maintenance of a stable international financial system has provided public officials with one of their greatest political and economic challenges. The fusion of globalization, innovation, speculation, and deregulation has produced a system that, in the words of Susan Strange, resembles nothing so much as "a vast casino."[1] This image of a casino, of a system whose operations are based on the luck of the players no less than their skill, pervades both the scholarly literature and popular culture.[2]

Over the past twenty years, it seemed on any number of occasions that the players' luck had finally run out. The breakdown of the Bretton Woods monetary system, the oil shocks, and the debt crisis all threatened public confidence in the financial marketplace, and raised the specter of a global crash. If the postwar world was to avoid the economic—and, by extension, political—fate of the 1930s, some framework for governing global financial markets had to be built.

I have argued in this book that states have, in fact, built such a framework; now I would like to assess the most prominent threats to its endurance and its applicability to other issue-areas. As I have said, it is a two-level structure, with international cooperation at the upper level and home country control below. States have pursued international agreements as part of an ongoing effort to reconcile their prudential and competitive concerns; in the absence of such cooperation, a regulatory "race to the bottom" might occur. At the same time, given that central banks remain national in character, regulatory and supervisory agreements are ultimately founded upon the principle of home country control of domestic financial institutions.

This structure of governance should puzzle those who believe that international banking now operates in some extranational realm, beyond the nation-state.[3] Indeed, I have tried to show in this book that such a conceptualization is at odds with reality. Banks are not extranational actors, but highly regulated firms which must identify the piece of territory they call home. Thus, even if banks *wanted* to operate in the absence of national supervision—and I have argued that they would not wish to do so, since states provide them with essential diplomatic and regulatory services—they are *prevented* from so doing by international agreements.

I have focused on international finance because, beyond any intrinsic interest that it might have held for readers, it provides a challenging case for those of us who continue to believe in the enduring utility of a state-oriented approach to economic relations. Finance is an issue-area in which state power appears to be relatively weak and ineffective. Modern technology allows banks and investment firms to send money across borders on a twenty-four-hour basis, and state surveillance of all the world's daily financial transactions is probably impossible to achieve. If, despite these unpromising background conditions, states have somehow managed to build a reasonably sound structure for the regulation and supervision of international financial markets, maybe this tells us something of more general importance about the political underpinnings of the global economy.

Extending the Argument

My findings regarding the state's response to globalization should, of course, be tested against a variety of issue-areas in order to assess their generality, and I would be the first to admit that only so much analytical power can be drawn from a study of international banking regulation. As a small first step in determining whether my argument has any broader significance, I have briefly examined two additional cases of international regulation: pollution from oil tankers, and telecommunications. The results of this cursory study suggest that many of the observations presented here are relevant to sectors other than finance.

International efforts to regulate pollution from oil tankers, for example, provide "for the retention of the flag state as the basic standard-setting jurisdiction."[4] This is somewhat counterintuitive on its surface, since it is coastal, "host" states that are usually subject to tanker pollution. But if the ultimate objective of international cooperation in this area is to establish a set of minimal standards for tanker safety that all shipowners must follow, home or flag state control is a necessity. The alternative of host or coastal state control would bring about not tighter supervision but chaos. This is so because tankers call on several different ports during a normal run, and pass through the coastal waters of many more countries; it would simply be impossible for oil tankers to adjust and readjust their fittings and operations for every country whose waters were traversed.

Despite general agreement on the retention of flag state control, however, struggles regarding enforcement of international standards still do occur between home and coastal states. As we would predict, these have become especially acute following environmental disasters of the *Torrey Canyon* and *Brea* varieties. (The *Torrey Canyon* was the supertanker that ran aground off Cornwall, England, in 1967, fouling beaches and damaging wildlife in Britain, France, and several other European countries. The *Brea* ran aground off Scotland in 1993, also with malign effects.) But even in the aftermath of such painful experiences, coastal states have not been able to do much about protecting their shores from oil tankers on a unilateral basis. A more effective approach has been to seek international agreements requiring flag states to ensure that their tankers meet minimal safety standards before they are allowed to sail. Powerful coastal states, such as the United States, have played a leadership role in these negotiations by placing their concerns on the international agenda, but they have normally not sought to shift regulatory responsibility from home to coastal states.

Turning to a very different example, we find that the regime in telecommunications is likewise based on "state control over international communications."[5] The durability of this regulatory philosophy, which has been in place since 1865, is especially surprising given the dramatic technological changes in this sector and the way in which major industrial nations have been dismantling traditional "natural monopolies" (firms that operate in sectors which would seem to require a monopoly producer), such as the Bell Telephone System. To be sure, as Peter Cowhey has demonstrated, many new regulations for international telecommunications have been proposed or adopted by states in response to these changes, with policy outcomes reflecting, in two-level fashion, both the relative power of the state in the issue-area and the influence of societal actors on the policymaking process. But it is unlikely that these new regulatory agreements will result in supranational control, even in the European Community; international (or, in the European case, regional) cooperation based on home country supervision of those who engage in telecommunications may be expected to endure.[6]

These examples suggest that something of a generic policy solution to economic globalization has emerged in those issue-areas which threaten to unleash cross-border externalities (that is, unwanted events like pollution or a financial crisis) in the event of a systems breakdown; the system could be an oil tanker, a bank, or a telephone network. This does not mean the formula that states have adopted is perfect; on the contrary, it more likely reflects a lowest-common-denominator solution on the part of the public and private sector actors involved. Perhaps supranational agencies would provide the global economy with more effective supervision of multinational firms and transactions, but international cooperation based on home country control provides a way for states to enjoy the benefits of interdependence while maintaining national responsibility for the sector in question.

Yet the evolution of regulatory cooperation among nation-states should not make us overconfident with respect to the global economy's ability to withstand future shocks. International agreements, such as the Basle Accord and the Concordat, may contribute to the stability of the marketplace during "normal" periods of economic activity, but they have proved a weak reed during periods of crises, or even in meeting scandals of the BCCI variety. In the absence of leadership by one or more states that are willing and able to play the role of crisis manager, we must therefore recognize that an international financial shock could cause the global economy to collapse. To put this point in its starkest terms, we might ask what would have happened had public officials allowed the market alone to develop a response to the debt crisis. Would we have achieved stability or chaos?

Moreover, despite increasing cooperation, economic conflicts among states have not ended, and they could become even sharper as economic competition replaces military competition in the post–Cold War world. As I have shown in this book, three sources of tension are particularly apparent. First, home country rules and regulations continue to differ from one country to the next, and in a competitive environment such rules can have powerful implications for domestic firms. They alter the cost structure that enterprises face and, in turn, the prices they must charge for their products.

Regulatory differences between countries are not, of course, the sole determinant of relative cost structures, or even necessarily the most important ones. But they are highly visible and easily comparable across countries, and they give private sector actors a good excuse for seeking a level playing field. When domestic political actors succeed in forcing public officials to seek remedies for their competitive ills through bilateral and multilateral arrangements, the result is international politics. These cross-border interactions may ultimately result in cooperative agreements, as with the Basle Accord, but in the absence of leadership and common interests they could lead instead in the direction of trade wars.

Second, home and host states continue to debate the appropriate division of supervisory and regulatory responsibilities between them, as was painfully revealed during the BCCI debacle. In the aftermath, the Basle Committee and the European Community have made various attempts to resolve matters, but they have only produced more confusion, since their guidelines are not the same; this is all the more troubling in that their memberships have significant overlap. Furthermore, history provides us with additional reasons not to expect too much progress on this issue. The Basle Concordat, for example, which was originally promulgated by the G-10 central bankers in 1974 as a statement of their common understanding with respect to home and host country responsibilities, has been revised three times over the past twenty years as part of an ongoing effort to determine the roles of supervisory authorities.

Finally, and building on these last two points, we can expect increasing tensions in the future between regional and international organizations when it comes to the question of who writes the rules for international trade and finance. I have focused on conflicts between the European Community and the Basle Committee, and I expect that these two will continue to occupy center stage in the realm of international finance. But as we head toward the millennium, new regional formations seem to be emerging, with roots in such current undertakings as the North American Free Trade Agreement and Asia-Pacific Economic Cooperation. If regionalism becomes a prominent feature of the world economy in the next century, we might well ask whether these arrangements will be supportive of economic globalization or at odds with it.

To put the issue in economic terms, the question is whether these regional groupings will be "trade creating" or "trade diverting" with respect to outsiders. Economists would argue that they will be trade creating to the extent that they generate gains in economic growth rates for their member states—gains that lead to increases in overall demand for world imports.[7] Political scientists would be more concerned with the security implications of bloc formation. Will the blocs cooperate with one another, or will they be confrontational?[8]

In short, the international structure of governance that has emerged in the financial marketplace, and in the world economy more generally, has reflected the convergence of a number of distinct features of postwar life. Politically, the most prominent features of this era include leadership by the United States in building international regimes for free trade and investment, and, concomitantly, the rejection of protectionism, in the United States and elsewhere, by economic interest groups with institutional linkages to the state; in this regard, it should be emphasized that financial actors have been particularly vocal internationalists since 1945. Economically, the growth of the world economy has been coupled with increasing competition, the spread of technology, and changes in the nature of the multinational enterprise, to produce a phenomenon that is widely known by the term "globalization." Together, these political and economic factors have created a world not of laissez-faire capitalism but of managed liberalism.

Although the structure of governance described in these pages has proved surprisingly durable over the past generation, it must not be taken for granted. A rise in protectionism, a shift to regionalism, and/or changes in the distribution of power around the world could generate forces that cause it to collapse. While it is possible that something just as effective would be built in its place, it is also possible that a "postglobal" world economy would be less stable and thus less inviting to free trade and investment flows.

If we can agree that efforts should be made to preserve international cooperation based on home country control, the next step is to determine what in particular public officials might do to help ensure that outcome. The findings presented in this book lead to the following modest recommendations.

First, public officials in the industrial countries should act to strengthen the supervisory capabilities of weak home states. As we have seen, a constant source of tension in financial markets has been caused by home states that lacked the capacity to supervise their global enterprises. This problem is likely to be compounded in coming years, with the explosion in the number of new states and the democratization and economic liberalization of those once under communist rule. If these states are to become full members of the world economy, they will have to develop the regulatory apparatus needed to supervise their firms' activities. The Group of Ten countries can and should play a leading role in educating public officials in these countries and in bringing them up to date with respect to best supervisory practices.

Second, public officials should combat protectionism and promote market opening. The case for free trade is not easy to sustain, especially during periods of economic downturn. It relies on a belief in the ability of markets to respond to systemic change in a way that increases social welfare. Naturally, this belief is readily contradicted by our knowledge of industries that have been shut down owing to foreign competition, leaving individuals and regions permanently devastated. But we also know that protectionism, while benefiting special interests, hurts society as a whole, and its global spread has plunged the world toward depression and conflict. Combatting protectionism and advocating free trade and investment flows are essential tasks for public officials, and they require more than the occasional expression of declaratory policy. With respect to finance in particular, despite the global trends discussed in this book, many countries still prevent foreign banks from establishing operations within their borders, and market access agreements should remain high on the agenda of trade negotiations. The drawn out Uruguay Round discussions of the General Agreement on Tariffs and Trade had liberalization of service industries as one of their focal points, but in the end they achieved few concrete results.

Third, public officials should use the market whenever possible to regulate multinational firms. Traditionally, regulation has been, with some exceptions, the province of the state. In recent years, however, we have learned that markets can provide a variety of these regulatory services with greater efficiency, once minimal guidelines and standards have been established. One example of market-based enforcement is provided by the Basle Accord, in which rating agencies and investment banks will play an important role in informing the public about which banks have achieved the required capital adequacy levels, and in providing the incentives for meeting these levels; as a consequence, there is no need for a large international bureaucracy to monitor the agreement.[9] In sum, while it is true that markets need structures of governance in order to function, they cannot operate efficiently when they are imprisoned by overregulation.

The evidence provided in this book suggests that our way of conceptualizing economic globalization is in need of fundamental reexamination. The world economy does not operate somewhere offshore, but instead functions within the political framework provided by nation-states. If financial markets operated in the absence of state interference, and on a truly laissez-faire basis, it is unlikely that the international system could have survived the shocks that it suffered during the 1970s and 1980s without significant political and economic disruption.

The United States has played a special role in the global economy, acting as lender of last resort and keeping its markets open for trade and investment, even during periods of world recession. Thus, should American leadership of the world economy weaken, the major challenge for public officials will be to develop some alternative form of international governance. While it is easy to sketch out a number of different possibilities, it is much harder to guess whether these new structures will prove as effective as the old one in maintaining the degree of international economic stability that we have enjoyed during the past two generations.

Yet one should not minimize the conflict that has existed even in the American-dominated world order. The industrial states, including the United States, may have promoted international cooperation since 1945, but they have also actively tried to promote the competitiveness of their own domestic firms and economies. The trick, as we have seen, has been to strike the proper balance, and in so doing maintain the foundations of global economic growth through increases in international trade and investment.

In the post–Cold War era, and lacking any security rationale for sustaining the ideology and practice of free trade, societal actors will in all likelihood increase their pressure on public officials to emphasize national competitiveness, perhaps through the adoption of protectionist or industrial policies. This, in turn, will inevitably create a new set of tensions in international economic relations, endangering the delicate balance between cooperation and competition that has somehow been maintained. As future leaders seek to resolve these tensions, they must ask whether any alternative structure holds as much promise for economic growth and world peace as the one built by the United States and its allies from the ashes of World War II.

Notes

1. Governments and Global Markets

Epigraph: J. M. Keynes, "National Self-Sufficiency," *Yale Review* (June 1933): 758.

1. See, for example, Robert Reich, "Who Is US?" *Harvard Business Review* 90 (January–February 1990): 53–64.
2. Cited in Andrew Walter, *World Power and World Money* (Hertfordshire, England: Harvester Wheatsheaf, 1991), p. 12.
3. Eugene Staley, *World Economy in Transition* (New York: Council on Foreign Relations, 1939), p. vii.
4. Richard N. Cooper, *The Economics of Interdependence* (New York: McGraw-Hill, 1968).
5. Raymond Vernon and Ethan Kapstein, "National Needs, Global Resources," in Vernon and Kapstein, eds., *Defense and Dependence in a Global Economy* (Washington, D.C.: CQ Press, 1992), p. 15.
6. Ibid.
7. Stephen Kobrin, "Transnational Integration, National Markets and Nation-States," Working Paper, Reginald Jones Center, Wharton School, August 1991.
8. Walter, *World Power and World Money*, p. 198.
9. Organization for Economic Cooperation and Development (hereafter referred to as OECD), *Banks under Stress* (Paris: OECD, 1992), p. 119.
10. Linda Corman, "Lands of Opportunity," *Fidelity Focus* (Fall 1992): 9.
11. Allen Myerson, "Turmoil in the Currency Markets," *New York Times*, 17 September 1992, p. D1.
12. See Janice Thomson and Stephen Krasner, "Global Transactions and the Consolidation of Sovereignty," in Robert Art and Robert Jervis, eds., *International Politics* (New York: HarperCollins, 1992), p. 310.

13. See, for example, Walter Wriston, *The Twilight of Sovereignty: How the Information Revolution Is Transforming Our World* (New York: Scribners, 1992).

14. Walter, *World Power and World Money*, p. 201.

15. See "Banks and Technology," *Economist*, 3 October 1992, pp. 21–24.

16. Charles Radin, "US Data Highway Gathers Speed," *Boston Globe*, 26 December 1992, p. 10.

17. For an articulation of this view, see John Gerard Ruggie, "Territoriality and Beyond: Problematizing Modernity in International Relations," *International Organization* 47 (Winter 1993): 139–174.

18. Thomson and Krasner, "Global Transactions," p. 310.

19. For a classic account of this issue with respect to the nineteenth century, see Karl Polanyi, *The Great Transformation* (Boston: Beacon Press, 1944). In the modern world, a simple example is provided by the rise of Japan and the economic challenge it poses for the United States; such a challenge was, of course, unthinkable during the late 1940s and early 1950s.

20. For another account of the state response to international finance, see Louis Pauly, *Opening Financial Markets: Banking Politics on the Pacific Rim* (Ithaca, N.Y.: Cornell University Press, 1988). Pauly compares the policies of the United States, Canada, Japan, and Australia in this issue-area.

21. During the summer of 1992 a Deutsche Bundesbank memo critical of British economic policy was leaked to the press, and the British government responded sharply. The *Financial Times* followed these events in particularly fine detail. It should be noted that the timing of the crisis was especially bad, given that many European countries were just then voting on the Maastricht Treaty, a major part of which revolved around the creation of a European central bank and single currency.

22. Henry Kaufman, "Fundamental Precepts Guiding Future Financial Regulation," address to the International Organization of Securities Commissions, London, 27 October 1992.

23. Robert Gilpin, *The Political Economy of International Relations* (Princeton: Princeton University Press, 1987), p. 241.

24. Ibid., p. 257.

25. Robert Reich, "Who Is US?"

26. For a critique of Reich's argument, see Ethan B. Kapstein, "We Are US: The Myth of the Multinational," *National Interest* (Winter 1991–1992): 55–62.

27. For an academic treatment of international cooperation, see Robert Keohane, *After Hegemony* (Princeton: Princeton University Press, 1984). I must stress that I do not define "international cooperation" solely in terms of *mutually beneficial* policy coordination among nation-states, since the nature of policy coordination is often misleading; what appears as mutually beneficial

from the perspective of one state may not be viewed as such from that of another, and as a result some policy analysts confuse "cooperation" with "coercion." For an example, see Wendy Dobson, *Economic Policy Coordination* (Washington, D.C.: Institute for International Economics, 1991).

28. For a review of these interactions, see Peter C. Hayward, "Prospects for International Cooperation by Bank Supervisors," *International Lawyer* 24 (Fall 1990): 787–801. The Group of Ten countries include the world's leading industrial economies.

29. This terminology is borrowed from the work of Robert Putnam, who speaks of "two-level games." My approach is somewhat different from that adopted by Putnam, Glenn Tobin, and others who use the two-level game model; perhaps the most obvious difference is the lack of discussion here on "winsets." For the now-classic article, see Putnam, "Diplomacy and Domestic Politics: The Logic of Two-Level Games," *International Organization* 42 (Summer 1988): 427–460. For a study that uses two-level games with respect to international financial regulation, see Glenn Tobin, "Global Money Rules" (diss., Harvard University, 1991).

30. There is a rich literature on this topic. See, for example, Stephen D. Krasner, *Defending the National Interest* (Princeton: Princeton University Press, 1978).

31. For a good summary of the institutionalist perspective, see G. John Ikenberry, "Conclusion: An Institutional Approach to American Foreign Economic Policy," *International Organization* 42 (Winter 1988): 219–243.

32. Raymond Vernon, personal communication, 26 February 1993.

33. Cited in James Q. Wilson, *The Politics of Regulation* (New York: Basic Books, 1980), p. 358.

34. Sam Peltzman, "Toward a More General Theory of Regulation," *Journal of Law and Economics* 19 (August 1976): 211–240.

35. Some observers, however, believe that central banks should *not* play a regulatory role, owing to the capture problem. Should they be viewed as captured actors, they could no longer claim "independence." See "A Central Bankers' Charter," *Economist*, 10 October 1992, pp. 16–17.

36. There is a great deal of literature, for example, on the rise and fall of hegemonic powers, but little on how these powers adapt to change. For important exceptions, however, see Robert Gilpin, *War and Change in World Politics* (New York: Cambridge University Press, 1981); Aaron Friedberg, *The Weary Titan* (Princeton: Princeton University Press, 1988); and Joseph Nye, *Bound to Lead* (New York: Basic Books, 1990).

37. Samuel Huntington, "Transnational Organizations in World Politics," *World Politics* 25 (April 1973): 363.

38. On the relationship between domestic politics and hegemony, see Robert Gil-

pin, "Economic Interdependence and National Security in Historical Perspective," in Klaus Knorr and Frank Trager, eds., *Economic Issues and National Security* (Lawrence, Kans.: Regents Press of Kansas, 1977), pp. 19–63.

39. Keohane, *After Hegemony*. Indeed, the study of international cooperation has in recent years been enriched by a debate among two competing paradigms over the role of international institutions and the regimes that they embody in world politics. One party views such institutional arrangements as more or less epiphenomenal, with little or no voice in state policy formation. Others hold that they may act as "intervening variables" between state interests and policy outcomes. On regime formation and maintenance, see the essays in Stephen Krasner, ed., *International Regimes* (Ithaca, N.Y.: Cornell University Press, 1983); for a "realist" counterargument, see Joseph Grieco, "Anarchy and the Limits of Cooperation," *International Organization* 42 (Summer 1988): 485–507. I argue that neither side has a monopoly on truth. My analysis reveals that the institutionalization of cooperation by bank supervisors *has* contributed to policy convergence among them, but that such cooperation cannot and should not be viewed as a substitute for hegemonic power, meaning leadership by a dominant state.

40. Furthermore, once standards have been set, states will become concerned with reputational effects, and will encourage their national banks to meet the terms of any international agreements; this situation will be reinforced by state actions, so as to deny market access to those players that do not meet these terms.

41. I thank C. Randall Henning of the Institute for International Economics for highlighting this point.

42. For the role of consensual knowledge in international cooperation, see Ernst Haas, "Why Collaborate?" *World Politics* 32 (April 1980): 357–405.

43. See John Pincus, *Economic Aid and International Cost Sharing* (Baltimore: Johns Hopkins University Press, 1965). For a treatment of the United Nations' latest efforts to cope with its financing difficulties, see the recent report of the "wise men," chaired by Paul Volcker, which was published as *Financing an Effective United Nations* (New York: Ford Foundation, 1993).

44. For a skeptical view of the role of international institutions during periods of crisis, see Robert Lieber, "Existential Realism," *Washington Quarterly* 16 (Winter 1993): 155–168.

45. I am not arguing, of course, that there is no room for international debate during periods of crisis; but I believe that such debate is unhelpful in the absence of action.

46. For a comparison of hegemonic and international responses to a series of

postwar energy crises, see Ethan B. Kapstein, *The Insecure Alliance: Energy Crises and Western Politics since 1944* (New York: Oxford University Press, 1990).

47. In the following chapters I trace the response of states to financial globalization by examining the most prominent international financial "crises" of the past two decades and the regulatory actions that states have taken during and after these periods. Admittedly, I use the term "crisis" in a more general way than do most economists (who themselves have developed no single, accepted definition): I define it as a shock to the financial system that requires extraordinary government intervention in order to maintain public confidence. I should also emphasize that crises do not always arise from the actions—perverse or otherwise—of market actors themselves. Indeed, as Martin Feldstein has remarked, "the major source of the increased risk in our economy has been a series of seemingly well intentioned government policies." Feldstein's point only emphasizes the importance of state action in the marketplace, for better or for worse. See Martin Feldstein, ed., *The Risk of Economic Crisis* (Chicago: University of Chicago Press, 1991).

48. See Barry Eichengreen, "Should the Maastricht Treaty Be Saved?" *Princeton Studies in International Finance* 74 (December 1992).

49. See David Baldwin, *Economic Statecraft* (Princeton: Princeton University Press, 1985).

50. See "The Global Firm: R.I.P.," *Economist*, 6 February 1993, p. 69.

51. For a good introduction to these debates, see "An Expanding Universe," *Economist*, 7–13 July 1990; this was the magazine's annual survey of the European Community.

52. See Raymond Vernon, *Sovereignty at Bay* (New York: Basic Books, 1971).

53. Charles P. Kindleberger, *The World in Depression, 1929–1939* (Berkeley: University of California Press, 1973).

54. Kenneth Spong, *Banking Regulation* (Kansas City, Kans.: Federal Reserve Bank of Kansas City, 1983), p. 6.

55. Alan Greenspan, "International Financial Integration," address to the Federation of Bankers Association of Japan, 14 October 1992.

56. Gilbert G. Johnson and Richard Abrams, *Aspects of the International Banking Safety Net* (Washington, D.C.: International Monetary Fund, 1983), p. 1.

57. Ibid.

58. Kindleberger, *The World in Depression*.

59. Jack Guttentag and Richard Herring, *The Lender of Last Resort in an International Context* (Princeton, N.J.: Princeton Essays in International Finance, 1983), p. 2.

60. Kerry Cooper and Donald Fraser, *Banking Deregulation and the New Competition in Financial Services* (Cambridge, Mass.: Ballinger, 1984).

61. "A New Awakening," *Economist,* 24 March 1984.

62. Benjamin J. Cohen, *In Whose Interest?* (New Haven, Conn.: Yale University Press, 1986), pp. 22–25.

63. I thank Benjamin J. Cohen of the University of California at Santa Barbara for highlighting this point.

64. Guttentag and Herring, *The Lender of Last Resort,* p. 3.

65. Laura Tyson and John Zysman, "American Industry in International Competition," in Tyson and Zysman, eds., *American Industry in International Competition* (Ithaca, N.Y.: Cornell University Press, 1983), p. 19.

66. Laura Tyson, "Competitiveness: An Analysis of the Problem and a Perspective on Future Policy," in Martin K. Starr, ed., *Global Competitiveness* (New York: Norton, 1988), p. 96.

67. C. Fred Bergsten, "Letter to the Editor," *New York Times,* 29 November 1992, p. 10.

68. Cited in Tyson, "Competitiveness," p. 97.

69. I would like to thank C. Randall Henning for making this important point.

70. Catherine England, "Introduction: The Uncertain Future of U.S. Banking," in England, ed., *Governing Banking's Future* (Boston: Kluwer, 1991), p. 3.

71. David D. Hale, "Global Finance and the Retreat to Managed Trade," *Harvard Business Review* (January–February 1990): 150.

72. U.S. Congress, Committee on Banking, Finance, and Urban Affairs, *Task Force on the International Competitiveness of U.S. Financial Institutions* (Washington, D.C.: GPO, 1990), p. 4.

73. American Bankers Association, *International Banking Competitiveness: Why It Matters* (Washington, D.C.: American Bankers Association, 1990), p. 1.

74. Federal Reserve Bank of New York, *International Competitiveness of U.S. Financial Firms* (New York: FRBNY, 1991), p. 173.

75. "Four U.S. Banks among World's Most Profitable," *USA Today,* 13 November 1992, p. 4B.

76. U.S. Congress, *Task Force on International Competitiveness,* p. 9.

77. See U.S. Treasury, *National Treatment Study,* a report issued annually since 1979.

78. U.S. Congress, *Task Force on International Competitiveness.*

79. See Ethan B. Kapstein, *The Political Economy of National Security* (New York: McGraw-Hill, 1992).

80. U.S. Congress, *Task Force on International Competitiveness,* p. 13.

81. See William Greider, *Secrets of the Temple* (New York: Simon and Schuster, 1987).

2. The Collapse of Bretton Woods

Epigraph: James Tobin, "Agenda for International Coordination of Macro-economic Policy," in Paul Volcker et al., eds., *International Monetary Cooperation: Essays in Honor of Henry C. Wallich* (Princeton, N.J.: Princeton Essays in International Finance, 1987).

1. Benjamin J. Cohen, *In Whose Interest?* (New Haven, Conn.: Yale University Press, 1986), p. 19.
2. On the interbank market, see Bank for International Settlements, "The International Interbank Market: A Descriptive Study," *BIS Economic Papers* 8 (July 1983); and Stephen V. O. Clarke, "American Banks in the International Interbank Market," *Monograph Series in Finance and Economics, 1983–1984* (New York: New York University Graduate School of Business, 1984).
3. Ralph Bryant, *International Financial Intermediation* (Washington, D.C.: Brookings Institution, 1987), p. 69.
4. Robert Aliber, "International Banking: A Survey," *Journal of Money, Credit, and Banking* 16 (November 1984): 663.
5. For the data, see "Special Supplement," *Euromoney* (March 1991): S16.
6. Bryant, *International Financial Intermediation,* p. 64.
7. John Karlik, "Some Questions and Brief Answers about the Eurodollar Market," in John Adams, ed., *The Contemporary International Economy* (New York: St. Martin's Press, 1979), p. 311.
8. Cohen, *In Whose Interest?* p. 19.
9. Ibid.
10. Karlik, "The Eurodollar Market," p. 312.
11. See Jeffry Alan Frieden, "Studies in International Finance: Private Interest and Public Policy in the International Political Economy" (diss., Columbia University, 1985).
12. For an elaboration of this point, see Benjamin J. Cohen, *Organizing the World's Money* (New York: Basic Books, 1977).
13. Frieden, *Studies in International Finance,* p. 149.
14. It is interesting to note that American officials have severed the domestic and international markets in other commodities as well, notably oil, where after 1957 oil import quotas limited U.S. imports of foreign petroleum; on this point see Kapstein, *The Insecure Alliance.*
15. Ethan B. Kapstein, *The Political Economy of National Security: A Global Perspective* (Columbia, S.C.: University of South Carolina Press, 1992), p. 78.
16. The story of the rise and fall of Bretton Woods has been told many times, and from several different angles. For an account that focuses on U.S. domestic politics, see Joanne Gowa, *Closing the Gold Window* (Ithaca, N.Y.: Cor-

nell University Press, 1983); see also John Odell, *U.S. International Monetary Policy* (Princeton, N.J.: Princeton University Press, 1982). For a systemic account, see Robert Gilpin, *The Political Economy of International Relations* (Princeton, N.J.: Princeton University Press, 1987). For a comprehensive and classic study by a leading political economist, see Benjamin J. Cohen, *Organizing the World's Money* (New York: Basic Books, 1977). On the Triffin dilemma, see Robert Triffin, *Gold and the Dollar Crisis* (New Haven, Conn.: Yale University Press, 1960).

17. See Cohen, *Organizing the World's Money*, pp. 114–117.

18. L. Oxelheim and C. Wihlborg, *Macroeconomic Uncertainty* (New York: John Wiley and Sons, 1987), p. 9.

19. See Citicorp, *Annual Report*, various years.

20. See Robert M. Dunn, Jr., *The Many Disappointments of Flexible Exchange Rates* (Princeton, N.J.: Princeton Essays in International Finance, 1983).

21. The Herstatt story is well told in John Cooper, *The Management and Regulation of Banks* (New York: St. Martin's Press, 1984), pp. 6, 23, 241; Richard Dale, *The Regulation of International Banking* (Cambridge: Woodhead-Faulkner, 1984), pp. 156–157; and Joan Spero, *The Failure of the Franklin National Bank* (New York: Columbia University Press, 1980), pp. 110–113.

22. Ibid.

23. G. G. Johnson, *Aspects of the International Banking Safety Net* (Washington, D.C.: International Monetary Fund, 1983), p. 3.

24. E. P. Davis, "Instability in the Euromarkets and the Economic Theory of Financial Crisis," *Bank of England Discussion Papers* 43 (October 1989): 17.

25. Cited ibid., p. 19.

26. Ibid.

27. On the Franklin, see Spero, *Failure of the Franklin National Bank;* and Dale, *Regulation of International Banking*, pp. 159–161.

28. Dale, *Regulation of International Banking*, p. 160.

29. Spero, *Failure of the Franklin National Bank*, p. 156.

30. Deutsche Bundesbank, *Banking Act of the Federal Republic of Germany* (Frankfurt, 1991), p. 13.

31. Spero, *Failure of the Franklin National Bank*, p. 154.

32. Cited ibid., p. 155.

33. Davis, "Instability in the Euromarkets," p. 19.

34. Interview with Sir George Blunden, London, 25 June 1991.

35. In fact, the committee normally takes the name of its chairman; thus it has been the "Blunden Committee," the "Cooke Committee," and so forth. For ease of identification, however, I refer to it throughout as the "Basle Committee."

36. On the origins of the Basle Committee, see Spero, *Failure of the Franklin National Bank,* pp. 159–166; interview with George Blunden, 25 June 1991; Basle Committee, *Report on International Developments in Banking Supervision, 1981* (Basle, 1982), p. 1; George Blunden, "Control and Supervision of the Foreign Operations of Banks," in J. Wadsworth, J. Wilson, and H. Fournier, eds., *The Development of Financial Institutions in Europe, 1956–1976* (Leyden: A. W. Sitjhoff, 1977); George Blunden, "International Cooperation in Banking Supervision," *Bank of England Quarterly Bulletin* (September 1977): 325–329; and W. Peter Cooke, "The Development of Cooperation between Bank Supervisory Authorities in the Group of Ten Countries, Luxembourg and Switzerland," *Proceedings of the International Conference of Banking Supervisors* (Washington, D.C., 1981).

37. Interview with George Blunden, 25 June 1991, London.

38. Blunden, "Control and Supervision," p. 194.

39. Ibid., p. 195.

40. Ibid., p. 194.

41. Henry Kaufman, "Fundamental Precepts Guiding Future Financial Regulation" (mimeo), 27 October 1992.

42. On the problems of providing the lender-of-last-resort function in a global economy, see Jack Guttentag and Richard Herring, "The Lender-of-Last-Resort Function in an International Context," *Princeton Essays in International Finance* 151 (May 1983).

43. Interview with George Blunden, 25 June 1991.

44. Cooke, "The Development of Cooperation between Bank Supervisors."

45. Ibid.

46. Ibid.

47. The former chairman of the House Committee on Banking, Ferdinand St. Germain, asked the General Accounting Office to look into the Basle Committee's activities in 1983. See GAO, *International Banking: International Coordination of Bank Supervision—The Record to Date* (Washington, D.C., 1986).

48. Cooke, "The Development of Cooperation between Bank Supervisors."

49. R. M. Pecchioli, *The Internationalisation of Banking: The Policy Issues* (Paris: OECD, 1983), pp. 103–104.

50. Karlik, "The Eurodollar Market," p. 322.

51. On these efforts, see Glenn Tobin, "Global Money Rules" (diss., Harvard University, 1991), pp. 166–186; and James P. Hawley, "Protecting Capital from Itself: U.S. Attempts to Regulate the Eurocurrency System," *International Organization* 38 (Winter 1984): 131–166.

52. Hawley, "Protecting Capital."

53. Glenn Tobin, "Global Money Rules," p. 150.

54. See Cooper, *Management and Regulation of Banks,* pp. 275–280, and Dale, *Regulation of International Banking,* pp. 161–163.

55. Cooper, *Management and Regulation of Banks,* p. 276.

56. G. G. Johnson, *Aspects of the International Banking Safety Net,* p. 3.

57. Cited in Cooper, *Management and Regulation of Banks,* p. 278.

58. Ibid.

59. Dale, *Regulation of International Banking,* p. 163.

3. The Politics of Petrodollar Recycling

Epigraph: Paul Volcker and Toyoo Gyohten, *Changing Fortunes* (New York: Times Books, 1992), p. 140.

1. For the history, see Ethan B. Kapstein, *The Insecure Alliance: Energy Crises and Western Politics since 1944* (New York: Oxford University Press, 1990), pp. 152–176.

2. Ibid., p. 165.

3. This chapter has been heavily influenced by the important work of David Spiro on petrodollar recycling; see Spiro, *Hegemony Unbound: Petrodollar Recycling and the Delegitimation of American Power* (Ithaca, N.Y.: Cornell University Press, 1994). I am grateful to Spiro for sharing his work with me.

4. W. W. Rostow, *The World Economy: History and Prospect* (Austin: University of Texas Press, 1978).

5. See Klaus Knorr, "The Limits of Economic and Military Power," and Raymond Vernon, "The Distribution of Power," both in Vernon, ed., *The Oil Crisis* (New York: Norton, 1976).

6. Cited in Simon Bromley, *American Hegemony and World Oil* (University Park, Pa.: Pennsylvania State University Press, 1991), p. 125.

7. Statistics reveal, however, that official aid from the United States to the developing world *did* increase between 1970 and 1975, rising from $3.2 billion to almost $5 billion. See Roger D. Hansen, ed., *U.S. Foreign Policy and the Third World: Agenda 1982* (New York: Praeger, 1982), p. 239.

8. Paul Volcker and Toyoo Gyohten, *Changing Fortunes* (New York: Times Books, 1992), p. 140.

9. Richard Mattione, *OPEC's Investments and the International Financial System* (Washington, D.C.: Brookings Institution, 1984), p. 26.

10. See Peter Katzenstein, ed., *Between Power and Plenty* (Madison: University of Wisconsin Press, 1978).

11. For a good overview, see Edward R. Fried and Charles L. Schultze, eds., *Higher Oil Prices and the World Economy* (Washington, D.C.: Brookings Institution, 1975).

12. David Spiro, "Policy Coordination in the International Political Economy: The Politics of Recycling Petrodollars" (diss., Princeton University, 1987), cited in Robert Gilpin, *The Political Economy of International Relations* (Princeton, N.J.: Princeton University Press, 1987), pp. 315–316.

13. U.S. Congress, Senate Committee on Foreign Relations, *International Debt, the Banks, and U.S. Foreign Policy* (Washington, D.C.: GPO, 1977); Mattione, *OPEC's Investments*, p. 26.

14. Mattione, *OPEC's Investments*, p. 36.

15. Edward Fried, "Financial Implications," in Joseph Yager and Eleanor Steinberg, eds., *Energy and U.S. Foreign Policy* (Cambridge, Mass.: Ballinger, 1974), pp. 295–296.

16. Committee on Economic Development, *International Economic Consequences of High-Priced Energy* (Washington, D.C.: CED, 1975), pp. 49–50.

17. George Blunden, "International Cooperation in Banking Supervision," *Bank of England Quarterly Bulletin* (September 1977): 326.

18. David Spiro, *Hegemony Unbound.*

19. Ibid., pp. 191–192.

20. Ibid., p. 252.

21. Ibid.

22. W. W. Rostow, *The World Economy* (Austin: University of Texas Press, 1978), p. 297. I thank Benjamin J. Cohen for emphasizing that bank and official loans went largely to different groups of countries, and were thus complementary.

23. Dankwart Rustow and John Mugno, *OPEC: Success and Prospects* (New York: New York University Press, 1976), p. 61.

24. David Lomax and P. Gutmann, *The Euromarkets and International Financial Policies* (New York: John Wiley, 1981), p. 7.

25. See P. A. Wellons, *Borrowing by Developing Countries on the Euro-Currency Market* (Paris: OECD, 1977), p. 32.

26. Ibid., p. 24.

27. John Williamson, "The International Financial System," in Fried and Schultze, *Higher Oil Prices*, p. 224.

28. Ibid., p. 218.

29. For the classic account, see Philip A. Wellons, *Passing the Buck: Banks, Governments and Third World Debt* (Boston: Harvard Business School Press, 1987).

30. Spiro, *Hegemony Unbound.*

31. Andrew Spindler, *The Politics of International Credit* (Washington, D.C.: Brookings Institution, 1984).

32. Wellons, *Passing the Buck,* p. 54.

33. See ibid. and David T. Llewellyn, "The International Monetary System since

1972: Structural Change and Financial Innovation," in Michael Posner, ed., *Problems of International Money, 1972–1985* (Washington, D.C.: International Monetary Fund, 1985), pp. 14–47.

34. Benjamin Friedman, *Postwar Changes in American Financial Markets* (Cambridge, Mass.: National Bureau of Economic Research, 1980), p. 71.

35. That calculation, it should be noted, was made more difficult by problems of data collection. According to two MIT economists, the Federal Reserve Board was receiving poor data during the early 1970s with respect to money supplies, GNP growth rates, and the effect of the oil price hikes on the economy. In particular, the Federal Reserve was slow to recognize the extent to which oil prices were leading to a domestic economic slowdown. See Rudiger Dornbusch and Stanley Fischer, *Macroeconomics* (New York: McGraw-Hill, 1981), p. 576.

36. Andrew H. Bartels, "Volcker's Revolution at the Fed," *Challenge* (September–October 1985): 35–42.

37. Volcker and Gyohten, *Changing Fortunes*, pp. 191–194.

38. Gershon Feder et al., "Projecting Debt Servicing Capacity of Developing Countries," *Journal of Financial and Quantitative Analysis* 16 (December 1981): 657.

39. David Lomax, *The Developing Country Debt Crisis* (New York: St. Martin's Press, 1986), p.32.

40. Ibid., p. 33.

41. Richard Cooper and Jeffrey Sachs, "Borrowing Abroad: The Debtor's Perspective," in Gordon Smith and John Cuddington, eds., *International Debt and the Developing Countries* (Washington, D.C.: World Bank, 1985), pp. 21–60.

42. Ibid.

43. "Lessons of the Debt Crisis," *Financial Times*, 30 July 1992, p. 12.

44. Dornbusch and Fischer, *Macroeconomics*, p. 580.

45. Robert Putnam and Nicholas Bayne, *Hanging Together: Cooperation and Conflict in the Seven-Power Summits* (Cambridge, Mass.: Harvard University Press, 1987), p. 37.

46. Hans-Eckart Scarrer, "Burdens of Debt and the New Protectionism," in Daniel Yergin and Martin Hillenbrand, *Global Insecurity* (Boston: Houghton Mifflin, 1982), p. 294.

47. Citicorp, *Annual Report, 1977*, p. 9.

48. See Kapstein, *The Insecure Alliance*, pp. 185–191.

49. Richard N. Cooper, International Energy Seminar, Harvard University, 20 April 1983.

50. International Monetary Fund, *International Capital Markets* (Washington, D.C.: IMF, 1980), p. 16.

51. Althea Duersten and Arpad von Lazar, "The Global Poor," in Yergin and Hillenbrand, *Global Insecurity*, p. 271.
52. Hans-Eckart Scharrer, "Burdens of Debt," ibid., p. 299.
53. International Monetary Fund, *International Capital Markets* (Washington, D.C.: IMF, 1983), p. 13.
54. Volcker and Gyohten, *Changing Fortunes*, p. 196.
55. Ibid., p. 198.
56. Ibid., p. 199.
57. "Central Banking," *Economist*, 22 September 1984, p. 56.
58. Ibid.
59. The quote is taken from Title 12, sec. 84 of the United States Code, as cited in Wellons, *Passing the Buck*, p. 101.
60. Ibid.
61. Wellons, *Passing the Buck*, p. 106.
62. I thank Benjamin J. Cohen for emphasizing this point.
63. Benjamin J. Cohen, *In Whose Interest? International Banking and American Foreign Policy* (New Haven, Conn.: Yale University Press, 1986), p. 40.

4. The Debt Crisis

Epigraph: Jeffrey Sachs, "Managing the LDC Debt Crisis," *Brookings Papers on Economic Activity* 4 (1986): 410.
1. "The Debt Crisis: R.I.P.," *Economist*, 12 September 1992, p. 15.
2. Benjamin J. Cohen, "What Ever Happened to the LDC Debt Crisis?" *Challenge* (May–June 1991): 47–51.
3. Jeffrey Sachs, "International Policy Coordination: The Case of the Developing Country Debt Crisis," in Martin Feldstein, ed., *International Policy Coordination* (Chicago: University of Chicago Press, 1988), p. 254.
4. See Carlos F. Diaz-Alejandro, "Latin American Debt: I Don't Think We Are in Kansas Anymore," *Brookings Papers on Economic Activity* 2 (1984): 355–356.
5. Sachs, "International Policy Coordination," p. 254.
6. For an early argument along these lines, see Miles Kahler, "Politics and International Debt: Explaining the Crisis," *International Organization* 39 (Summer 1985): 357–382.
7. David Spiro, *Hegemony Unbound: Petrodollar Recycling and the Delegitimation of American Power* (Ithaca, N.Y.: Cornell University Press, 1994).
8. Richard Kohl, "The Causes of the Third World Debt Crisis" (diss., University of California at Berkeley, 1989), p. 50.
9. Ibid., p. 88.
10. Kohl, "The Causes of the Third World Debt Crisis," p. 53.

11. For reviews, see ibid.; see also Robert Devlin, *Debt and Crisis in Latin America* (Princeton, N.J.: Princeton University Press, 1989).

12. Jeffrey Sachs, "External Debt and Macroeconomic Performance in Latin America and East Asia," *Brookings Papers on Economic Activity* 2 (1985): 523–564.

13. Devlin, *Debt and Crisis,* pp. 5–6.

14. Statement by Elinor Constable, in U.S. Congress, House of Representatives, *International Bank Lending* (Washington, D.C.: GPO, 1983), p. 58.

15. See, for example, David Lomax, *The Developing Country Debt Crisis* (New York: St. Martin's Press, 1986); Devlin, *Debt and Crisis;* and Karen Lissakers, *Banks, Borrowers and the Establishment* (New York: Basic Books, 1991).

16. Benjamin J. Cohen, *In Whose Interest?* (New Haven, Conn.: Yale University Press, 1986), p. 212.

17. Clive Crook, "The Limits of Cooperation," *Economist,* 26 September 1987, p. 49.

18. International Monetary Fund, *International Capital Markets* (Washington, D.C.: IMF, 1986), p. 48.

19. Cohen, *In Whose Interest?* p. 218.

20. World Bank, *World Development Report, 1988* (New York: Oxford University Press, 1988), p. 4.

21. This is a point made by Jeffrey Sachs in "Managing the LDC Debt Crisis."

22. The story of the Mexican weekend is well told in William Grieder, *Secrets of the Temple* (New York: Simon and Schuster, 1987), pp. 517–521.

23. Ibid., p. 518.

24. For a contrasting view that focuses on the role of big banks in keeping small banks in the game, see Charles Lipson, "Bankers' Dilemmas: Private Cooperation in Rescheduling Sovereign Debts," *World Politics* 37 (October 1985): 200–225.

25. Cohen, *In Whose Interest?* p. 214.

26. See William Cline, *International Debt and the Stability of the World Economy* (Washington, D.C.: Institute for International Economics, 1983); and Thomas Enders and Richard Mattione, *Latin America: The Crisis of Debt and Growth* (Washington, D.C.: Brookings Institution, 1984).

27. Volcker and Gyohten, *Changing Fortunes,* p. 201.

28. For a comparative analysis, see Louis Pauly, "Institutionalizing a Stalemate: National Financial Policies and the International Debt Crisis," *Journal of Public Policy* 10 (1991): 23–43.

29. Technically, the Mexican rescheduling was dated August 1983.

30. For a complete list of the major reschedulings, see International Monetary Fund, *International Capital Markets, 1986,* p. 122, table 46.

31. William Rhodes, "The Disaster That Didn't Happen," *Economist,* 12 September 1992, p. 22.

32. R. T. McNamar, "Evolution of the International Debt Challenge," in Martin Feldstein, ed., *International Economic Cooperation* (Chicago: University of Chicago Press, 1988), p. 306.

33. U.S. Congress, Senate Committee on Banking, *Proposed Solutions to International Debt Problem,* 98th Cong., 1st sess., 11 April 1983, p. 95.

34. The text may be found in U.S. Congress, House Committee on Banking, Finance and Urban Affairs, *International Bank Lending,* 98th Cong., 1st sess., 20–21 April 1983, p. 234.

35. On this provision, and on ILSA generally, see Cynthia Lichtenstein, "The U.S. Response to the International Debt Crisis: The International Lending Supervision Act of 1983," *Virginia Journal of International Law* 25 (1985): 401–435. As I will discuss later, Lichtenstein misses a central part of the ILSA story.

36. U.S. Congress, *International Bank Lending,* p. 183.

37. Cited in Barry Blechman, "The Congressional Role in U.S. Military Policy," *Political Science Quarterly* 106 (Spring 1991): 17–32.

38. Jeffrey Sachs, "Managing the LDC Debt Crisis," p. 406.

39. Volcker and Gyohten, *Changing Fortunes,* p. 206.

40. H. A. Holley, *Developing Country Debt* (London: Routledge and Kegan Paul, 1987), p. 46.

41. Raymond Vernon, Deborah Spar, and Glenn Tobin, *Iron Triangles and Revolving Doors: Cases in U.S. Foreign Economic Policymaking* (New York: Praeger, 1991), p. 87.

42. On the background, see Peter Dombrowski, "U.S. Policies toward the International Expansion of American Banks, 1965–1990" (diss., University of Maryland, 1990), pp. 179–195. For a review, see International Monetary Fund, *International Capital Markets* (Washington, D.C.: IMF, February 1986), pp. 16–18.

43. William Ogden, "The Need for Change in Managing LDC Debt," in Feldstein, ed., *International Policy Coordination,* p. 285.

44. Percy Mistry, "Third World Debt: Beyond the Baker Plan," *Banker* (September 1987): 1–7. This paper was a World Bank document prepared by a senior financial adviser to president Barber Conable.

45. Ibid.

46. See Richard S. Weinert, "Swapping Third World Debt," *Foreign Policy* (Winter 1986–1987): 85–97.

47. For a thorough analysis, see Graham Bird, *Loan-Loss Provisions and Third-World Debt* (Princeton, N.J.: Princeton Essays in International Finance, 1989).

48. Rhodes, "The Disaster That Didn't Happen."
49. On the Brady plan, see Karen Lissakers, *Banks, Borrowers and the Establishment* (New York: Basic Books, 1991), pp. 227–248; Vernon, Spar, and Tobin, *Iron Triangles and Revolving Doors,* ch. 4; and Dombrowski, *U.S. Policies,* ch. 6.
50. Cited in Lissakers, *Banks,* p. 236.
51. The story is well told in Vernon, Spar, and Tobin, ch. 4.
52. I thank Randall Henning for emphasizing this point.
53. Jean-Claude Berthélemy and Robert Lensink, "An Assessment of the Brady Plan Agreements," *OECD Development Center Technical Papers* 67 (Paris: OECD, 1992).
54. I thank Louis Pauly of the University of Toronto for highlighting this point.
55. "Solution Passes the Test of Time," *Financial Times,* 30 July 1992, p. 4.
56. I thank Benjamin J. Cohen for emphasizing this point.

5. International Cooperation

Epigraph: William M. Isaac, "Capital: Yes, It Is Important," in *Proceedings: International Conference of Banking Supervisors* (Rome, September 13–14, 1984). At this time Isaac was chairman of the Federal Deposit Insurance Corporation.
1. Louis Pauly, "Institutionalizing a Stalemate: National Financial Policies and the International Debt Crisis," *Journal of Public Policy* 10 (1991): 23–43.
2. Basle Committee, *International Convergence of Capital Measurement and Capital Standards* (Basle: Basle Committee, 1988).
3. Portions of this chapter are drawn from my earlier writing on the Basle Accord. See Ethan B. Kapstein, "Resolving the Regulator's Dilemma: International Coordination of Banking Regulations," *International Organization* 43 (Spring 1989): 323–347; idem, "Between Power and Purpose: Central Bankers and the Politics of Regulatory Convergence," *International Organization* 46 (Winter 1992): 264–287; and idem, *Supervising International Banks: Origins and Implications of the Basle Accord* (Princeton, N.J.: Princeton Essays in International Finance, 1991).
4. Raj Bhala and Ethan Kapstein, "The Basle Accord and Financial Competition," *Harvard Business Review* 90 (January–February 1990): 158–159.
5. For a good historical overview, see Sandra Ryan, *History of Bank Capital Adequacy Analysis* (Washington, D.C.: FDIC, 1969).
6. In the best Washington tradition, this act was in fact passed as "Title IX" of a large housing bill.
7. Interview with Federal Reserve Board staff member, Cambridge, Mass., 20 May 1991.

8. Paul Volcker and Donald Regan, "Improving International Bank Capital Standards," 30 May 1984, mimeograph.

9. Basle Committee, *Report on International Developments in Banking Supervision* (Basle: Basle Committee, 1985).

10. For a good recounting of the Continental Illinois crisis, see William Greider, *Secrets of the Temple* (New York: Simon and Schuster, 1987), pp. 625–637.

11. Cohen, *In Whose Interest?* p. 295.

12. On the fringe banks, see Margaret Reid, *The Secondary Banking Crisis, 1973–1975* (London: Macmillan, 1982).

13. Bernard Wesson, *Risk and Capital Adequacy in Banking* (London: Institute of Banking, 1985).

14. William Seidman, "Bank Supervision in the United States," in Richard Dale, ed., *Financial Deregulation* (Cambridge: Woodhead-Faulkner, 1986), p. 78.

15. Federal Reserve Board, "Capital Maintenance: Supplemental Adjusted Capital Measure," 24 January 1986, mimeograph.

16. American Bankers Association, "Comments to the Federal Reserve Board," 23 May 1986, mimeograph.

17. Glenn Tobin, "Global Money Rules" (diss., Harvard University, 1991), p. 221.

18. As cited by a public official interviewed by Glenn Tobin, 4 May 1990.

19. "Why the Transatlantic Deal Must Be Extended," *Financial Times*, 7 May 1987, p. 3.

20. Paul Volcker, "Capital Trends and Federal Reserve Guidelines Program," *Federal Reserve Bulletin* (June 1987): 435–440.

21. Peter Hayward, "Prospects for International Cooperation by Bank Supervisors," *International Lawyer* 24 (Fall 1990): 787–801.

22. Bank of Boston, "Comments to the Federal Reserve Board," 11 May 1987, mimeograph.

23. An interview provided this information concerning Delors' complaint. Other interviews revealed that Cooke himself was disappointed that the Bank of England and the Federal Reserve System went the bilateral route, rather than continuing to work through the Basle Committee. Thus, he agreed with Delors' pronouncement.

24. Barbara Rehm, "NY Fed Chief Lists Ways Japan Can Open Markets," *American Banker*, 7 May 1987.

25. Hayward, "Prospects for International Cooperation."

26. Glenn Tobin, "International Capital Adequacy: A Case Study" (Cambridge, Mass.: Harvard University Kennedy School of Government, 1990).

27. Basle Committee, *Report on International Developments* (Basle: Basle Committee, 1987).

28. Ibid.

29. Hayward, "Prospects for International Cooperation."

30. Federal Reserve Board, "Risk-Based Capital," 1 August 1988 (mimeo).

31. Hayward, "Prospects for International Cooperation."

32. U.S. Treasury, *Modernizing the Financial System* (Washington, D.C.: GPO, 1991).

33. Sherman J. Maisel, *Risk and Capital Adequacy in Commercial Banks* (Chicago: University of Chicago Press, 1981).

34. Graham Bird, *Loan-Loss Provisions and Third World Debt* (Princeton, N.J.: Princeton Essays in International Finance, 1989).

35. It should be noted that by 1993, the Basle Committee had not yet agreed on how to define these assets in terms of their market risk. Once banks must account for market risk, the incentive to hold these securities will diminish.

36. See Brian J. Hall, "How Has the Basle Accord Affected Bank Portfolios?" Harvard University Department of Economics, 24 May 1993.

37. "Banks Find Their Sources of Capital Are Drying Up," *Wall Street Journal*, 9 October 1990, p. C1.

38. "Japanese Banks: Wanna Buy a Loan?" *Economist*, 15 September 1990, p. 89.

39. "Banks Find Their Sources of Capital Are Drying Up," *Wall Street Journal*, 9 October 1990, p. C1.

40. Basle Committee, *Report on International Developments* (Basle: Basle Committee, 1990).

41. Ibid.

42. Noel Tichy and Ram Charan, "Citicorp Faces the World: An Interview with John Reed," *Harvard Business Review* 90 (November–December 1990): 137.

43. Paul Duke and David Hilder, "Squeezed Lenders," *Wall Street Journal*, 1 November 1990, p. A1.

44. Nathaniel Nash, "Treasury Now Favors Creation of Huge Banks," *New York Times*, 7 June 1987, p. 1.

6. Regional Cooperation

Epigraph: Margaret Thatcher, cited in Nicholas Colchester, "Europe's Internal Market," *Economist*, 8 July 1989, p. 41.

1. For the efficiency gains, see the series of reports by Price Waterhouse titled *The Costs of Non-Europe* (Luxembourg: European Commission, 1988).

2. For the classic account, see Richard N. Cooper, *The Economics of Interdependence* (New York: McGraw-Hill, 1968).

3. John Goodman and Louis Pauly, "The New Politics of International Capital Mobility," paper presented to the annual meeting of the American Political Science Association, San Francisco, 30 August to 1 September 1990.

4. I thank John Goodman of the Harvard Business School for highlighting this point.

5. Wayne Sandholtz and John Zysman, "Recasting the European Bargain," *World Politics* 42 (Fall 1989), p. 95.

6. Press Release, European Commission, 9 January 1974.

7. On the history, see Jean Bonnardin, "The Development of Cooperation between Bank Supervisory Authorities in the European Economic Community," *Proceedings: International Conference of Banking Supervisors,* Washington, D.C., September 24–25, 1981.

8. Bonnardin, "The Development of Cooperation."

9. For early reviews, see Raymond Vernon, "The Schuman Plan," *American Journal of International Law* 47 (April 1953): 183–202; and Inis Claude, *Swords into Plowshares* (New York: Random House, 1956).

10. See Andrew Moravcsik, "Negotiating the Single European Act: National Interests and Conventional Statecraft in the European Community," *International Organization* 45 (Winter 1991): 19–56.

11. See Rob Dixon, *Banking in Europe: The Single Market* (New York: Routledge, 1991), p. 55.

12. See the U.K. Treasury report, "Banking: Towards Integration," in *Trade and Industry,* 6 January 1978, p. 18.

13. Banque de Bruxelles, "European Banks: The Endeavour of the EEC Commission," Brussels, 5 May 1974.

14. Benjamin J. Cohen, "European Financial Integration and National Banking Interests," in P. Guerrieri and P. Padoan, eds., *The Political Economy of European Integration* (Savage, Md.: Barnes and Noble Books, 1989), pp. 145–169.

15. Ibid.

16. Bonnardin, "Development of Cooperation."

17. U.K. Treasury, "Banking: Towards Integration."

18. Christopher Tugendhat, "The Development of Banking Policy in the European Community," address to the Financial Times Conference on Domestic Banking, London, 28 June 1977.

19. First Banking Coordination Directive, 77/780/EEC, 12 December 1977.

20. Tugendhat, "The Development of Banking Policy."

21. European Documentation, *The European Financial Common Market* (Luxembourg: European Communities, 1989).

22. Tugendhat, "The Development of Banking Policy."

23. R. Pecchioli, *The Internationalisation of Banking* (Paris: OECD, 1983).

24. Ibid.

25. See Andrew Moravcsik, "Negotiating the Single European Act: National Interests and Conventional Statecraft in the European Community," *International Organization* 45 (Winter 1991): 19–56.

26. Interviews at EC Headquarters, Brussels, July 1991.
27. On the role of the European Court of Justice in the integration process, see Anne-Marie Burley and Walter Mattli, "Europe before the Court: A Political Theory of Legal Integration," *International Organization* 47 (Winter 1993): 43–76.
28. For a review of mutual recognition in the EC, see Kalyso Nicolaides, "Legal Precedent and Political Innovation in the European Community: Explaining the Emergence of Managed Mutual Recognition," Kennedy School of Government, Harvard University, March 1993, manuscript.
29. On the various ECJ rulings I have relied on Jim Murray, "The 1992 Initiative: Revolution or Culmination?" Harvard University, 15 January 1993, manuscript.
30. European Documentation, *European Financial Common Market.*
31. See "Special Supplement," *Euromoney* (March 1992): 22.
32. British Bankers Association, *The EC Banking Directives of 1989* (London: BBA, 1990).
33. British Bankers Association, *EC Banking Directives*, p. 7.
34. Caroline Bradley, "1992: The Case of Financial Services," *Northwestern Journal of International Law and Business* 12 (Spring–Summer 1991): 124–162.
35. Bradley, "1992: The Case of Financial Services."
36. James Blitz, "London's Role in Forex Threatened," *Financial Times*, 10 August 1992, p. 15.
37. U.S. Department of State, *Financial Services and the European Community's Single Market Program* (Washington, D.C.: Department of State, 1989).
38. British Bankers Association, *EC Banking Directives*.
39. Cited ibid., p. 26.
40. Ibid.
41. Government Accounting Office, *European Community: U.S. Financial Services' Competitiveness under the Single Market Program* (Washington, D.C.: GPO, 1990), p. 60.
42. Ibid.
43. Ibid., p. 25.
44. Interviews with officials of the Banking Federation, Brussels, July 1991.
45. Interviews in Brussels, July 1991. See also Philippe Vigneron and Aubry Smith, "The Concept of Reciprocity in Community Legislation: The Example of the Second Banking Directive," *Journal of International Banking Law* 5 (1990): 181–191.
46. Bradley, "1992: The Case of Financial Services," p. 153.
47. "Europe's Capital Markets," *Economist*, 16 December 1989.
48. Interviews in Brussels, July 1991.

49. Letter, Corrigan to Brittan, 4 June 1992.
50. For more on this distinction, see John Zysman, *Governments, Markets and Growth* (Ithaca, N.Y.: Cornell University Press, 1983).
51. Ibid.
52. Interviews with British officials, London, 11 December 1992.
53. Jacques Thierry, "Banking in Europe after 1992," in Z. Mikdashi, ed., *New Strategies and Perspectives in Banking*, p. 143.
54. Ibid.
55. U.S. Department of State, *Financial Services*.

7. BCCI and Beyond

Epigraph: Brian Quinn, February 5, 1992; cited in House of Commons, Treasury and Civil Service Committee, *Banking Supervision and BCCI: International and National Regulation* (London: HMSO, 1992), p. 54.

1. Cited in "The Dirtiest Bank of All," *Time*, 29 July 1991, p. 21. See also the account given in James Ring Adams and Douglas Frantz, *A Full-Service Bank* (New York: Pocket Books, 1991).
2. For such an analysis, see Jim Hoagland, "A Saga of Joint Ventures, Starring Bankers and Spies," *International Herald Tribune*, 22 July 1991, p. 6.
3. Peter Truell and Larry Gurwin, "False Profits," *Newsweek*, 7 December 1992, p. 49.
4. For a study of crime and international finance, see U.S. Congress, Senate Committee on Governmental Affairs, *Crime and Secrecy: The Use of Offshore Banks and Companies* (Washington, D.C.: GPO, 1983).
5. For an argument along these lines that examines state efforts to shut down transnational criminal activities such as piracy and the slave trade, see Ethan Nadelmann, "Global Prohibition Regimes: The Evolution of Norms in International Society," *International Organization* 44 (Autumn 1990): 479–526.
6. The story of BCCI is well told in House of Commons, *Banking Supervision and BCCI*; and U.S. Congress, Senate Committee on Foreign Relations, *The BCCI Affair* (Washington, D.C.: GPO, 1992).
7. Cited in House of Commons, *Banking Supervision and BCCI*, p. viii.
8. For an in-depth study of BCCI's exploitation of powerful Americans, see U.S. Congress, *The BCCI Affair*.
9. U.S. Congress, *The BCCI Affair*, p. 456.
10. Lord Justice Bingham, *Inquiry into the Supervision of the Bank of Credit and Commerce International* (London: HMSO, 1992).
11. House of Commons, *Banking Supervision and BCCI*, p. xiv.
12. This, indeed, was the conclusion of Bingham's *Inquiry*.

13. Bingham, *Inquiry*, p. 45.
14. House of Commons, *Banking Supervision and BCCI*, p. ix.
15. The history is well documented in U.S. Congress, *The BCCI Affair*.
16. See ibid., pp. 163–164.
17. For the memos, see ibid., pp. 175–176.
18. Ibid., p. 193.
19. Ibid., p. 195.
20. Ibid., p. 198.
21. A page-turning account of Operation C-Chase is found in Adams and Frantz, *A Full-Service Bank*.
22. See ibid.; and U.S. Congress, *The BCCI Affair*, pp. 247–290.
23. Bingham, *Inquiry*, p. 62.
24. Cited in House of Commons, *Banking Supervision and BCCI*, p. xi.
25. Cited ibid., p. xiv.
26. See, for example, Richard Dale, "Someone Must Be in Charge," *Financial Times*, 22 July 1991, p. 12.
27. Jacques Maisonrouge, "The Mythology of Multinationalism," *Columbia Journal of World Business* 9 (Summer 1974): 12.
28. "Whipping Boys: Foreign Banks in America," *Economist*, 23 May 1992, p. 89.
29. The text of the act and of the entire hearings can be found in U.S. Congress, Senate Hearing 102–379, 23 May 1991.
30. See "A Central Bankers' Charter," *Economist*, 10 October 1992, pp. 16–17.
31. See David Mulford, "Testimony before the House Committee on Banking, Finance and Urban Affairs," 11 June 1991.
32. "Whipping Boys," *Economist*.
33. U.S. Congress, *The BCCI Affair*, p. 455.
34. Basle Committee, *Report on International Developments in Banking Supervision*, no. 8 (Basle: Basle Committee, 1992), pp. 4–5.
35. House of Commons, *Banking Supervision and BCCI*, p. ix.
36. Ibid., p. ix.
37. As cited in Kenneth Waltz, *Man, the State, and War* (New York: Columbia University Press, 1954), pp. 167–168.
38. Basle Committee, *Minimum Standards for the Supervision of International Banking Groups and Their Cross-Border Establishments* (Basle: Basle Committee, 1992).
39. Bingham, *Inquiry*, p. 28.
40. The report is found in House of Commons, *Banking Supervision and BCCI*, pp. 92–95; and in Sir Leon Brittan, "Banking Supervision in the European Community," *Financial Times*, 29 July 1992, p. 3.
41. House of Commons, *Banking Supervision and BCCI*, p. 45.

42. "Luxembourg Rules Out Stricter Banking Rules," *International Herald Tribune,* 12 July 1991, p. 13.
43. "Deposit Insurance: Euro-Muddle," *Economist,* 19 December 1992, p. 74.
44. House of Commons, *Banking Supervision and BCCI,* p. 94.

8. Assessing the Response to Globalization

Epigraph: Raymond Vernon, *Sovereignty at Bay* (New York: Basic Books, 1971), p. 284.
1. Susan Strange, *Casino Capitalism* (New York: Basil Blackwell, 1986), p. 1.
2. See, for example, Tom Wolfe, *The Bonfire of the Vanities,* in which the lead character, an investment banker, makes his fortune by developing "Giscard" gold bonds.
3. The term is taken from John Gerard Ruggie. See Ruggie, "Territoriality and Beyond: Problematizing Modernity in International Relations," *International Organization* 47 (Winter 1993): 139–174.
4. R. Michael M'Gonigle and Mark W. Zacher, *Pollution, Politics, and International Law* (New York: Columbia University Press, 1979), p. 250; and Ronald B. Mitchell, *Intentional Oil Pollution at Sea: Environmental Policy and Treaty Compliance* (Cambridge, Mass.: MIT Press, 1994).
5. See Peter F. Cowhey, "The International Telecommunications Regime: The Political Roots of Regimes for High Technology," *International Organization* 44 (Spring 1990): 169–199.
6. Ibid. The telecommunications sector is, of course, enormously complex, and different international rules and standards have been created for different industry segments.
7. I thank Lisa Martin for highlighting this point.
8. It is possible, for example, that two of the regional groupings would have a military alliance in order to balance against the third, and thereby maintain relatively open markets with respect to one another.
9. Of course, critics of the accord argue that it provides a perfect example of overregulation; my discussion here, however, focuses on the role that the market will play in regulatory enforcement.

Bibliography

Government Reports and Official Documents

Bank for International Settlements. "The International Interbank Market." *BIS Economic Papers* 8 (1983).

Basle Committee on Banking Supervision. *International Convergence of Capital Measurements and Capital Standards.* Basle, July 1988.

—— *Minimum Standards for International Banking Groups and Their Cross-Border Establishments.* Basle, June 1992.

—— *Report on International Developments in Banking Supervision.* Annual report since 1981.

Berthélemy, Jean-Claude, and Robert Lensink. "An Assessment of the Brady Plan Agreements." *OECD Development Center Technical Papers* 67 (May 1992).

Bingham, Lord Justice. *Inquiry into the Supervision of the Bank of Credit and Commerce International.* London: HMSO, 1992.

Blunden, George. "International Cooperation in Banking Supervision." *Bank of England Quarterly* (September 1977).

Cooke, W. Peter. "The Development of Cooperation between Bank Supervisory Authorities in the G-10 Countries." *Proceedings of the International Conference of Banking Supervisors.* Washington, D.C., September 24–25, 1981.

Davis, E. P. "Instability in the Euromarkets and the Economic Theory of Financial Crisis." *Bank of England Discussion Papers* 43 (October 1989).

Deutsche Bundesbank. *Banking Act of the Federal Republic of Germany.* Frankfurt, 1991.

European Documentation. *The European Financial Common Market.* Luxembourg: European Communities, 1989.

Federal Reserve Bank of New York. *International Competitiveness of U.S. Financial Firms.* New York, May 1991.

Federal Reserve Board. "Capital Maintenance: Supplemental Adjusted Capital Measure." Washington, D.C., January 1986.

International Monetary Fund. *International Capital Markets*. Annual report.

Johnson, Gilbert G., and R. Abrams. *Aspects of the International Banking Safety Net*. Washington, D.C.: International Monetary Fund, March 1983.

Organization for Economic Cooperation and Development. *Banks under Stress*. Paris, 1992.

────── *The Internationalisation of Banking: The Policy Issues*. Paris, 1983.

Posner, Michael, ed. *Problems of International Money: 1972–1985*. Washington, D.C.: International Monetary Fund, 1985.

Price Waterhouse. *The Cost of Non-Europe*. Luxembourg: European Commission, 1988.

Ryan, Sandra. "History of Bank Capital Adequacy Analysis." Federal Deposit Insurance Corporation Working Paper 69-4. Washington, D.C.: FDIC, 1969.

Smith, Gordon, and John Cuddington, eds. *International Debt and the Developing Countries*. Washington, D.C.: World Bank, 1985.

Spong, Kenneth. *Banking Regulation*. Kansas City, Kans.: Federal Reserve Bank of Kansas City, 1983.

United Kingdom, House of Commons, Treasury and Civil Service Committee. *Banking Supervision and BCCI: International and National Regulations*. London: HMSO, 1992.

U.S. Congress, House Committee on Banking, Finance, and Urban Affairs. *Task Force on the International Competitiveness of U.S. Financial Institutions*. Washington, D.C.: GPO, 1990.

────── *International Bank Lending*. Washington, D.C.: GPO, 1983.

U.S. Congress, Senate Committee on Banking. *Proposed Solutions to the International Debt Problem*. Washington, D.C.: GPO, 1983.

U.S. Congress, Senate Committee on Foreign Relations. *International Debt, the Banks and U.S. Foreign Policy*. Washington, D.C.: GPO, 1977.

────── *The BCCI Affair*. Washington, D.C.: GPO, 1992.

U.S. Congress, Senate Committee on Governmental Affairs. *Crime and Secrecy: The Use of Offshore Banks and Companies*. Washington, D.C.: GPO, February 1983.

U.S. Department of State. *Financial Services and the EC's Single Market Program*. Washington, D.C.: Department of State, 1989.

U.S. Department of the Treasury. *National Treatment Study*. Annual report since 1979.

U.S. General Accounting Office. *U.S. Financial Services' Competitiveness under the Single Market Program*. Washington, D.C.: GPO, 1990.

────── *International Banking: International Coordination of Banking Supervision*. Washington, D.C.: GPO, 1986.

Volcker, Paul. "Capital Trends and Federal Reserve Guidelines Program." *Federal Reserve Bulletin* (June 1987).

Wellons, P. A. *Borrowing by Developing Countries in the Euro-Currency Market.* Paris: OECD, 1977.

World Bank. *World Development Report.* Annual report.

Books, Articles, and Dissertations

Adams, James Ring, and Douglas Frantz. *A Full Service Bank.* New York: Pocket Books, 1991.

Adams, John, ed. *The Contemporary International Economy.* New York: St. Martin's Press, 1979.

Aliber, Robert. "International Banking: A Survey." *Journal of Money, Credit and Banking* 16 (November 1984).

American Bankers Association. *International Banking Competitiveness: Why It Matters.* Washington, D.C.: American Bankers Association, 1990.

Baldwin, David. *Economic Statecraft.* Princeton, N.J.: Princeton University Press, 1985.

Bird, Graham. *Loan-Loss Provisions and Third World Debt.* Princeton, N.J.: Princeton Essays in International Finance, 1989.

Blunden, George. "Control and Supervision of the Foreign Operations of Banks." In J. Wilson et al., eds., *The Development of Financial Institutions in Europe, 1956–1976.* Leyden: A. W. Sitjihoff, 1977.

Bradley, Caroline. "1992: The Case of Financial Services." *Northwestern Journal of International Law and Business* 12 (Spring–Summer 1991).

British Bankers Association. *The EC Banking Directives of 1989.* London: British Bankers Association, 1990.

Bromley, Simon. *American Hegemony and World Oil.* University Park: Pennsylvania State University Press, 1991.

Bryant, Ralph. *International Financial Intermediation.* Washington, D.C.: Brookings Institution, 1987.

Burley, Anne-Marie, and Walter Mattli. "Europe before the Court: A Political Theory of Legal Integration." *International Organization* 47 (Winter 1993).

Clarke, Stephen V. O. *American Banks in the International Interbank Market.* Monograph Series in Finance and Economics. New York: New York University Graduate School of Business, 1984.

Cline, William. *International Debt and the Stability of the World Economy.* Washington, D.C.: Institute for International Economics, 1983.

Cohen, Benjamin J. *Organizing the World's Money.* New York: Basic Books, 1977.

———— *In Whose Interest?* New Haven, Conn.: Yale University Press, 1986.

———— "What Ever Happened to the LDC Debt Crisis?" *Challenge* (May–June 1991).

Committee on Economic Development. *International Economic Consequences of High-Priced Energy*. Washington, D.C.: Committee on Economic Development, 1975.

Cooper, John. *The Regulation and Management of Banks*. New York: St. Martin's Press, 1984.

Cooper, Kerry, and Donald Fraser. *Banking Deregulation and the New Competition in Financial Services*. Cambridge, Mass.: Ballinger, 1984.

Cooper, Richard N. *The Economics of Interdependence*. New York: McGraw-Hill, 1968.

Cowhey, Peter F. "The International Telecommunications Regime: The Political Roots of Regimes for High Technology." *International Organization* 44 (Spring 1990).

Dale, Richard, ed. *The Regulation of International Banking*. Cambridge: Woodhead-Faulkner, 1984.

———— ed. *Financial Deregulation*. Cambridge: Woodhead-Faulkner, 1986.

Diaz-Alejandro, Carlos. "Latin American Debt: I Don't Think We Are in Kansas Anymore." *Brookings Papers on Economic Activity* 2 (1984).

Dobson, Wendy. *Economic Policy Coordination*. Washington, D.C.: Institute for International Economics, 1991.

Dombrowski, Peter. "U.S. Policies toward the International Expansion of American Banks, 1965–1990." Diss., University of Maryland, 1990.

Dunn, Robert M. *The Many Disappointments of Flexible Exchange Rates*. Princeton, N.J.: Princeton Essays in International Finance, 1983.

Eichengreen, Barry. *Should the Maastricht Treaty Be Saved?* Princeton, N.J.: Princeton Studies in International Finance, 1992.

Enders, Thomas, and Richard Mattione. *Latin America: The Crisis of Debt and Growth*. Washington, D.C.: Brookings Institution, 1984.

England, Catherine. *Governing Banking's Future*. Boston: Kluwer, 1991.

Feder, Gershon, et al. "Projecting Debt Servicing Capacity of Developing Countries." *Journal of Financial and Quantitative Analysis* 16 (December 1981).

Feldstein, Martin, ed. *International Policy Coordination*. Chicago: University of Chicago Press, 1988.

———— *The Risk of Economic Crisis*. Chicago: University of Chicago Press, 1991.

Fried, Edward R., and Charles Schultze, eds. *Higher Oil Prices and the World Economy*. Washington, D.C.: Brookings Institution, 1975.

Frieden, Jeffry Alan. "Studies in International Finance: Private Interest and Public Policy in the International Political Economy." Diss., Columbia University, 1985.

Friedman, Benjamin. *Postwar Changes in American Financial Markets*. Cambridge, Mass.: National Bureau of Economic Research, 1980.

Gilpin, Robert. *The Political Economy of International Relations*. Princeton, N.J.: Princeton University Press, 1987.

Goodman, John. *Monetary Sovereignty*. Ithaca, N.Y.: Cornell University Press, 1992.

—— and Louis Pauly. "The New Politics of International Capital Mobility." Paper Presented to the American Political Science Association, San Francisco, 1990.

Gowa, Joanne. *Closing the Gold Window*. Ithaca, N.Y.: Cornell University Press, 1983.

Greenspan, Alan. "International Financial Integration." Remarks before the Bankers Association of Japan, 14 October 1992.

Greider, William. *Secrets of the Temple*. New York: Simon and Schuster, 1987.

Grieco, Joseph. "Anarchy and the Limits of Cooperation." *International Organization* 42 (Summer 1988).

Guerrieri, P., and P. Padoan, eds. *The Political Economy of European Integration*. Savage, Md.: Barnes and Noble Books, 1989.

Guttentag, Jack, and Richard Herring. *The Lender of Last Resort in an International Context*. Princeton, N.J.: Princeton Essays in International Finance, 1983.

Haas, Ernst. "Why Collaborate?" *World Politics* 32 (April 1980).

Hale, David. "Global Finance and the Retreat to Managed Trade." *Harvard Business Review* (January–February 1990).

Hansen, Roger D., ed. *U.S. Foreign Policy and the Third World: Agenda 1982*. New York: Praeger, 1982.

Hawley, James P. "Protecting Capital from Itself: U.S. Attempts to Regulate the Eurocurrency System." *International Organization* 38 (Winter 1984).

Hayward, Peter. "Prospects for International Cooperation by Bank Supervisors." *International Lawyer* 24 (Fall 1990).

Holley, H. A. *Developing-Country Debt*. London: Routledge and Kegan Paul, 1987.

Huntington, Samuel P. "Transnational Organizations in World Politics." *World Politics* 25 (April 1973).

Ikenberry, G. John. "An Institutional Approach to American Foreign Economic Policy." *International Organization* 42 (Winter 1988).

Kahler, Miles. "Politics and International Debt: Explaining the Crisis." *International Organization* 39 (Summer 1985).

Kapstein, Ethan B. "Resolving the Regulator's Dilemma: International Coordination of Banking Regulations." *International Organization* 43 (Spring 1989).

—— *The Insecure Alliance*. New York: Oxford University Press, 1990.

———— *Supervising International Banks: Origins and Implications of the Basle Accord.* Princeton, N.J.: Princeton Essays in International Finance, 1991.

———— *The Political Economy of National Security: A Global Perspective.* Columbia, S.C.: University of South Carolina Press, 1992.

———— "We Are US: The Myth of the Multinational." *National Interest* (Winter 1991–1992).

———— "Between Power and Purpose: Central Bankers and the Politics of Regulatory Convergence." *International Organization* 46 (Winter 1992).

———— and Raj Bhala. "The Basle Accord and Financial Competition." *Harvard Business Review* (January–February 1990).

Katzenstein, Peter, ed. *Between Power and Plenty.* Madison, Wis.: University of Wisconsin Press, 1978.

Kaufman, Henry. "Fundamental Precepts Guiding Future Financial Regulation." Remarks before the International Organization of Securities Commissions, London, 27 October 1992.

Keohane, Robert. *After Hegemony.* Princeton, N.J.: Princeton University Press, 1984.

Keynes, John Maynard. "National Self-Sufficiency." *Yale Review* (June 1933).

Kindleberger, Charles P. *The World in Depression, 1929–1939.* Berkeley: University of California Press, 1973.

Knorr, Klaus, and Frank Trager, eds. *Economic Issues and National Security.* Lawrence: Regents Press of Kansas, 1977.

Kobrin, Stephen. "Transnational Integration, National Markets and Nation-States." Working Paper, Reginald Jones Center, Wharton School of Business, August 1991.

Kohl, Richard. "The Causes of the Third World Debt Crisis." Diss., University of California at Berkeley, 1973.

Krasner, Stephen D. *Defending the National Interest.* Princeton, N.J.: Princeton University Press, 1978.

———— ed. *International Regimes.* Ithaca, N.Y.: Cornell University Press, 1983.

Lichtenstein, Cynthia. "The U.S. Response to the International Debt Crisis: The International Lending Supervision Act of 1983." *Virginia Journal of International Law* 25 (1985).

Lieber, Robert. "Existential Realism." *Washington Quarterly* 16 (Winter 1993).

Lipson, Charles. "Bankers' Dilemmas: Private Cooperation in Rescheduling Sovereign Debts." *World Politics* 37 (October 1985).

Lissakers, Karen. *Banks, Borrowers and the Establishment.* New York: Basic Books, 1991.

Lomax, David, and P. Gutman. *The Euromarkets and International Financial Policies.* New York: John Wiley and Sons, 1981.

Maisel, Sherman J. *Risk and Capital Adequacy in Commercial Banks*. Chicago: University of Chicago Press, 1981.

Maisonrouge, Jacques. "The Mythology of Multinationalism." *Columbia Journal of World Business* 9 (Summer 1974).

Mattione, Richard. *OPEC's Investments and the International Financial System*. Washington, D.C.: Brookings Institution, 1984.

Mistry, Percy. "Third World Debt: Beyond the Baker Plan." *Banker* (September 1987).

Mitchell, Ronald B. *Intentional Oil Pollution at Sea: Environmental Policy and Treaty Compliance*. Cambridge, Mass.: MIT Press, 1994.

Moravcsik, Andrew. "Negotiating the Single European Act: National Interests and Conventional Statecraft in the European Community." *International Organization* 45 (Winter 1991).

Nadelmann, Ethan. "Global Prohibition Regimes: The Evolution of Norms in International Society." *International Organization* 44 (Autumn 1990).

Nye, Joseph. *Bound to Lead*. New York: Basic Books, 1990.

Odell, John. *U.S. International Monetary Policy*. Princeton, N.J.: Princeton University Press, 1982.

Oxelheim, L., and C. Wihlborg. *Macroeconomic Uncertainty*. New York: John Wiley and Sons, 1987.

Pauly, Louis. *Opening Financial Markets: Banking Politics on the Pacific Rim*. Ithaca, N.Y.: Cornell University Press, 1988.

——— "Institutionalizing a Stalemate: National Financial Policies and the International Debt Crisis." *Journal of Public Policy* 10 (1991).

Peltzman, Sam. "Toward a More General Theory of Regulation." *Journal of Law and Economics* 19 (August 1976).

Pincus, John. *Economic Aid and International Cost Sharing*. Baltimore, Md.: Johns Hopkins University Press, 1965.

Polanyi, Karl. *The Great Transformation*. Boston: Beacon Press, 1944.

Putnam, Robert. "Diplomacy and Domestic Politics: The Logic of Two-Level Games." *International Organization* 42 (Summer 1988).

——— and Nicholas Bayne. *Hanging Together: Cooperation and Conflict in the Seven Power Summits*. Cambridge, Mass.: Harvard University Press, 1987.

Reich, Robert. "Who Is US?" *Harvard Business Review* (January–February 1990).

Reid, Margaret. *The Secondary Banking Crisis, 1973–1975*. London: Macmillan, 1982.

Rostow, W. W. *The World Economy: History and Prospect*. Austin: University of Texas Press, 1978.

Ruggie, John Gerard. "Territoriality and Beyond: Problematizing Modernity in International Relations." *International Organization* 47 (Winter 1993).

Rustow, Dankwart, and John Mugno. *OPEC: Success and Prospects*. New York: New York University Press, 1976.

Sachs, Jeffrey. "Managing the LDC Debt Crisis." *Brookings Papers on Economic Activity* 4 (1986).

Sandholtz, Wayne, and John Zysman. "Recasting the European Bargain." *World Politics* 42 (Fall 1989).

Spero, Joan. *The Failure of the Franklin National Bank*. New York: Columbia University Press, 1980.

Spindler, Andrew. *The Politics of International Credit*. Washington, D.C.: Brookings Institution, 1984.

Spiro, David. *Hegemony Unbound*. Ithaca, N.Y.: Cornell University Press, 1994.

Staley, Eugene. *World Economy in Transition*. New York: Council on Foreign Relations, 1939.

Starr, Martin K., ed. *Global Competitiveness*. New York: Norton, 1988.

Strange, Susan. *Casino Capitalism*. New York: Basil Blackwell, 1986.

Thomson, Janice, and Stephen Krasner. "Global Transactions and the Consolidation of Sovereignty." In Robert Art and Robert Jervis, eds., *International Politics*. New York: HarperCollins, 1992.

Tobin, Glenn. "Global Money Rules." Diss., Harvard University, 1991.

Triffin, Robert. *Gold and the Dollar Crisis*. New Haven, Conn.: Yale University Press, 1960.

Tyson, Laura, and John Zysman. *American Industry in International Competitiveness*. Ithaca, N.Y.: Cornell University Press.

Vernon, Raymond. *Sovereignty at Bay*. New York: Basic Books, 1971.

———— ed. *The Oil Crisis*. New York: Norton, 1976.

———— et al. *Iron Triangles and Revolving Doors: Cases in U.S. Foreign Economic Policy*. New York: Praeger, 1991.

———— and Ethan B. Kapstein. *Defense and Dependence in a Global Economy*. Washington, D.C.: CQ Press, 1992.

Vigneron, Philippe, and Aubry Smith. "The Concept of Reciprocity in Community Legislation: The Example of the Second Banking Directive." *Journal of International Banking Law* 5 (1990).

Volcker, Paul, ed. *International Monetary Cooperation: Essays in Honor of Henry C. Wallich*. Princeton, N.J.: Princeton Essays in International Finance, 1987.

———— and Toyoo Gyohten. *Changing Fortunes*. New York: Times Books, 1992.

Walter, Andrew. *World Power and World Money*. Hertfordshire, England: Harvester Wheatsheaf, 1991.

Weinert, Richard. "Swapping Third World Debt." *Foreign Policy* (Winter 1986).

Wellons, Philip A. *Passing the Buck: Governments and Third World Debt*. Boston: Harvard Business School Press, 1987.

Wesson, Bernard. *Risk and Capital Adequacy in Banking*. London: Institute of Banking, 1985.

Wilson, James Q., ed. *The Politics of Regulation*. New York: Basic Books, 1980.

Wolfe, Tom. *The Bonfire of the Vanities*. New York: Farrar, Straus and Giroux, 1987.

Wriston, Walter. *The Twilight of Sovereignty: How the Information Revolution Is Transforming Our World*. New York: Scribners, 1992.

Yager, Joseph, and Eleanor Steinberg, eds. *Energy and U.S. Foreign Policy*. Cambridge, Mass.: Ballinger, 1974.

Yergin, Daniel, and Martin Hillenbrand. *Global Insecurity*. Boston: Houghton Mifflin, 1982.

Zysman, John. *Governments, Markets and Growth*. Ithaca, N.Y.: Cornell University Press, 1983.

Index